Financial statements

Tutorial

David Cox

Published by Osborne Books Limited
Unit 1B Everoak Estate
Bromyard Road, Worcester WR2 5HP
Tel 01905 748071
Email books@osbornebooks.co.uk
Website www.osbornebooks.co.uk

Design by Laura Ingham

Printed by CPI Group (UK) Limited, Croydon, CRO 4YY, on environmentally friendly, acid-free paper from managed forests.

British Library Cataloguing in Publication Data
A catalogue record for this book is available from the British Library

ISBN 978 1909173 255

Contents

Acknowledgements

The publisher wishes to thank the following for their help with the reading and production of the book: Jean Cox, Jon Moore, Wesley Ogden, and Cathy Turner. Thanks are also due to Alison Aplin for her technical editorial work and to Laura Ingham for her designs for this series.

The publisher is indebted to the Association of Accounting Technicians for its help and advice to our authors and editors during the preparation of this text. Thanks also go to the International Accounting Standards Board.

Author

David Cox is a Certified Accountant with more than twenty years' experience teaching accountancy students over a wide range of levels. Formerly with the Management and Professional Studies Department at Worcester College of Technology, he now lectures on a freelance basis and carries out educational consultancy work in accountancy studies. He is author and joint author of a number of textbooks in the areas of accounting, finance and banking.

Introduction

what this book covers

This book has been written specifically to cover the 'Financial statements' Unit which is mandatory for the revised (2013) AAT Level 4 Diploma in Accounting.

The book contains a clear text with worked examples and case studies, chapter summaries and key terms to help with revision. Each chapter has a wide range of activities, many in the style of the computer-based assessments used by AAT.

year dates, negative amounts

Note that year dates are shown in the book as either 20-1 or 20X1; negative money amounts are shown with either brackets, eg (£1,000), or with a minus sign, eg −£1,000.

International Financial Reporting Standards (IFRS) terminology

This book is fully compliant with IFRS terminology. A glossary of IFRS terms is given on page 31.

Osborne Workbooks

Osborne Workbooks contain practice material which helps students achieve success in their assessments. *Financial statements Workbook* contains a number of paper-based practice exams in the style of the computer-based assessment. Please visit www.osbornebooks.co.uk for further details and access to our online shop.

Web directory

There are a number of websites which will help to supplement your studies of limited company financial statements.

information and accountancy news

www.accountancyage.com	– news and information service – regular newsletter
www.accountingweb.co.uk	– news and information – includes a students' discussion forum
www.bis.gov.uk	– Department for Business, Innovation and Skills – a large website with links to various sections of the Department
www.companieshouse.gov.uk	– gives information about forming and running companies – provides details of how to obtain copies of company financial statements and other statutory information
www.hmrc.gov.uk	– HM Revenue & Customs – details of income taxes, corporation tax and VAT
www.ifrs.org	– the International Accounting Standards Board – gives a summary of international financial reporting standards
www.iasplus.com	– gives details of international financial reporting standards – news and information – includes a 'pocket guide' to international financial reporting standards
www.opsi.gov.uk	– Office of Public Sector Information – access to Acts of Parliament
www.pqmagazine.co.uk	– website of PQ (part-qualified) magazine – lively articles on a wide range of accountancy topics – a Study Zone section

accountancy associations

A selection of accountancy bodies and associations is given below, with their website addresses. As well as details of members' and students' services, they give information on assessment and examination schemes. Some sites also provide a news and information service.

www.aat.org.uk	–	The Association of Accounting Technicians
www.acca.org.uk	–	The Association of Chartered Certified Accountants
www.cimaglobal.com	–	The Chartered Institute of Management Accountants
www.cipfa.org.uk	–	The Chartered Institute of Public Finance and Accountancy
www.icaew.com	–	The Institute of Chartered Accountants in England and Wales
www.icas.org.uk	–	The Institute of Chartered Accountants of Scotland

firms of accountants

A selection of accountancy firms is given below. As well as advertising the firms and their services, a number of sites include technical information and notes on recent developments in accounting.

www.deloitte.com	–	Deloitte
www.ey.com	–	EY (formerly known as Ernst & Young)
www.grant-thornton.co.uk	–	Grant Thornton
www.kpmg.co.uk	–	KPMG
www.pwc.com	–	PwC (formerly PricewaterhouseCoopers)
	–	includes a 'pocket guide' to international financial reporting standards

published financial statements

Most large public limited companies include their published financial statements on their websites – search for 'financial statements' or 'investor centre'. Here are a few links:

www.tescoplc.com

www.j-sainsbury.co.uk/investor-centre

www.annualreport.marksandspencer.com/financialstatements

www.osbornebooks.co.uk – additional study material

The Resources Section of the Osborne Books website www.osbornebooks.co.uk will be used to give information about changes and updating of the topics covered in this book.

1 Purpose of financial statements

this chapter covers...

This book builds on earlier studies of financial accounting and is solely concerned with the financial statements of limited companies.

In this chapter we begin our studies by considering the

- *general purpose of financial reporting*
- *elements of financial statements*
- *accounting equation*
- *development of the regulatory framework of accounting*
- *Conceptual Framework for Financial Reporting*
- *accounting concepts*

INTRODUCTION TO LIMITED COMPANIES

For most students, this is the first time that you will have studied the financial statements of limited companies. It is appropriate, therefore, to put limited companies in context. In previous studies you will have prepared the financial statements of sole traders and will then have moved on to those of partnerships. The transition from sole trader to partnership financial statements is not too big a step with, instead of one person owning the business, two or more owners. The step from sole traders/partnerships to limited companies is rather greater as we deal with incorporated – ie formed into a corporation (company) – businesses, where the owners are members (shareholders) of the company.

private sector organisations

Companies – together with sole traders and partnerships – are private sector (as compared with public sector organisations – such as local authorities, central government, the National Health Service – and other not-for-profit organisations – such as societies and charities). The following diagram illustrates the types of private sector organisations:

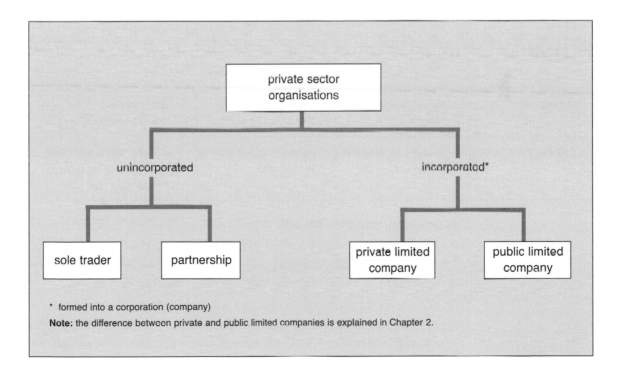

* formed into a corporation (company)

Note: the difference between private and public limited companies is explained in Chapter 2.

sole traders, partnerships and limited companies

Limited companies are more complex businesses to set up and to run. Chapter 2 explains the advantages of forming a company, the difference between private and public limited companies, and the types of shares issued. Chapter 3 covers limited company published financial statements – which are available to shareholders and are filed at Companies House. The following table illustrates the key differences between sole traders, partnerships and limited companies:

	sole trader	partnership	limited company
ownership	• owned by the sole trader	• owned by the partners	• owned by the shareholders
legal status	• the sole trader is the business	• the partners are the business	• separate legal entity from its owners
members	• one	• between 2 and 20 (normal maximum)	• minimum of one shareholder; no maximum
liability	• unlimited liability, for debts of business	• partners normally liable for entire partnership debt	• shareholders can only lose their investment
legislation	• none	• Partnership Act 1890	• Companies Acts
regulation	• none	• written or oral partnership agreement	• Articles of Association
management	• owner takes all decisions	• all partners normally take an active part	• directors and authorised employees
financial statements	• private – not available to the public	• private – not available to the public	• must be filed at Companies House where available to the public

In particular, note from the table that:

■ the Companies Acts of 1985, 1989 and 2006 regulate the setting up and running of limited companies

■ a company is a separate legal entity from its shareholder owners

■ companies are managed by directors who are themselves shareholders

■ companies – unlike sole traders and partnerships – must file their annual financial statements with Companies House, where they are available for public inspection

LIMITED COMPANIES

A walk or a drive around any medium-sized town will reveal evidence of a wide variety of businesses formed as limited companies – banks, shops, restaurants, hotels, bus and train operators, delivery firms. Many of their names will be well known – HSBC Bank plc, Tesco PLC, Marks & Spencer plc, etc – and to be found in most towns and cities; others will be known only in their own area – Wyvern Wool Shop Limited, Don's DIY Limited, etc. The letters 'plc' stand for public limited company – this can be a large company whose shares might (but not always) be traded on the stock markets. The word 'limited' refers to a private limited company – often a smaller company than a plc, but whose shares are not quoted on the stock markets. In fact there are far more private limited companies than there are plcs. In Chapter 2, we will look further into the differences between the types of companies.

Virtually all limited companies can be described as being in the **private sector** where they are owned by shareholders who are looking for the company to make profits. A small number of limited companies are set up by not for-profit organisations – such as societies and charities – to provide mutual services for their members and the community.

objectives of companies

For most limited companies the profit motive is commonly the most important objective. Profit is measured as the excess of income over expenses; sufficient profit needs to be generated each year to enable the owners (shareholders) to be paid dividends on their shares. Often there is a conflict within business between short-term profit and long-term profit: for example, a major investment in training will reduce this year's profit, but may well help to increase profit in future years. Once the profit motive has been satisfied, and particularly as a company increases in size, a range of other objectives is developed: examples include environmental issues – taking initiatives to improve the environment through becoming more energy efficient and reducing waste – and being a good employer – adding value to the output by providing better facilities and better training for the workforce.

FINANCIAL STATEMENTS AND THEIR PURPOSES

financial statements

The three main financial statements used by limited companies for financial reporting are:

■ a **statement of profit or loss and other comprehensive income** to measure the financial performance of the company for a particular time period (the accounting period)

■ a **statement of financial position**, to list the assets, liabilities and equity (capital) at the end of the accounting period

■ a **statement of cash flows**, to link profit with changes in assets and liabilities, and the effect on the cash of the company

The statement of profit or loss and statement of cash flows usually cover a twelve-month accounting period (but do not necessarily run to 31 December – the end of the calendar year); the statement of financial position shows the assets, liabilities and equity of the company at the end of the accounting period.

objective of financial reporting

What is the objective of financial reporting?

'The objective of general purpose financial reporting is to provide financial information about the reporting entity that is useful to existing and potential investors, lenders and other creditors in making decisions about providing resources to the entity.'

This definition is taken from the *Conceptual Framework for Financial Reporting* issued by the International Accounting Standards Board (see page 14).

Note the following from the definition:

■ **general purpose financial reporting** – provides financial information about the reporting entity

■ **financial information** – is given about the financial position, performance and changes in financial position of the reporting entity

■ **entity** – an organisation, such as a limited company, whose activities and resources are kept separate from those of the owner(s)

■ **existing and potential investors, lenders and other creditors** – financial statements are used by a number of interested parties (see below)

■ **making decisions** – information from the financial statements is used to help in making decisions about investment or potential investment in the entity, eg to buy or sell a company's shares, to make a loan to the company, and to provide other forms of credit

LIMITED COMPANY FINANCIAL STATEMENTS: INTERESTED PARTIES

Who is interested?	What are they interested in?	Why are they interested?
Existing and potential investors	• Is the company making a profit? • Can the company pay its way? • What was the sales revenue figure?	• To assess the stewardship of management • To see how much money can be paid in dividends • To see if the company will continue in the foreseeable future • To see if the company is expanding or declining
Lenders	• Has the company made a profit? • What amount is currently loaned? • What is the value of the assets?	• To check if the company will be able to pay finance costs and make loan repayments • To assess how far the lender is financing the company • To assess the value of security available to the lender
Suppliers	• Can the company pay its way? • What is the value of the assets?	• To decide whether to supply goods and services to the company • To assess if the company is able to pay its debts
Employees and trade unions	• Has the company made a profit? • Can the company pay its way?	• To assess whether the company is able to pay wages and salaries • To consider the stability of the company in offering employment opportunities in the future
Customers	• Is the company profitable? • What is the value of the assets? • Can the company pay its way?	• To see if the company will continue to supply its products or services • To assess the ability of the company to meet warranty liabilities, and provision of spare parts
Competitors	• Is the company profitable? • What is the sales revenue figure? • How efficiently is the company using its resources? • Can the company pay its way?	• For comparison purposes with their own performance • To consider the possibility of acquisition of the company
Government and government agencies	• Has the company made a profit? • What was the sales revenue figure?	• To calculate the tax due • To ensure that the company is registered for VAT and completes VAT returns on time • To provide a basis for government regulation and statistics • To see how grants provided have been spent
The public	• Is the company profitable? • Can the company pay its way?	• To assess employment prospects • To assess the contribution to the economy
Managers	• Is the company making a profit? • Can the company pay its way? • How efficiently is the company using its resources?	• To see if the company is expanding or declining • To see if the company will continue in the foreseeable future • To examine the efficiency of the company and to make comparisons with other, similar, companies

users of financial statements

There is a wide variety of users – both internal and external – of financial statements of limited companies, as shown by the table on the previous page. Study this table and then read the text that follows.

Internal users include company directors and managers, employees.

External users include existing and potential shareholders, lenders, suppliers and customers, competitors, government agencies, the public, etc.

Whilst each user is interested in a number of different aspects, as the diagram on the previous page shows, most users will assess the stewardship of the management of the company. By stewardship, we mean that the management of a company is accountable for the safe-keeping of the company's resources, and for their proper, efficient and profitable use.

contents of the financial statements

As financial statements are the principal means of communicating accounting information to users they must provide details of:

financial position

- they provide information about the economic resources used by the company
- they provide information about the liquidity, use of resources, and financial position of the company

financial performance

- they assess the stewardship of management
- they make possible an assessment of the effectiveness of the use of the company's resources in achieving its objectives, eg in profitability
- they allow comparison to be made with the financial performance from previous accounting periods

changes in financial position

- they provide information about the investing, financing and operating activities of the company
- they enable an assessment of the ability of the company to generate cash and how such cash flows will be used

ELEMENTS OF FINANCIAL STATEMENTS

Elements of financial statements are the 'building blocks' from which financial statements are constructed – that is, they are the classes of items which comprise financial statements.

The five main elements of financial statements are as follows:

- assets
- liabilities
- equity
- income
- expenses

Note that the elements are broad classes and, in practice, financial statements will include a number of sub-classifications – eg assets will be classified between non-current and current, each of which will be further detailed (see Chapters 2 and 3). The intention is that the company will give sufficient information to users to enable them to make economic decisions.

The way in which the elements link together in the financial statements of profit or loss and financial position, together with definitions, is shown in the diagrams on the next page.

importance of elements of financial statements

The importance of the elements of financial statements is that they define the items which can be included in financial statements. The elements are appropriate for the financial statements of limited companies:

- a statement of profit or loss and other comprehensive income to show income and expenses for the accounting period
- a statement of financial position to show assets, liabilities and equity at a particular date
- a statement of cash flows to reflect the elements of the statement of comprehensive income, together with changes to the elements shown on the statement of financial position

Study the diagrams on the next page in conjunction with the note below.

Tutorial note:

Pay particular attention to the definitions of the five elements, together with profits or losses, which are given in the diagram on the next page. If asked these in an assessment, it is important in an answer to give a full definition. For example, if asked to define an asset, you will need to say more than 'something owned'; instead, pick out and explain the three key parts of the definition:

- a resource controlled by the entity
- as a result of past events
- from which future economic benefits are expected

Applying these key parts to two example assets:

current asset: inventories

- the entity can sell them to customers, or use them in the manufacture of products
- the inventories were bought in the past
- cash will be received when the inventories, or the manufactured products, are sold

non-current asset: machine

- the entity can decide when and how to use the asset
- the asset was bought in the past
- the asset can be used to manufacture products which can be sold and cash received

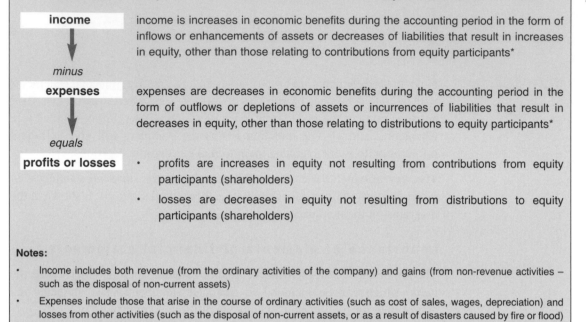

statement of profit or loss and other comprehensive income

income income is increases in economic benefits during the accounting period in the form of inflows or enhancements of assets or decreases of liabilities that result in increases in equity, other than those relating to contributions from equity participants*

minus

expenses expenses are decreases in economic benefits during the accounting period in the form of outflows or depletions of assets or incurrences of liabilities that result in decreases in equity, other than those relating to distributions to equity participants*

equals

profits or losses
- profits are increases in equity not resulting from contributions from equity participants (shareholders)
- losses are decreases in equity not resulting from distributions to equity participants (shareholders)

Notes:

- Income includes both revenue (from the ordinary activities of the company) and gains (from non-revenue activities – such as the disposal of non-current assets)

- Expenses include those that arise in the course of ordinary activities (such as cost of sales, wages, depreciation) and losses from other activities (such as the disposal of non-current assets, or as a result of disasters caused by fire or flood)

- Items of income and expenses that do not arise from ordinary activities are reported separately within the statement of profit or loss and other comprehensive income

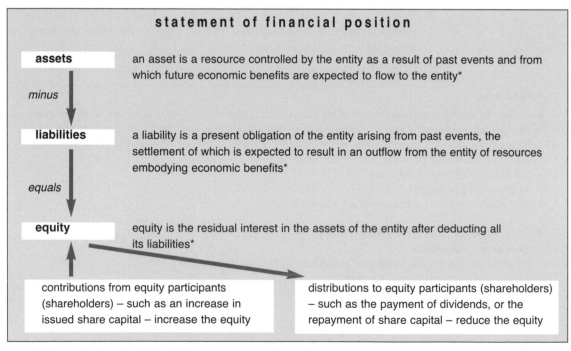

statement of financial position

assets an asset is a resource controlled by the entity as a result of past events and from which future economic benefits are expected to flow to the entity*

minus

liabilities a liability is a present obligation of the entity arising from past events, the settlement of which is expected to result in an outflow from the entity of resources embodying economic benefits*

equals

equity equity is the residual interest in the assets of the entity after deducting all its liabilities*

contributions from equity participants (shareholders) – such as an increase in issued share capital – increase the equity

distributions to equity participants (shareholders) – such as the payment of dividends, or the repayment of share capital – reduce the equity

* definitions taken from *Conceptual Framework for Financial Reporting* – see page 14.

THE ACCOUNTING EQUATION

The accounting equation underlies the statement of financial position of a limited company and relates to the following elements:

assets *minus* liabilities *equals* equity

Equity increases with

- profits from the revenue activities of the company
- other comprehensive income, eg revaluation of assets
- contributions from the shareholders, eg an issue of shares

Equity decreases with

- losses from the revenue activities of the company
- losses from other activities, eg the devaluation of assets
- distributions to shareholders, eg the payment of dividends

In the statement of financial position of a limited company, the equity is represented by the share capital and reserves of the company. The statement of profit or loss links to the statement of financial position where profits are added to, or losses are deducted from, equity – thus the statement of profit or loss explains how the change in equity came about, together with any contributions by, or distributions made to, the shareholders – capital introduced or repaid. (The statement of changes in equity – see page 61 – shows such items and their effect on equity.)

To summarise, equity is represented by:

- capital from shareholders
- retained earnings from the statement of profit or loss
- other reserves

THE REGULATORY FRAMEWORK OF ACCOUNTING

The regulatory framework forms the 'rules' of accounting. When drafting company financial statements, accountants seek to follow the same set of rules – thus enabling broad comparisons to be made between the financial results of different companies.

The regulatory framework comprises

- accounting standards
- company law
- Conceptual Framework for Financial Reporting

This body of accounting standards and other guidance is often referred to as *Generally Accepted Accounting Practice (GAAP)*.

The historical development of the regulatory framework in the UK dates from the first Companies Act in 1862 through to the main Companies Acts of the last thirty years in 1985, 1989 and 2006. Accounting standards have been developed over the last forty years to provide a framework for accounting. A more recent development has been the adoption by large UK companies of international financial reporting standards.

The diagram below explains the development of the regulatory framework in the UK since 1970.

Historical development of the regulatory framework in the UK

1970	1980	1990	2000	2010

Statements of Standard Accounting Practice (SSAPs) and Financial Reporting Standards (FRSs)

Companies Act

1985   1989   2006

International Accounting Standards (IASs) and International Financial Reporting Standards (IFRSs)

1989   revised 2010
Conceptual Framework for Financial Reporting

2005
International
financial reporting
standards adopted
by UK companies

accounting standards

Over the last forty years, a number of accounting standards have been produced to provide a framework for accounting and to reduce the variety of accounting treatments which companies may use in their financial statements.

Statements of Standard Accounting Practice (SSAPs) and **Financial Reporting Standards (FRSs)**, which are issued by the Financial Reporting Council, are the UK domestic accounting standards. They are used by smaller limited companies.

International financial reporting standards – in the form of **International Accounting Standards (IASs)** and **International Financial Reporting Standards (IFRSs)** – have been developed by the International Accounting Standards Board since 1973 with the aim of harmonising international financial reporting. All large companies in the European Union prepare their financial statements in accordance with international financial reporting standards, and the standards are being adopted increasingly on a worldwide basis.

A list of the international financial reporting standards that are required for AAT's *Financial Statements* Assessment is given on page 94. Note that IASs are the older standards, which are being replaced with IFRSs – the collective term usually used for both is 'international financial reporting standards'. (A full list of the reporting standards is available at www.ifrs.org.)

purposes of accounting standards

The purposes of using accounting standards are:

- to provide a framework for preparing and presenting financial statements – the 'rules' of accounting
- to standardise financial statements so that the same accounting rules apply to all companies
- to reduce the variations of accounting treatments used in financial statements – thus making 'window dressing' more difficult
- to help to ensure high quality financial accounting for users through the application of the qualitative characteristics of useful financial information
- to enable compliance with the Companies Acts and audit requirements that financial statements have been prepared in accordance with accounting standards
- to allow users of financial statements to make inter-firm comparisons in the knowledge that all the financial statements have been prepared using the same standards

Company Law

Limited companies are regulated by the Companies Acts of 1985, 1989 and 2006. In particular, the Acts require that directors of a company state that the financial statements have been prepared in accordance with applicable accounting standards and, if there have been any material departures, must give details and the reasons for such departures.

Conceptual Framework for Financial Reporting

Although not an accounting standard, the *Conceptual Framework for Financial Reporting* has been developed by the International Accounting Standards Board to set out the concepts that underlie the preparation and presentation of financial statements for external users. Its purpose is to:

- assist in the development and review of international financial reporting standards

- assist in promoting harmonisation of standards by reducing the number of permissible alternative accounting treatments

- help preparers of accounts to deal with issues not yet covered by the standards

- help users of accounts to interpret the information in financial statements which have been prepared in accordance with the standards

We look in more detail at the *Conceptual Framework for Financial Reporting* in the next section.

CONCEPTUAL FRAMEWORK FOR FINANCIAL REPORTING

As we have seen, the *Conceptual Framework for Financial Reporting* is not itself an accounting standard. It sets out the concepts which underlie the preparation and presentation of financial statements for external users. It helps the development of future international financial reporting standards and the review of existing standards.

It deals with the objective of financial reporting, the qualitative characteristics of useful financial information and the definition, recognition and measurement of the elements of financial statements.

users of financial information

The *Conceptual Framework for Financial Reporting* identifies the primary users of financial information as:

- investors, both existing and potential
- lenders
- other creditors

These users will make use of the financial reports of an entity in order to help in making decisions, such as:

- when to buy, hold or sell shares in the company
- to assess the stewardship of the management of the company

- to assess the ability of the company to pay its suppliers and employees
- to assess the security available for loans made to the company
- to determine the distributable profits and dividends of the company
- to obtain figures for use in national statistics
- to assess the amount of tax payable on the profits of the company
- to regulate the activities of the company

Other users of financial reports include:

- the management of the reporting entity
- regulators
- members of the public (other than investors, lenders and other creditors)

the objective of financial reporting

As we saw earlier (page 6), the objective of financial reporting is *'to provide information about the reporting entity that is useful to existing and potential investors, lenders and other creditors in making decisions about providing resources to the entity'*.

Financial reports provide information about the reporting entity's **financial position** through a statement of financial position. Financial reports also show the **performance** of the entity, usually presented in a statement of profit or loss and other comprehensive income, and the **changes in financial position**, shown by a statement of cash flows.

Financial statements do not provide all the information users may need since they only show the financial effects of what has happened in the past and exclude a lot of non-financial information. Users work with financial statements to assess the stewardship of management and to make decisions.

underlying assumptions

When preparing financial statements, it is assumed they are prepared on the basis that the entity is a going concern.

Going concern means that financial statements are prepared on the assumption that the entity will continue in business for the foreseeable future. Thus there is no intention to liquidate or reduce the size of the business – if this was the case, the financial statements would have to be prepared on a different basis.

At the same time, it is important that financial performance reflects the principles of **accrual accounting**. Using the accrual basis means that the effects of transactions are recognised when they occur (and not when cash is received or paid) and they are recorded in the accounting records and reported in the financial statements of the periods to which they relate.

qualitative characteristics of useful financial information

The qualitative characteristics identify the types of information that are likely to be most useful to users of financial statements for making decisions. The *Conceptual Framework for Financial Reporting* identifies:

- fundamental qualitative characteristics
    - relevance
    - faithful representation
- enhancing qualitative characteristics
    - comparability
    - verifiability
    - timeliness
    - understandability

The diagram below shows these characteristics.

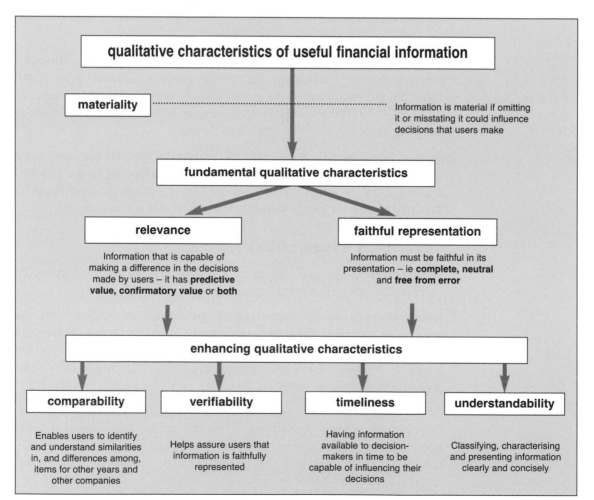

relevance

The diagram shows that, for information to be relevant, it must.

- be capable of making a difference in the decisions made by users
- have predictive value, which helps users to predict future outcomes
- have confirmatory value, which helps users to confirm previous evaluations

faithful representation

For the faithful representation of information it must:

- correspond to the effect of transactions or events
- as far as possible be **complete** (to include all information necessary for a user), **neutral** (without bias), and **free from error** (no errors in the description or process)

enhancing qualitative characteristics

- **comparability** enables users to identify and understand similarities in, and differences among, items for other years and other companies – a comparison relates to at least two items
- **verifiability** helps assure users that information is faithfully represented – can be direct (eg counting cash) or indirect (eg calculating inventory valuations using a method such as first-in, first-out)
- **timeliness** means having information available to decision-makers in time to be capable of influencing their decisions – generally the older the information is the less useful it is
- **understandability** means that information is classified, characterised and presented clearly and concisely – financial reports are prepared on the basis that users and their advisers have a reasonable knowledge of business and economic activities

materiality

Under the heading of qualitative characteristics, the *Conceptual Framework for Financial Reporting* also refers to **materiality**. Although materiality is rarely defined in law or accounting standards, the preparer of financial statements must make judgements as to whether or not an item is material. As the *Conceptual Framework* says: 'Information is material if omitting it or misstating it could influence the decisions that users make on the basis of financial information about a specific reporting entity.' It goes on to say: 'Materiality is an entity-specific aspect of relevance based on the nature or magnitude, or both, of the items to which the information relates in the context of an individual entity's financial report.' Thus materiality depends very much on the size of the business: a large company may consider that items of less than £1,000 are not material; a small company will use a much lower figure. What is material, and what is not, becomes a matter of judgement, based on the overall relevance of the financial information.

the elements of financial statements

Elements of financial statements are the classes of items that financial statements comprise. They have been discussed in detail earlier in this chapter (page 8).

financial position – the statement of financial position

The principal elements are assets, liabilities and equity.

An **asset** is a resource controlled by the entity as a result of past events and from which future economic benefits are expected to flow.

A **liability** is a present obligation of the entity arising from past events, the settlement of which is expected to result in an outflow of resources.

Equity is the residual interest in the assets of the entity after deducting all its liabilities. It includes funds contributed by shareholders, retained earnings, and other gains and losses.

financial performance – the statement of profit or loss

Profits or **losses** are increases or decreases in equity not resulting from contributions from shareholders. They are the result of comparing income and expenses. Note that profit is frequently used as a measure of performance – see Chapter 7, Interpretation of Financial Statements.

Income is an increase in economic benefits in the form of inflows or enhancements in assets that increase equity.

Expenses are decreases in economic benefits in the form of outflows or depletions of assets or the incurring of liabilities that decrease equity.

recognition in financial statements

Recognition is the process of including an element (ie assets, liabilities, equity, income, expenses) in the statements of financial position or profit or loss. An item should be recognised:

■ if it is probable that future economic benefits will flow to or from the entity; and
■ it has a cost or value that can be reliably measured.

measurement bases

Measurement is the process of determining the money amounts at which the elements are to be recognised and carried in the financial statements.

A number of different measurement bases are useful – sometimes in varying combinations – in financial statements. They include:

■ **historical cost** – assets are recorded at the amount paid, or the fair value (see page 96) at the time of acquisition; liabilities are recorded at the amount expected to be paid

- **current cost** – what it would cost to replace assets and liabilities at today's prices
- **realisable (settlement) value** – what the assets could be sold for, and the amount required to settle the liabilities, today
- **present value** – assets and liabilities are valued at the present discounted values of their future cash inflows and outflows

ACCOUNTING CONCEPTS

There are a number of accounting concepts which form the 'bedrock' of the preparation of financial statements. Some are included in the *Conceptual Framework for Financial Reporting* (see previous section), while others are discussed further in IAS 1, entitled *Presentation of Financial Statements* – see Chapter 3.

Accounting concepts are illustrated in the diagram on the next page and include:

business entity

This refers to the fact that financial statements record and report on the activities of one particular entity. They do not include the personal assets and liabilities of those who play a part in owning or running the entity.

materiality

Some items are of such low value that it is not worth recording them separately in the accounting records, ie they are not 'material'. Examples include

- small expense items grouped together as sundry expenses
- small end-of-year items of office stationery not valued for the purpose of financial statements
- low-cost non-current assets being charged as an expense in the statement of profit or loss

Materiality is important in the preparation of financial statements – see page 17.

going concern

This presumes that the entity to which the financial statements relate will continue in the foreseeable future, ie there is no intention to reduce significantly the size of the entity or to liquidate it. Values based on break-up (realisable) amounts tend not to be relevant to users seeking to assess the entity's ability to generate cash or to adapt to changing circumstances.

Going concern is the underlying assumption in the preparation of financial statements – see page 15.

accruals

This means that income and expenses are matched so that they concern the same goods or services and the same time period. The statement of profit or loss shows the amount of income that should have been received and the amount of expense that should have been incurred.

Accrual accounting is important in the preparation of financial statements – see page 15.

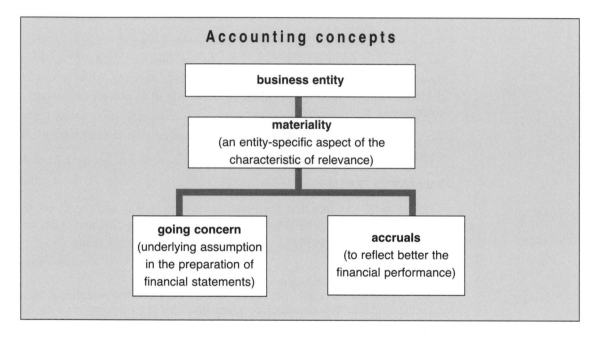

Chapter Summary

- Limited companies are a common form of business unit.

- There are two main types of limited companies:
  - public limited companies (plc)
  - private limited companies (ltd)

- Virtually all limited companies are in the private sector, where they are owned by shareholders.

- The profit motive is commonly the most important objective of companies.

- The three main financial statements used by limited companies are a statement of profit or loss and other comprehensive income, a statement of financial position and a statement of cash flows.

- There is a wide variety of users of financial statements – investors, employees, lenders, suppliers, customers, competitors, government, the public.

- The elements of financial statements are: assets, liabilities, equity, income, expenses.

- The regulatory framework of accounting comprises
  - accounting standards
  - company law
  - Conceptual Framework for Financial Reporting

- International financial reporting standards have been developed with the aim of harmonising international financial reporting. They comprise International Accounting Standards (IASs) and International Financial Reporting Standards (IFRSs).

- The *Conceptual Framework for Financial Reporting* sets out the concepts that underlie the preparation and presentation of financial statements for external users.

- Accounting concepts form the 'bedrock' of the preparation of financial statements; they include: business entity, materiality, going concern and accruals.

limited company	business entity in the private sector, generally owned by shareholders who are looking for profits
stewardship	management of a company is accountable for the safe-keeping of the company's resources, and for their proper, efficient and profitable use
making decisions	existing and potential investors, lenders and other creditors make use of financial reporting to make decisions about providing resources to the entity
elements of financial statements	the building blocks from which financial statements are constructed
accounting equation	assets *minus* liabilities *equals* equity
IAS	International Accounting Standard
IFRS	International Financial Reporting Standard
financial position	information is provided in a statement of financial position
financial performance	information is provided in a statement of profit or loss and other comprehensive income
changes in financial position	information is provided in a statement of cash flows

Activities

1.1   Which **ONE** of the following statements is correct?

		✓
(a)	assets = equity – liabilities	
(b)	equity = assets + liabilities	
(c)	equity = assets – liabilities	
(d)	liabilities = assets + equity	

1.2   Which **ONE** of the following statements is correct?

		✓
(a)	profits or losses = assets + income	
(b)	profits or losses = income – expenses \	
(c)	income = expenses – profits or losses	
(d)	expenses = income + profits or losses	

1.3   Which **ONE** of the following options is correct?

	Assets £	Liabilities £	Equity £	✓
(a)	80,250	35,000	45,000	
(b)	75,400	15,100	90,500	
(c)	68,350	26,800	41,550	
(d)	96,850	37,500	49,350	

1.4   Which **ONE** of the following options is correct?

	Income £	Expenses £	Profit/(Loss) £	✓
(a)	76,400	73,900	2,500	
(b)	47,800	43,200	(4,600)	
(c)	55,100	56,200	1,100	
(d)	33,400	18,300	51,700	

1.5 You are to fill in the missing figures for the following businesses:

	Assets £	Liabilities £	Equity £
Business A	70,800	....	39,200
Business B	....	27,300	64,700
Business C	105,100	46,600	....
Business D	98,900	....	50,300

1.6 You are to fill in the missing figures for the following businesses:

	Income £	Expenses £	Profit/(Loss) £
Business M	56,300	39,700	....
Business N	77,400	....	(8,300)
Business O	....	51,600	12,800
Business P	94,900	....	(4,100)

1.7 The statement of financial position of a company shows the following:

Assets £10,000 – Liabilities £4,500 = Equity £5,500

The company subsequently makes two transactions:

(1) it purchases inventories for £2,500 on credit

(2) it sells the inventories purchased in (1) for £3,500 cash

Required:

(a) Explain what each of the terms 'assets', 'liabilities' and 'equity' means.

(b) Explain the effect of each of the two transactions on the elements in the statement of financial position.

(c) State the accounting equation for the business after the two transactions have taken place.

(d) Draft a simple statement of profit or loss for the two transactions.

1.8 Explain the purpose of the three main financial statements used by limited companies for financial reporting.

statement of profit or loss and other comprehensive income

statement of financial position

statement of cash flows

1.9 **(a)** State the objective of financial reporting as defined by the *Conceptual Framework for Financial Reporting.*

(b) State the three user groups identified by the *Conceptual Framework for Financial Reporting.*

1.

2.

3.

1.10 **(a)** Define the terms asset and liability in accordance with the definitions in the *Conceptual Framework for Financial Reporting.*

asset

liability

(b) Show how the definitions of asset and liability apply to inventories and trade payables.

inventories

trade payables

1.11 Define the terms income and expenses in accordance with the definitions in the *Conceptual Framework for Financial Reporting*.

income

expenses

1.12 **(a)** From the *Conceptual Framework for Financial Reporting* state the two fundamental qualitative characteristics that make financial information useful.

1.

2.

(b) Explain what is meant by each of the two fundamental qualitative characteristics identified above.

1.13 The *Conceptual Framework for Financial Reporting* identifies four enhancing qualitative characteristics that make financial information useful. From the following list, which are the four enhancing qualitative characteristics?

	✓
verifiability	
materiality	
going concern	
timeliness	
understandability	
faithful representation	
comparability	
relevance	

1.14 Write in the accounting concept which relates to each of the statements below.

Statement	Accounting concept
(a) Some items are of such low value that it is not worth recording them separately in the accounting records.	
(b) The financial statements record and report on the activities of one particular entity.	
(c) Income and expenses are matched so that they concern the same goods or services and the same time period.	
(d) The presumption is that the entity to which the financial statements relate will continue in the foreseeable future.	

1.15 The directors of Machier Limited have asked you a number of questions about financial statements. Prepare notes for the directors answering the following questions:

(a) What are the elements in a statement of financial position of a company? State which of the balances in the statement of financial position of Machier Limited (shown below) fall under each element.

(b) How are the elements related in the accounting equation? Show numerically that the accounting equation is maintained in the statement of financial position of Machier Limited.

Machier Limited	
Statement of financial position as at 31 March 20-9	
	£000
Non-current assets	4,282
Current assets	
Inventories	448
Trade receivables	527
Cash	–
	975
Total assets	5,257
Share capital	200
Share premium	100
Retained earnings	1,408
Total equity	1,708
Non-current liabilities: loan	2,800
Current liabilities	
Trade payables	381
Tax	165
Bank overdraft	203
	749
Total liabilities	3,549
Total equity and liabilities	5,257

1.16 The *Conceptual Framework for Financial Reporting* states that:

'The objective of general purpose financial reporting is to provide financial information about the reporting entity that is useful to existing and potential investors, lenders and other creditors in making decisions about providing resources to the entity.'

You are to:

(a) State which financial statement provides information on

- financial position

- financial performance

- changes in financial position

(b) State what is meant by the term 'entity'.

(c) Suggest a decision that might be made by each user of financial statements and which is helped by information contained in the financial statements.

for your notes

2 Introduction to limited company financial statements

this chapter covers...

In this chapter we focus on the financial statements of limited companies and look at:

- *accounting terminology used in limited company financial statements*

- *the advantages of forming a limited company*

- *the differences between a private limited company, a public limited company, and a company limited by guarantee*

- *the information contained in a company's Articles of Association*

- *the differences between ordinary shares and preference shares*

- *the concept of reserves, and the difference between capital reserves and revenue reserves*

- *the layout of limited company financial statements for 'internal use'*

ACCOUNTING TERMINOLOGY USED IN FINANCIAL STATEMENTS

The accounting terminology used in limited company financial statements follows the terms used in international financial reporting standards (IFRS). This is shown in the left-hand column of the table below. Other terms which are sometimes used in sole trader and partnership financial statements are shown in the right-hand column. In this book we use IFRS terminology throughout as this is the practice in the published financial statements of all larger limited companies.

Accounting terminology

IFRS terms	Other terms
Statement of profit or loss	*Profit and loss account*
Revenue	Turnover (sales)
Profit from operations	Operating profit
Statement of financial position	*Balance sheet*
Non-current assets	Fixed assets
Property, plant and equipment	Tangible assets
Inventories	Stocks
Trade receivables	Trade debtors
Cash and cash equivalents (see page 160)	Cash at bank and in hand
Trade payables	Trade creditors
Non-current liabilities	Long-term liabilities
Total equity	Capital and reserves
Retained earnings	Profit and loss balance
Non-controlling interest (see page 245)	Minority interest

Please note that from your previous studies you will be familiar with the terms 'trade receivables' and 'trade payables'; in limited company financial statements these are usually referred to as 'trade receivables and other receivables' and 'trade payables and other payables'.

In this chapter we will study the 'internal use' financial statements, rather than being concerned with the detailed requirements of international financial reporting standards; however, we will use IFRS terminology throughout. The published financial statements of limited companies are studied in Chapter 3.

ADVANTAGES OF FORMING A LIMITED COMPANY

A limited company is a separate legal entity, owned by shareholders and managed by directors.

The limited company is often chosen as the legal status of a business for a number of reasons:

limited liability

The shareholders (members) of a company can only lose the amount of their investment, being the money paid already, together with any money unpaid on their shares (unpaid instalments on new share issues, for example). Thus, if the company became insolvent (went 'bust'), shareholders would have to pay any unpaid instalments to help pay the liabilities. As this happens very rarely, shareholders are usually in a safe position: their personal assets, unless pledged as security to a lender (as in the case of a director/shareholder), are not available to pay the company's liabilities.

separate legal entity

A limited company is a separate legal entity from its owners. Anyone taking legal action proceeds against the company and not the individual shareholders.

ability to raise finance

A limited company can raise substantial funds from outside sources by the issue of shares:

- for the larger public company – from the public and investing institutions on the Stock Exchange or similar markets
- for the smaller company – privately from venture capital companies, relatives and friends

Companies can also raise finance by means of debentures (see page 37).

membership

A member of a limited company is a person who owns at least one share in that company. A member of a company is the same as a shareholder.

other factors

A limited company is usually a much larger business unit than a sole trader or partnership. This gives the company a higher standing and status in the business community, allowing it to benefit from economies of scale, and making it of sufficient size to employ specialists for functions such as production, marketing, finance and human resources.

THE COMPANIES ACTS

Limited companies are regulated by the Companies Acts of 1985, 1989 and 2006.

Under the Acts there are two main types of limited company: the larger public limited company (abbreviated to 'Plc'), which is defined in the Act, and the smaller company, traditionally known as a private limited company (abbreviated to 'Ltd'), which is any other limited company. A further type of company is limited by guarantee.

public limited company (Plc)

A company may become a public limited company if it has:

■ issued share capital of over £50,000

■ at least two members (shareholders) and at least two directors

A public limited company may raise capital from the public on the Stock Exchange or similar markets – the new issues and privatisations of recent years are examples of this. A public limited company does not have to issue shares on the stock markets, and not all do so.

private limited company (Ltd)

The private limited company is the most common form of limited company and is defined by the Companies Act 2006 as 'any company that is not a public company'. Many private limited companies are small companies, often in family ownership. A private limited company has:

- no minimum requirement for issued share capital
- at least one member (shareholder) and at least one director who may be the sole shareholder

The shares are not traded publicly, but are transferable between individuals, although valuation will be more difficult for shares not quoted on the stock markets.

company limited by guarantee

A company limited by guarantee is not formed with share capital, but relies on the guarantee of its members to pay a stated amount in the event of the company's insolvency. Examples of such companies include charities, and artistic and educational organisations.

GOVERNING DOCUMENTS OF COMPANIES

There are a number of documents required by the Companies Act in the setting-up of a company. One essential governing document is the **Articles of Association**, which:

- provides the constitution of the company
- regulates the affairs of the company to the outside world
- sets out the rules for running the company, including the powers of directors and the holding of company meetings

TYPES OF SHARES ISSUED BY LIMITED COMPANIES

The **authorised share capital** – also known as the nominal or registered capital – is the maximum share capital that the company is allowed to issue. For companies formed prior to the Companies Act 2006, the statement of authorised share capital is given in a governing document of the company called the Memorandum of Association. Under the terms of the Companies Act 2006 there is no requirement for a company to have authorised capital – however, many companies will have been formed under earlier company legislation.

Where a company has an amount stated for authorised capital it can increase the amount by passing a resolution at a general meeting of the shareholders. This will enable a company that has already issued the amount of the authorised capital to expand the business by issuing more shares.

Authorised share capital can be shown on the statement of financial position (or as a note to the accounts) 'for information', but is not added into the total of the statement of financial position, as it may not be the same amount as the **issued share capital**. By contrast, the issued share capital – showing the classes and number of shares that have been issued – is included in the equity section of the statement of financial position.

The authorised and issued share capital may be divided into a number of classes or types of share; the main types are **ordinary shares** and, less commonly, **preference shares**.

ordinary (equity) shares

These are the most commonly issued class of share which carry the main 'risks and rewards' of the business: the risks are of losing part or all of the value of the shares if the business loses money or becomes insolvent; the rewards are that they take a share of the profits – in the form of **dividends** – after allowance has been made for all expenses of the business, including finance costs (eg loan and debenture interest), tax, and after preference dividends (if any). When a company makes large profits, it will have the ability to pay higher dividends to the ordinary shareholders; when losses are made, the ordinary shareholders may receive no dividend.

Companies rarely pay out all of their profits in the form of dividends; most retain some profits as reserves. These can always be used to enable a dividend to be paid in a year when the company makes little or no profit, always assuming that the company has sufficient cash in the bank to make the payment. Ordinary shareholders, in the event of the company becoming insolvent, will be the last to receive any repayment of their investment: other liabilities will be paid off first.

Ordinary shares usually carry voting rights – thus shareholders have a say at the annual general meeting and at any other shareholders' meetings.

preference shares

Whereas ordinary share dividends will vary from year-to-year, preference shares usually carry a fixed percentage rate of dividend – for example, five per cent of nominal value. Their dividends are paid in preference to those of ordinary shareholders; but they are only paid if the company makes profits. In the event of the company ceasing to trade, the preference shareholders will also receive repayment of capital before the ordinary shareholders.

Preference shares do not normally carry voting rights.

nominal and market values of shares

Each share has a **nominal value** – or par value – which is entered in the accounts. Shares may be issued with nominal values of 5p, 10p, 25p, 50p or £1, or indeed for any amount. Thus a company with an authorised share capital of £100,000 might divide this up into:

100,000 ordinary shares of 50p each	£50,000
50,000 five per cent preference shares of £1 each	£50,000
	£100,000

Note that some shares are issued with no par value.

The nominal value usually bears little relationship to the **market value**. The market value is the price at which issued – or 'secondhand' – shares are traded. Share prices of a quoted public limited company may be listed in the *Financial Times* and other business newspapers.

issue price

This is the price at which shares are issued to shareholders by the company – either when the company is being set up, or at a later date when it needs to raise more funds. The issue price is either **at par** (ie the nominal value), or above nominal value. In the latter case, the amount of the difference between issue price and nominal value is known as a **share premium** (see page 40): for example – nominal value £1.00; issue price £1.50; therefore share premium is 50p per share.

LOANS AND DEBENTURES

In addition to money provided by shareholders, who are the owners of the company, further funds can be obtained by borrowing in the form of loans or debentures:

- **Loans** are monies borrowed by companies from lenders – such as banks – on a medium or long-term basis. Generally repayments are made throughout the period of the loan, but can often be tailored to suit the needs of the borrower. Invariably lenders require security for loans so that, if the loan is not repaid, the lender has an asset – such as property – that can be sold.

 Smaller companies are sometimes also financed by directors' loans.

- **Debentures** are formal certificates issued by companies raising long-term finance from lenders and investors. Debenture certificates issued by large public limited companies are often traded on the Stock Exchange. Debentures are commonly secured against assets such as property that, in the event of the company ceasing to trade, could be sold and used to repay the debenture holders.

Loans and debentures usually carry fixed rates of interest that must be paid, just like other overheads, whether a company makes profits or not. Loan and debenture interest is shown in the statement of profit or loss as 'finance costs'. In the event of the company ceasing to trade, loan and debenture-holders would be repaid before any shareholders. On the statement of financial position, loans and debentures are usually shown as non-current liabilities.

STATEMENT OF PROFIT OR LOSS AND OTHER COMPREHENSIVE INCOME

The statement of profit or loss and other comprehensive income of a limited company is very similar to the statement of profit or loss of a sole trader or partnership. However there are two overhead items commonly found in the statement of profit or loss of a limited company that are not found in the statements of other business types:

- **directors' remuneration** – as directors are employed by the company, the amount paid to them appears amongst the overheads of the company

- **debenture interest** – as already noted, when debentures are issued by companies, the interest is shown under the heading of 'finance costs'

The statement of profit or loss and other comprehensive income shows the profit for the year (although other items – such as the revaluation of property – are shown after profit in order to show the total comprehensive income of the company – see page 60). Limited company financial statements require a further statement – a statement of changes in equity – to show how the profit for the year has been distributed and to provide a link to the statement of financial position. The statement of changes in equity will be covered in more detail in Chapter 3. For the time being, we will use the following layout to demonstrate some of the changes in equity:

Statement of changes in equity

Retained earnings*	£
Balance at start of year	x
Profit for the year from continuing operations	x
Transfers from other reserves	x
	x
Dividends paid	(x)
Transfers to other reserves	(x)
Balance at end of year	x

*   retained earnings is a revenue reserve – see page 40

Notes:

■ dividends paid – all dividends **paid** during the accounting period; these include **interim dividends** (usually paid just over half-way through the financial year) and the previous year's **final dividends** (proposed at the end of the previous year, but paid early in the current financial year)

■ transfers to and from other reserves – see below

■ the balance at the end of the year is shown on the statement of financial position as 'retained earnings' in the total equity section

The diagram on pages 42 and 43 shows the statement of profit or loss (for internal use) of Orion Limited as an example.

STATEMENT OF FINANCIAL POSITION

The statements of financial position of limited companies follow a similar layout for those of sole traders and partnerships, but the total equity section is more complex with the issued shares and various reserves. The diagram on pages 44 and 45 shows the statement of financial position (for internal use) of Orion Limited as an example (published accounts are covered in the next chapter).

The layout of a statement of financial position usually includes lines for amounts to be shown for **total assets** and **total liabilities**. The total assets comprise the non-current assets and current assets, while the total liabilities comprise non-current liabilities and current liabilities – both totals are arrowed in the example statement of financial position on page 45. In this way, the accounting equation of assets minus liabilities equals equity can be proven.

RESERVES

A limited company rarely distributes all its profits to its shareholders. Instead, it will often keep part of the profits earned each year in the form of reserves. As the statement of financial position of Orion Limited shows (page 45), there are two types of reserves:

■ capital reserves, which are created as a result of non-trading activities

■ revenue reserves, which include retained earnings from the statement of profit or loss

capital reserves

Examples of capital reserves (which cannot be used to fund dividend payments, ie they are non-distributable) include:

■ **Revaluation reserve.** This occurs when a non-current asset, most probably property, is revalued (in an upwards direction). The amount of the revaluation is recorded as other comprehensive income (see page 60) and placed in a revaluation reserve on the statement of financial position where it increases the value of the shareholders' investment in the company. Note, however, that this is purely a 'book' adjustment – no cash has changed hands.

In the example below a company revalues its property upwards by £250,000 from £500,000 to £750,000.

STATEMENT OF FINANCIAL POSITION (EXTRACTS)

	£
Before revaluation	
Non-current asset: property at cost	500,000
Share capital: ordinary shares of £1 each	500,000
After revaluation	
Non-current asset: property at revaluation	750,000
Share capital: ordinary shares of £1 each	500,000
Capital reserve: revaluation reserve	250,000
Total equity	750,000

■ **Share premium account.** An established company may issue additional shares to the public at a higher amount than the nominal value. For example, Orion Ltd (page 45) may seek finance for further expansion by issuing additional ordinary shares. Although the shares have a nominal value of £1 each, because Orion is a well-established company, the shares are issued at £1.50 each. Of this amount, £1 is recorded in the issued share capital section, and the extra 50p is the share premium.

revenue reserves

Revenue reserves are profits generated from trading activities; they have been retained in the company to help build the company for the future. Revenue reserves include the balance of retained earnings from the statement of changes in equity (see page 38). Also, there may be named revenue reserve accounts, such as **general reserve**, or a revenue reserve for a specific purpose, such as **reserve for the replacement of plant and equipment**. Transfers to or from these named revenue reserve accounts are made in the statement of changes in equity. Revenue reserves are distributable, ie they can be used to fund dividend payments.

reserves: profits not cash

It should be noted that reserves – both capital and revenue – are not cash funds to be used whenever the company needs money, but are in fact represented by assets shown on the statement of financial position. The reserves record the fact that the assets belong to the shareholders via their ownership of the company.

STATEMENT OF PROFIT OR LOSS – TERMINOLOGY

The two terms 'statement of profit or loss' and 'statement of profit or loss and other comprehensive income' are in common use throughout the AAT Assessment and this book.

Generally in the book we have used the 'profit or loss and other comprehensive income' term in text which describes aspects of financial statements; the exceptions are in the chapters for interpretation of financial statements and consolidated financial statements – where the 'profit or loss' term is used – on the grounds that these assessment topics do not usually feature other comprehensive income.

For the headings of financial statements, where the profit or loss statement finishes with the line 'Profit for the year from continuing operations' then the heading used is 'Statement of profit or loss'. Where the profit or loss statement lists other comprehensive income and finishes with the line 'Total comprehensive income for the year (see Chapter 3) then the heading used is 'Statement of profit or loss and other comprehensive income'.

In practice, in the AAT Assessment, most headings are already completed as part of the pro-forma layouts.

EXAMPLE FINANCIAL STATEMENTS

On pages 42 to 45 are set out the statement of profit or loss and statement of financial position for Orion Limited, a private limited company. Note that these are the 'internal use' financial statements – the detailed layouts required by international financial reporting standards are covered in Chapter 3.

Explanations of the financial statements are set out in each case on the left-hand page.

year dates, negative amounts

Note that year dates are shown in the book as either 20-1 or 20X1; negative money amounts are shown with either brackets, eg (£1,000), or with a minus sign, eg –£1,000.

ACCESSIBILITY OF FINANCIAL STATEMENTS

Limited company financial statements are far more readily accessible to interested parties than the financial statements of sole traders and partnerships:

- all limited companies must submit financial statements to Companies House where they are available for public inspection

- a copy of the financial statements is available to all shareholders, together with a report on the company's activities during the year

- the statements of profit or loss and financial position of larger public limited companies are commented on and discussed in the media

- the financial statements of larger public limited companies are freely available to potential investors, lenders and other interested parties – the web directory, at the beginning of the book, lists some companies whose financial statements are available online

The **overheads** of a limited company are usually split between distribution costs and administrative expenses.

The company has recorded a **profit from operations** of £49,000, before deduction of finance costs (such as debenture interest, bank and loan interest).

Tax, the corporation tax that a company has to pay, based on its profits, is shown. We shall not be studying the detailed calculations for corporation tax in this book. It is, however, important to see how the tax is recorded in the financial statements.

Profit for the year from continuing operations, ie after deducting finance costs and tax is taken to the statement of changes in equity.

The **statement of changes in equity** demonstrates how profit for the year is added to the brought forward balance of retained earnings (a revenue reserve), while dividends paid during the year are deducted. The resultant balance of retained earnings at the end of the year is shown in the equity section of the statement of financial position. There is more on the statement of changes in equity in Chapter 3.

ORION LIMITED

Statement of profit or loss for the year ended 31 December 20-3

	£	£
Continuing operations		
Revenue		725,000
Opening inventories	45,000	
Purchases	381,000	
	426,000	
Closing inventories	−50,000	
Cost of sales		−376,000
Gross profit		349,000
Overheads:		
Distribution costs	−75,000	
Administrative expenses	225,000	
Profit from operations		49,000
Finance costs (debenture interest)		−6,000
Profit before tax		43,000
Tax		−15,000
Profit for the year from continuing operations		28,000

Statement of changes in equity

	£
Retained earnings	
Balance at 1 January 20-3	41,000
Profit for the year	28,000
	69,000
Dividends paid	−20,000
Balance at 31 December 20-3	49,000

The **non-current assets** section of a limited company statement of financial position usually distinguishes between:

intangible non-current assets, which do not have material substance but belong to the company and have value, eg goodwill (the amount paid for the reputation and connections of a business that has been taken over), patents and trademarks; the intangible non-current assets are amortised (depreciated) and/or are subject to impairment reviews.

property, plant and equipment, which are tangible (ie have material substance) non-current assets and are depreciated over their useful lives and may be subject to impairment reviews.

Authorised share capital, where applicable, can be included on the statement of financial position 'for information', but is not added into the total, as it may not be the same amount as the issued share capital. It can also be disclosed as a note to the accounts.

Issued share capital shows the shares that have been issued. In this statement of financial position, the shares are described as being fully paid, meaning that the company has received the full amount of the value of each share from the shareholders. Sometimes shares will be partly paid, eg ordinary shares of £1, but 75p paid. This means that the company can make a call on the shareholders to pay the extra 25p to make the shares fully paid.

Capital reserves are created as a result of non-trading activities and are non-distributable. Changes are recorded through the statement of profit or loss and other comprehensive income.

Revenue reserves are retained earnings from the statement of changes in equity and are distributable.

Total equity represents the stake of the ordinary shareholders in the company. It comprises ordinary share capital, plus capital and revenue reserves.

Non-current liabilities are those where repayment is more than twelve months from the date of the statement of financial position, eg loans and debentures.

As well as the usual **current liabilities**, where payment is due within twelve months of the date of the statement of financial position, this section also contains the amount of tax payable within the next twelve months.

ORION LIMITED
Statement of financial position as at 31 December 20-3

ASSETS Non-current assets	Cost £	Impairment/ Dep'n to date £	Net £
Intangible			
Goodwill	50,000	20,000	30,000
Property, plant and equipment			
Freehold land and buildings	280,000	40,000	240,000
Machinery	230,000	100,000	130,000
Fixtures and fittings	100,000	25,000	75,000
	660,000	185,000	475,000
Current assets			
Inventories			50,000
Trade and other receivables			38,000
Cash and cash equivalents			21,000
			109,000
Total assets			584,000
EQUITY AND LIABILITIES			
Equity			
Authorised share capital			
600,000 ordinary shares of £1 each			600,000
Issued share capital			
400,000 ordinary shares of £1 each, fully paid			400,000
Capital reserve			
Share premium			30,000
Revenue reserve			
Retained earnings			49,000
Total equity			479,000
Non-current liabilities			
10% debentures			60,000
			60,000
Current liabilities			
Trade and other payables			30,000
Tax liability			15,000
			45,000
Total liabilities			105,000
Total equity and liabilities			584,000

Note: The amounts shown for total assets and total liabilities (arrowed above) confirm the accounting equation of assets minus liabilities equals equity, here £584,000 – £105,000 = £479,000.

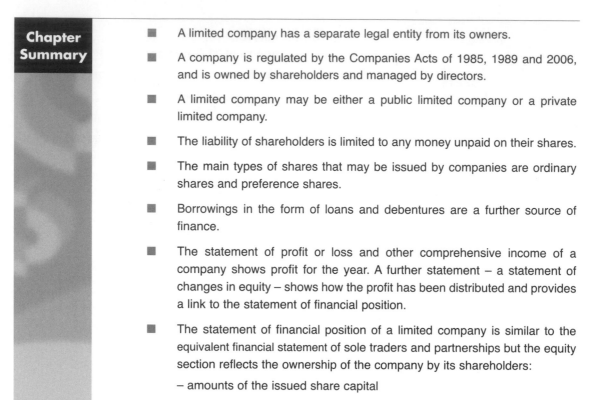

Chapter Summary

■   A limited company has a separate legal entity from its owners.

■   A company is regulated by the Companies Acts of 1985, 1989 and 2006, and is owned by shareholders and managed by directors.

■   A limited company may be either a public limited company or a private limited company.

■   The liability of shareholders is limited to any money unpaid on their shares.

■   The main types of shares that may be issued by companies are ordinary shares and preference shares.

■   Borrowings in the form of loans and debentures are a further source of finance.

■   The statement of profit or loss and other comprehensive income of a company shows profit for the year. A further statement – a statement of changes in equity – shows how the profit has been distributed and provides a link to the statement of financial position.

■   The statement of financial position of a limited company is similar to the equivalent financial statement of sole traders and partnerships but the equity section reflects the ownership of the company by its shareholders:

  – amounts of the issued share capital

  – details of capital reserves and revenue reserves

Key Terms

limited company	a separate legal entity owned by shareholders and managed by directors
limited liability	shareholders of a company are liable for company debts only to the extent of any money unpaid on their shares
shareholder	person who owns at least one share in a limited company; a shareholder is also a member of a company
public limited company	a company, registered as a plc, with an issued share capital of over £50,000 and at least two members and at least two directors; it may raise funds on the stock markets
private limited company	any limited company with share capital that is not a public company
Articles of Association	the document that provides the constitution of the company, regulates the affairs of the company to the outside world, and sets out the rules for running the company

ordinary shares	commonly issued type of shares which take a share in the profits of the company, in the form of dividends, but which also carry the main risks
preference shares	shares which carry a fixed rate of dividend paid, subject to sufficient profits, in preference to ordinary shareholders; in event of repayment of capital, rank before the ordinary shareholders
debentures	issued by companies raising long-term finance; debenture interest is a finance cost in the statement of profit or loss
nominal value	the par value of the shares entered in the financial statements
issue price	the price at which shares are issued to shareholders by the company
market value	the price at which shares are traded
directors' remuneration	amounts paid to directors as employees of the company; an overhead in the statement of profit or loss
corporation tax	tax paid by a company on its profit
statement of changes in equity	statement which shows how the profit for the year has been distributed and provides a link to the retained earnings figure shown in the statement of financial position
dividends	amounts paid to shareholders from the profit of the company; an interim dividend is paid just over half-way through a financial year; a final dividend is paid early in the following year
issued share capital	the classes and number of shares that have been issued by the company
reserves	profits retained by the company; two main types: – capital reserves, created as a result of non-trading activities, are non-distributable – revenue reserves, eg retained profits from the statement of profit or loss, are distributable
revaluation reserve	capital reserve created by the upwards revaluation of a non-current asset, most usually property; cannot be used to fund dividend payments
share premium account	capital reserve created by the issue of shares at a price higher than nominal value, the excess being credited to share premium; cannot be used to fund dividend payment

Activities

- Blank photocopiable pro-formas in the format used in AAT Assessments – of the statement of profit or loss and other comprehensive income and the statement of financial position are included in the Appendix – it is advisable to enlarge them to full A4 size. Blank workings sheets are also included in the Appendix.
- Pro-formas and workings sheets are also available to download from www.osbornebooks.co.uk

2.1 Show whether the following statements about a public limited company are true or false?

✓

Statement	True	False
(a) There is no minimum requirement for issued share capital.		
(b) There must be at least two members (shareholders).		
(c) There must be at least one director.		
(d) The company does not have to issue shares on the stock markets.		
(e) The Articles of Association regulate the affairs of the company to the outside world.		

2.2 Distinguish between:

(a)	ordinary shares and preference shares
(b)	nominal value and market value of shares
(c)	capital reserves and revenue reserves

2.3 Explain where the following items appear in a limited company's financial statements:

(a)	debenture interest
(b)	directors' remuneration
(c)	corporation tax
(d)	dividends paid
(e)	revaluation reserve
(f)	goodwill

2.4   Which **ONE** of the following items would not appear in the statement of profit or loss and other comprehensive income of a limited company?

		✓
(a)	tax	
(b)	dividends paid	
(c)	finance costs	
(d)	cost of sales	

2.5   Which **ONE** of the following would not appear in the statement of financial position of a limited company?

		✓
(a)	tax liability	
(b)	retained earnings	
(c)	opening inventories	
(d)	closing inventories	

2.6   Which **ONE** of the following items is a revenue reserve of a limited company?

		✓
(a)	revaluation reserve	
(b)	retained earnings	
(c)	share premium	
(d)	share capital	

2.7   Which **ONE** of the following items is a capital reserve of a limited company?

		✓
(a)	general reserve	
(b)	retained earnings	
(c)	reserve for replacement of plant and equipment	
(d)	share premium	

2.8 Distinguish between:

(a) non-current liabilities

(b) current liabilities

Give an example of each.

2.9 What does 'total assets' comprise on a company statement of financial position?

		✓
(a)	non-current assets, plus current assets, less current liabilities	
(b)	non-current assets, plus current assets, plus equity	
(c)	non-current assets, plus current assets	
(d)	current assets, less current liabilities	

2.10 What does 'total equity and liabilities' comprise on a company statement of financial position?

		✓
(a)	issued share capital, plus share premium	
(b)	issued share capital, plus capital and revenue reserves	
(c)	issued share capital, plus capital and revenue reserves, plus non-current liabilities	
(d)	issued share capital, plus capital and revenue reserves, plus non-current liabilities, plus current liabilities	

2.11 A new company issues 300,000 ordinary shares of 50p each at a premium of 25 per cent. What amount will be shown as the total of the equity section of the company's statement of financial position?

		✓
(a)	£300,000	
(b)	£150,000	
(c)	£37,500	
(d)	£187,500	

> **Tutorial note:**
>
> Activities 2.12, 2.13 and 2.14 require the preparation of limited company year end financial statements from a trial balance and further information. When answering these Activities, please refer to the example financial statements shown on pages 43 and 45 of this chapter.
>
> You may also find it helpful to use the layouts and workings sheets given in the Appendix – full use of these will be explained in the next chapter.

2.12 Nelson Ltd prepares its financial statements to 31 March each year. At 31 March 20-2 its trial balance was as follows:

	Debit	Credit
	£000	£000
Administrative expenses	285	
Share capital		500
Trade and other receivables	570	
Cash and cash equivalents	35	
Share premium		140
Distribution costs	420	
Plant and equipment – cost	950	
– accumulated depreciation at 1 April 20-1		320
Retained earnings at 1 April 20-1		245
Purchases	960	
Inventories at 1 April 20-1	140	
Trade and other payables		260
Revenue		1,935
Dividends paid	40	
	3,400	3,400

Further information:

- Inventories at 31 March 20-2 cost £180,000.

- The corporation tax charge for the year has been calculated as £15,000.

- Depreciation of plant and equipment is to be provided for the year at 20% on a straight-line basis, and is to be apportioned 40% to administrative expenses and 60% to distribution costs.

- All of the operations are continuing operations.

Required:

Prepare the financial statements of Nelson Ltd for the year ended 31 March 20-2.

2.13 Wentworth Ltd prepares its financial statements to 31 March each year. At 31 March 20-5 its trial balance was as follows:

	Debit	Credit
	£000	£000
Administrative expenses	340	
Share capital		600
Trade and other receivables	230	
Cash and cash equivalents	95	
Share premium		80
Distribution costs	175	
Finance costs	25	
Dividends paid	110	
Plant and equipment – cost	1,200	
– accumulated depreciation at 1 April 20-4		360
Retained earnings at 1 April 20-4		330
Purchases	1,220	
Inventories at 1 April 20-4	210	
Trade and other payables		110
Revenue		2,125
	3,605	3,605

Further information:

- Inventories at 31 March 20-5 cost £190,000.

- The corporation tax charge for the year has been calculated as £15,000.

- Distribution costs of £20,000 prepaid at 31 March 20-5 are to be allowed for.

- Depreciation of plant and equipment is to be provided for the year at 15% on a straight-line basis, and is to be apportioned as follows:

	%
Cost of sales	50
Administrative expenses	25
Distribution costs	25

- All of the operations are continuing operations.

Required:

Prepare the financial statements of Wentworth Ltd for the year ended 31 March 20-5.

2.14 Blenheim Ltd prepares its financial statements to 31 March each year. At 31 March 20-4 its trial balance was as follows:

	Debit	Credit
	£000	£000
Share capital		2,500
Land and buildings - value/cost	3,500	
– accumulated depreciation at 1 April 20-3		125
Plant and equipment - cost	800	
accumulated depreciation at 1 April 20-3		300
Purchases	2,100	
Revenue		3,650
Distribution costs	650	
Administrative expenses	420	
Accruals		50
Interest paid	90	
Trade and other receivables	190	
Trade and other payables		170
Retained earnings at 1 April 20-3		495
Inventories at 1 April 20-3	230	
6% bank loan repayable 20-9		1,500
Cash and cash equivalents	670	
Dividends paid	140	
	8,790	8,790

Further information:

- Trade receivables include a debt of £8,000 which is to be written off. Bad (irrecoverable) debts are to be classified as administrative expenses.

- Inventories at 31 March 20-4 cost £250,000.

- Depreciation on buildings of £500,000, included in the land and buildings figure, is to be provided for the year at 5 per cent on a straight-line basis and is to be allocated to administrative expenses.

- Depreciation on plant and equipment is to be provided at the rate of 20% for the year on a reducing balance basis, and apportioned equally between distribution costs and administrative expenses.

- The corporation tax charge for the year has been calculated as £35,000.

- Distribution costs of £10,000 owing at 31 March 20-4 are to be provided for.

- All of the operations are continuing operations.

Required:

Prepare the financial statements of Blenheim Ltd for the year ended 31 March 20-4.

3 Published financial statements of limited companies

this chapter covers...

In this chapter we focus on the published financial statements of limited companies and look at:

- *the purpose and components of financial statements*

- *the format of published financial statements*

- *dealing with dividends in the financial statements*

- *interpretation of the auditors' report*

- *the accounting policies followed by a particular company*

- *bonus issues and rights issues of shares*

Towards the end of the chapter (page 72) we see how a trial balance for a company is converted into the layout of published financial statements.

INTRODUCTION

All limited companies have shareholders. Each shareholder owns a part of the company and, although they do not take part in the day-to-day running of the company (unless they are also directors), they are entitled to know the financial results of the company.

Every limited company, whether public or private, is required by law to produce financial statements, which are also available for anyone to inspect if they so wish. We need to distinguish between the **statutory accounts** and the **annual report and accounts**. The **statutory accounts** are required to be produced under company law, and a copy is filed with the Registrar of Companies where it is available for public inspection.

The **annual report and accounts** – often referred to as the **corporate report** – is available to every shareholder and contains:

- statement of profit or loss and other comprehensive income

- statement of financial position

- statement of cash flows

- statement of changes in equity

- notes to the financial statements, including a statement of the company's accounting policies

- directors' report

- auditors' report

DUTIES AND RESPONSIBILITIES OF DIRECTORS

The directors of a limited company are elected by the shareholders to manage the company on their behalf. The directors are put in a position of trust by the shareholders to be responsible for the stewardship of the company's financial information.

The directors of a limited company have a duty to ensure that the provisions of the Companies Acts which relate to accounting records and statements are followed. The main provisions of the Acts are that:

- a company's accounting records must:
  - show and explain the company's transactions
  - disclose with reasonable accuracy at any time the financial position of the company

- enable the directors to ensure that the company's statements of profit or loss and other comprehensive income and financial position give a true and fair view of the company's financial position

■ a company's accounting records must contain:
  - day-to-day entries of money received and paid, together with details of the transactions
  - a record of the company's assets and liabilities
  - details of inventories held at the end of the year

■ a company's financial statements must be prepared in accordance with the Companies Act and with either UK accounting standards or international financial reporting standards (note that, in this book, we will study only financial statements which comply with IFRSs)

■ the directors must report annually to the shareholders on the way they have run the company on behalf of the shareholders

Every company director has a responsibility to ensure that the statutory accounts are produced and filed with the Registrar of Companies within a set time. The filing deadlines after the end of the accounting period are:

■ nine months for a private limited company

■ six months for a public limited company

There are penalties (fines) for late filing and, if the financial statements are too late, a company can be struck off the companies register.

The annual financial statements must be approved by the company's board of directors and the copy of the statement of financial position filed with the Registrar of Companies must be signed by one of the directors on behalf of the board. The directors must prepare a directors' report – this must be approved by the board and the copy to be filed with the Registrar of Companies signed on behalf of the board by a director (or the company secretary). The statutory accounts must be laid before the company at the annual general meeting, and they must be circulated beforehand to shareholders, debenture holders and any other persons entitled to attend the meeting.

IAS 1 – PRESENTATION OF FINANCIAL STATEMENTS

The objective of this accounting standard is to set out how financial statements should be presented to ensure comparability with previous accounting periods and with other entities. The standard states that *'the objective of financial statements is to provide information about the financial position, financial performance and cash flows of an entity that is useful to a wide range of users in making economic decisions'.*

Note that this definition is very similar to that stated in the *Conceptual Framework for Financial Reporting* – see the definition given on page 6 of this book.

Financial statements also show the results of management's stewardship of the resources entrusted to it. The statements provide information about an entity's:

■ assets

■ liabilities

■ equity

■ income and expenses, including gains and losses

■ contributions by, and distributions to, owners in their capacity as owners

■ cash flows

Such information – along with other information in the notes – assists users of financial statements in assessing the entity's future cash flows.

complete set of financial statements

IAS 1 states that a complete set of financial statements comprises:

■ statement of financial position

■ statement of profit or loss and other comprehensive income

■ statement of changes in equity

■ statement of cash flows

■ accounting policies and explanatory notes

■ comparative information for the preceding period

Note that IAS 1 states that:

■ all of the financial statements are to be given equal prominence

■ the statement of profit or loss and other comprehensive income can be presented
  – either as a single statement (which is how it appears in AAT Assessments)
  – or a profit or loss section, immediately followed by a separate statement of comprehensive income

overall considerations

The financial statements must present fairly the financial position, financial performance, and cash flows of an entity. The application of international financial reporting standards – supported by appropriate additional disclosures – is presumed to result in financial statements that achieve a fair presentation. IAS 1 requires that an entity whose financial statements comply with the standards should make an explicit and unreserved statement of such compliance in the notes.

IAS 1 requires compliance with a number of accounting concepts (see also pages 19-20) and other considerations:

- **going concern** – when an entity's financial statements are prepared in accordance with international financial reporting standards, the presumption is that the entity is a going concern, ie it will not cease to trade in the immediate future

- **accrual basis of accounting** – financial statements, except for cash flow information, are prepared under the accruals concept, ie income and expenses are matched to the same accounting period

- **materiality and aggregation** – each material class of similar items is to be presented separately in the financial statements, eg the classification of assets as non-current and current

- **offsetting** – generally it is not permitted to set off assets and liabilities, or income and expenses against each other in order to show a net figure, eg cash at bank is not netted off against a bank overdraft

- **frequency of reporting** – financial statements are prepared at least annually; however, when the reporting period changes, the financial statements will be for a period longer or shorter than one year and the entity must give the reason for the change and disclose that the amounts in the financial statements are not entirely comparable with those of previous periods

- **comparative information** – a requirement to show the figures from previous periods for all amounts shown in the financial statements in order to help users of the statements

structure and content – general principles

IAS 1 sets out the detailed disclosures to be shown on the face of the statement of profit or loss and other comprehensive income, statement of financial position, and statement of changes in equity. We shall be covering these later in this chapter.

There are some general principles that the standard requires. These include the identification of:

- the financial statements, which are to be distinguished from other information in the corporate report
- the name of the reporting entity

- whether the financial statements are for an individual entity or for a group (see Chapter 8)
- the period covered by the financial statements, eg for the year ended 31 December 20-6
- the currency of the financial statements, £s, €s, etc
- the level of rounding used for money amounts, thousands, millions, etc

STATEMENT OF PROFIT OR LOSS AND OTHER COMPREHENSIVE INCOME

The published statement of profit or loss and other comprehensive income does not have to detail every single overhead or expense incurred by the company – to do so would be to disclose important management information to competitors. Instead, the main items are summarised; however, IAS 1 requires that certain items must be detailed on the face of the statement, including:

- revenue
- finance costs
- share of the profit or loss of associates (see Chapter 8)
- tax expense
- other comprehensive income for the year (eg the revaluation of property)

Further detail may be needed to give information relevant to an understanding of financial performance.

Note that items of income and expense are not to be presented as extraordinary items, either on the face of the income statement or in the notes. When items are material, their nature and amount is to be disclosed separately.

The statement of profit or loss and other comprehensive income shows the:

- profit or loss
- total other comprehensive income
- comprehensive income for the year, ie the total of profit or loss and other comprehensive income (which is taken to the statement of changes in equity – see page 61)

Expenses in the statement of profit or loss and other comprehensive income must be analysed either by nature (raw materials, employee costs, depreciation, etc) or by function (cost of sales, distribution costs, administrative expenses, etc) – depending on which provides the more

XYZ PLC
Statement of profit or loss and other comprehensive income
for the year ended 31 December 20-9

	£000
Continuing operations	
Revenue	30,000
Cost of sales	−16,000
Gross profit	14,000
Distribution costs	−5,000
Administrative expenses	−4,000
Profit/(loss) from operations	5,000
Finance costs	−1,000
Profit/(loss) before tax	4,000
Tax	−1,500
Profit/(loss) for the year from continuing operations	2,500
Other comprehensive income for the year	
Gain on revaluation of property	500
Total comprehensive income for the year	3,000

Notes:
- IAS 1 does not permit items of income and expense to be described as 'extraordinary items'.
- All material items of income and expense are to be disclosed separately, either on the face of the statement of profit or loss and other comprehensive income or in the notes – examples include disposals of property, plant and equipment, disposals of investments, litigation settlements.
- In this example expenses are analysed by function – cost of sales, distribution costs, administrative expenses, etc. This is the analysis used in AAT Assessments.

reliable and relevant information. The analysis by nature is often appropriate for manufacturing companies, while the analysis by function is commonly used by trading companies. The example statement of comprehensive income of XYZ PLC on the next page (with sample figures) shows an analysis by function. Note that AAT Assessments only assess analysis by function.

Much of the detail shown in the statement of profit or loss and other comprehensive income is summarised. For example:

- revenue incorporates the figures for sales and sales returns

- cost of sales includes opening inventories, purchases, purchases returns, carriage inwards and closing inventories

- distribution costs include warehouse costs, post and packing, delivery drivers' wages, running costs of vehicles, depreciation of vehicles, etc

- administrative expenses include office costs, rent and rates, heating and lighting, depreciation of office equipment, etc

It is suggested that you study a recent statement of profit or loss and other comprehensive income for a large public limited company. The web directory at the beginning of this book lists some sources but all large plcs will have their financial statements available through their websites – search for 'financial statements' or 'investor centre'.

STATEMENT OF CHANGES IN EQUITY

IAS 1, *Presentation of Financial Statements,* requires that a statement of changes in equity is one of the components of financial statements. As its name implies, it shows the changes that have taken place to the shareholders' stake in the company – not only the profit or loss from continuing operations, but also other comprehensive income (such as the gain on the upward revaluation of property).

The information to be given in the statement of changes in equity is:

- total comprehensive income for the period (or profit for the year, if there is no other comprehensive income)
- for each item shown in the statement of changes in equity, a reconciliation between opening and closing balances which shows the reason for the change resulting from profit or loss, other comprehensive income and share capital
- the dividends paid to shareholders during the period

An example statement of changes in equity of XYZ PLC follows (with sample figures):

XYZ PLC
Statement of changes in equity for the year ended 31 December 20-9

	Share capital	Retained earnings	Share premium	Revaluation reserve	Total equity
	£000	£000	£000	£000	£000
Balance at 1 January 20-9	3,000	2,400	200	–	5,600
Changes in equity for the year					
Total comprehensive income*	–	2,500	–	500	3,000
Dividends	–	–600	–	–	–600
Issue of share capital	1,000	–	200	–	1,200
Balance at 31 December 20-9	4,000	4,300	400	500	9,200

* 'Profit for the year', if no other comprehensive income.

STATEMENT OF FINANCIAL POSITION

IAS 1, *Presentation of Financial Statements,* specifies the items to be shown on the statement of financial position as a minimum. The Standard does not, however, state the order in which the items are to be presented.

The items to be shown on the face of the statement of financial position include:

- property, plant and equipment
- investment property
- intangible assets
- financial assets (excluding investments, cash and receivables)
- investments accounted for using the equity method
- inventories
- trade and other receivables
- cash and cash equivalents
- trade and other payables
- provisions
- financial liabilities
- tax liabilities
- issued capital and reserves

In their statements of financial position, IAS 1 requires most companies to separate out current and non-current assets and liabilities. IAS 1 does, however, permit a presentation based on liquidity where it provides information that is reliable and more relevant – the order of liquidity of assets and liabilities is often used by banks and other financial institutions.

Current assets are

- cash or cash equivalents
- those to be realised, sold or used within the normal operating cycle
- assets held for trading and expected to be realised within twelve months

All other assets are non-current.

Examples of current assets are trade and other receivables, inventories, and cash and cash equivalents.

Current liabilities are:

- those expected to be settled within the normal operating cycle
- liabilities held for trading and expected to be settled within twelve months
- where the company does not have an unconditional right to defer payment beyond twelve months

All other liabilities are non-current.

Examples of current liabilities are trade and other payables, tax payable and bank overdraft.

Further detail can be given – either on the statement of financial position or in the notes. Examples include:

- property, plant and equipment may be shown by different classes – such as land and buildings, machinery, motor vehicles, office equipment, etc
- trade and other receivables may be split into amounts due from trade customers, prepayments, etc
- inventories can be sub classified into raw materials, work-in-progress, finished goods, etc
- share capital and reserves can be shown by the various classes of shares and reserves

In particular, IAS 1 requires the following disclosures about share capital (either on the statement of financial position or in the notes):

- the number of shares authorised
- the number of shares issued and fully paid, and issued but not fully paid
- the par value per share, or that the shares have no par value

---

Tutorial note:

IAS 1 does not set out a required format for the statement of financial position. An example of a statement of financial position of XYZ PLC which complies with IAS 1 is shown on the next page (with sample figures). Here assets are presented first, balanced against equity and liabilities.

XYZ PLC
Statement of Financial Position as at 31 December 20-9

	£000
ASSETS	
Non-current assets	
Intangible – Goodwill	50
Property, plant and equipment	9,750
	9,800
Current assets	
Inventories	1,190
Trade and other receivables	1,600
Cash and cash equivalents	10
	2,800
Total assets	12,600
EQUITY AND LIABILITIES	
Equity	
Share capital	4,000
Share premium	400
Revaluation reserve	500
Retained earnings	4,300
Total equity	9,200
Non-current liabilities	
Bank loans	1,600
	1,600
Current liabilities	
Trade and other payables	900
Tax payable	850
Bank overdrafts and loans	50
	1,800
Total liabilities	3,400
Total liabilities and equity	12,600

Note: The amounts shown for total assets and total liabilities confirm the accounting equation of assets minus liabilities equals equity, here £12,600 – £3,400 = £9,200.

It is suggested that you study a recent statement of financial position for a large public limited company – the web directory at the beginning of this book lists some sources.

DEALING WITH DIVIDENDS IN THE FINANCIAL STATEMENTS

Dividends are distributions to the shareholders, who own the company, as a return on their investment. Many companies pay dividends twice a year – an **interim dividend**, which is usually paid just over halfway through the financial year, and a **final dividend** which is paid early in the next financial year. The interim dividend is based on the profits reported by the company during the first half of the year, while the final dividend is based on the profits reported for the full year. The final dividend is proposed by the directors but has to be approved by shareholders at the Annual General Meeting of the company. Thus the financial calendar for a company with a financial year end of 31 December 20-9 might take the following form:

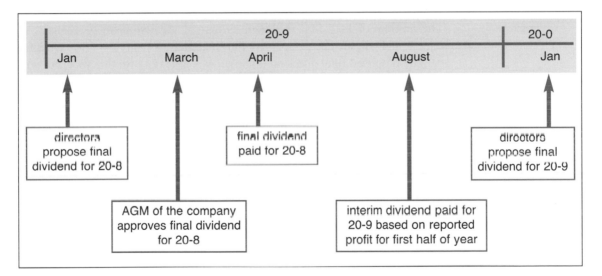

Only the dividends paid during the year can be recorded in the financial statements (see IAS 10, *Events after the Reporting Period*, page 146). In the above example, the dividends paid in April 20-9 (final dividend for the previous year) and August 20-9 (interim dividend for the current year) are recorded in the financial statements. The proposed final dividend for the year ended 31 December 20-9 is disclosed as a note to the financial statements, stating that it is subject to approval by the shareholders at the company's Annual General Meeting. An example of the note for dividends in the published financial statements of XYZ PLC follows (with sample figures):

XYZ PLC
DIVIDENDS
Note for published financial statements
for the year ended 31 December 20-9

	£000
Amounts recognised as distributions to equity holders during the year:	
• **Final dividend** for the year ended 31 December 20-8 of 7.5p per share	450
• **Interim dividend** for the year ended 31 December 20-9 of 2.5p per share	150
	600
Proposed final dividend for the year ended 31 December 20-9 of 8p per share	480

The proposed final dividend is subject to approval by shareholders at the Annual General Meeting and has not been included as a liability in these financial statements

---

The amount of £600,000 is shown as part of the statement of changes in equity, and will also be recorded in the statement of cash flows (see Chapter 6). The proposed final dividend is shown as a note only for this year, but will form part of dividends paid for next year.

The reason for treating proposed dividends in this way is that, until they are approved at the AGM, they are not liabilities of the company and should not, therefore, be shown in the financial statements.

DIRECTORS' REPORT

The directors' report includes review of the activities of the company over the past year and of likely developments in the future.

STATEMENT OF CASH FLOWS

IAS 7 requires that limited companies must include, in their financial statements, a statement of cash flows, which we will look at in detail in Chapter 6. Such a statement shows an overall view of money flowing in and out during an accounting period. It links profit with changes in assets and liabilities and the effect on the cash of the company.

AUDITORS' REPORT

Larger companies must have their financial statements audited by external auditors, who are appointed by the shareholders. The auditors' report, which is printed in the published financial statements, is the culmination of their work. The three main sections of the auditors' report are:

■ **respective responsibilities of directors and auditors** – the directors are responsible for preparing the financial statements, while the auditors are responsible for forming an opinion on the financial statements

■ **basis of opinion** – the framework of auditing standards within which the audit was conducted, other assessments, and the way in which the audit was planned and performed

■ **opinion** – the auditors' view of the company's financial statements

The opinion is 'unqualified' if the auditors are of the opinion that:

■ the financial statements have been prepared properly, and

■ they give a true and fair view of the company's affairs in accordance with company law and international financial reporting standards, and

■ the information given in the directors' report is consistent with the financial statements

The auditors' report may be 'qualified' if the auditors feel that certain parts of the financial statements have not been dealt with correctly and that this is important enough to be brought to the attention of the Registrar of Companies and other users of the financial statements, such as investors or suppliers.

Note that small and medium-sized private companies are exempt from audit requirements.

ACCOUNTING POLICIES

Accounting policies are the specific accounting methods selected by the directors and used by a company – such as the method of depreciation – in the preparation of financial statements. IAS 1, *Presentation of Financial Statements,* requires companies to disclose the accounting policies used as part of the notes to the financial statements. In selecting and applying accounting policies:

■ where an accounting policy is given in an accounting standard (IAS and IFRS) for a particular transaction, then that policy must apply

- where there is no accounting standard to give guidance, the management of the company must use its judgement to give information that is useful to users – eg investors, lenders, creditors – in making decisions

A company selects its accounting policies to fit the qualitative characteristics of useful financial information set out in the *Conceptual Framework for Financial Reporting* (see pages 16-17):

- relevance – giving information to users that is capable of making a difference in the decisions made by users

- faithful representation – giving information to users that is faithful in its presentation

- comparability – enabling users to make comparisons with information from previous accounting periods

- verifiability – assuring users that information is faithfully represented

- timeliness – providing information to users in time to be capable of influencing their decisions

- understandability – presenting information to users clearly and concisely

Once adopted by a company, accounting policies are to be applied consistently for similar transactions – unless a standard allows differing policies to be applied to categories of items. Changes of accounting policies can only occur:

- if the change is required by an accounting standard; or

- if the change results in the financial statements providing more relevant information that faithfully represents the effects of transactions on the financial statements

When there are changes in accounting policies, they are to be applied retrospectively. Any changes require the figure for equity and other figures from the statement of profit or loss and other comprehensive income and the statement of financial position to be altered for previous financial statements – subject to the practicalities of calculating the relevant amounts.

NOTES TO THE FINANCIAL STATEMENTS

IAS 1, *Presentation of Financial Statements,* requires a number of notes to the financial statements. These include:

- information about the basis of preparation of the financial statements and the specific accounting policies used

- disclosure of information required by international financial reporting standards that is not already included in the statements of profit or loss and other comprehensive income, changes in equity, financial position, or cash flows

■ the provision of additional information that is relevant to an understanding of the financial statements

Notes are to be presented systematically, with cross-referencing from the financial statements to the relevant note.

Included in the notes is to be a summary of significant accounting policies followed, including:

■ the measurement basis (or bases) – eg historical cost basis – used in preparing the financial statements, and

■ the other accounting policies used that are relevant to an understanding of the financial statements.

With regard to dividends, there must be disclosed in the notes the amount of dividends proposed or declared before the financial statements were authorised for issue but not recognised as a distribution to shareholders during the period, and the related amount per share (see page 66 for an example of this note).

BONUS ISSUES AND RIGHTS ISSUES

Limited companies – and particularly plcs – quite often increase their capital by means of either **bonus issues** or **rights issues** of shares. Whilst both of these have the effect of increasing the number of shares in issue, they have quite different effects on the structure of the company statement of financial position.

bonus issues

A bonus issue is made when a company issues free shares to existing shareholders; it does this by using reserves that have built up and capitalising them (ie they are turned into permanent share capital). The bonus issue is distributed on the basis of existing shareholdings – for example, one bonus share for every two shares already held.

With a bonus issue no cash flows in or out of the company. The shareholders are no better off: with more shares in issue the stock market price per share will fall in proportion to the bonus issue, ie the company's assets are now spread among a greater number of shares.

Bonus issues are made in order to acknowledge the fact that reserves belong to shareholders. Often a build-up of reserves occurs because a company hasn't the cash to pay dividends, so a bonus issue is a way of passing the reserves to shareholders.

Note that capital or revenue reserves can be used for bonus issues. If there is a choice, then capital reserves are used first – this is because it is one of the few uses of a capital reserve, which cannot be used to fund the payment of dividends.

rights issues

A rights issue is used by a company seeking to raise further finance through the issue of shares. Instead of going to the considerable expense of offering additional shares to the public, it is cheaper to offer shares to existing shareholders at a favourable price (usually a little below the current market price). As with a bonus issue the extra shares are offered in proportion to the shareholders' existing holding. The shareholder may take up the rights by subscribing for the shares offered; alternatively the rights can often be sold on the stock market.

Case Study

SEVERN PLC AND WYE PLC: BONUS ISSUES AND RIGHTS ISSUES

situation

The following are the summary statements of financial position of Severn plc and Wye plc:

	Severn £	Wye £
Non-current assets	300,000	300,000
Current assets (including bank)	100,000	100,000
Total assets	400,000	400,000
Ordinary shares of £1 each	200,000	200,000
Retained earnings	200,000	200,000
Total equity	400,000	400,000

Severn is planning a one-for-two bonus issue.

Wye is seeking finance for a capital expenditure programme through a one-for-two rights issue at a price of £1.80 per share (the current market price is £2.10).

solution

After the issues, the statements of financial position appear as:

	Severn	Wye
	£	£
Non-current assets	300,000	300,000
Current assets (including bank)	100,000	280,000
Total assets	400,000	580,000
Ordinary shares of £1 each	300,000	300,000
Share premium	–	80,000
Retained earnings	100,000	200,000
Total equity	400,000	580,000

The changes are:

Severn   Retained earnings are reduced by £100,000, whilst share capital is increased by the same amount; the ordinary share capital is now more in balance with non-current assets; no cash has been received.

Wye   The bank balance has increased by £180,000, being 100,000 shares (assuming that all shareholders took up their rights) at £1.80; share capital has increased by £100,000, whilst 80p per share is the share premium, ie £80,000 in total. The company now has the money to finance its capital expenditure programme. There are also significant retained earnings which could be used for a bonus issue in the future.

The statement of changes in equity for each company are:

Severn: Statement of changes in equity

	Issued share capital	Share premium	Retained earnings	Total
	£	£	£	£
At start	200,000	–	200,000	400,000
Issue of bonus shares	100,000	–	–100,000	–
After share issue	300,000	–	100,000	400,000

Wye: Statement of changes in equity

	Issued share capital	Share premium	Retained earnings	Total
	£	£	£	£
At start	200,000	–	200,000	400,000
Issue of shares at a premium	100,000	80,000	–	180,000
After share issue	300,000	80,000	200,000	580,000

PREPARING FOR ASSESSMENT

In AAT Assessments there are two tasks which require financial statements to be drafted. There are two types of assessment: either two tasks which use a trial balance as a starting point, or two tasks which focus on the statement of cash flows (see Chapter 6). In the case of the former you will be provided with a limited company's trial balance and additional information:

■ in the first task you will be required to draft a statement of profit or loss and other comprehensive income and a statement of changes in equity

■ in the second task you will be required to draft a statement of financial position

For both of these tasks the same trial balance and additional information apply. Blank layouts are provided and, in the AAT Assessment, you select narrative items from pick lists and enter money amounts into gap fill boxes. Pro-formas for workings are also provided, as appropriate, in the assessment and partial marks can be obtained from these in the event of errors being made in the main layouts for the statements. Note that pro-formas for layouts and workings – in the format used in AAT Assessments – are provided in the Appendix of this book.

In the Case Study which follows we see how the statement of profit or loss and other comprehensive income, the statement of changes in equity and the statement of financial position are prepared from a trial balance and additional information – ie the two tasks for this type of AAT Assessment.

Note: the second type of assessment - which focuses on the statement of cash flows – is described in Chapter 6.

Case Study

ALBANY LIMITED: PREPARING THE FINANCIAL STATEMENTS FROM A TRIAL BALANCE

situation

You have been asked to help prepare the financial statements of Albany Ltd for the year ended 30 June 20X2. The company's trial balance as at 30 June 20X2 and further information is shown opposite.

Albany Ltd		
Trial balance as at 30 June 20X2		
	Debit	Credit
	£000	£000
Share capital		5,000
Share premium		1,500
Trade and other payables		1,872
Land and buildings – cost	8,500	
– accumulated depreciation at 1 July 20X1		424
Plant and equipment – cost	5,800	
– accumulated depreciation at 1 July 20X1		2,900
Trade and other receivables	4,235	
Prepayments	15	
5% bank loan repayable 20X7		4,000
Cash and cash equivalents	385	
Retained earnings at 1 July 20X1		3,875
Interest paid	200	
Sales revenue		25,840
Purchases	12,965	
Distribution costs	5,468	
Administrative expenses	2,933	
Inventories at 1 July 20X1	4,285	
Dividends paid	625	
	45,411	45,411

Further information:

- The inventories at the close of business on 30 June 20X2 cost £5,162,000.

- Land, which is not depreciated, is included in the trial balance at a value of £3,000,000. It is to be revalued at £3,500,000 and this revaluation is to be included in the financial statements for the year ended 30 June 20X2.

- Depreciation is to be provided for the year to 30 June 20X2 as follows:

Buildings	2% per annum	Straight line basis
Plant and equipment	20% per annum	Reducing balance basis

Depreciation is to be apportioned as follows:

	%
Cost of sales	40
Distribution costs	40
Administrative expenses	20

- Trade receivables include a debt of £10,000 which is to be written off. Bad (irrecoverable) debts are to be classified as administrative expenses.

- Distribution costs of £18,000 owing at 30 June 20X2 are to be provided for.

- The corporation tax charge for the year has been calculated as £1,475,000.

- All of the operations are continuing operations.

required

(a) Draft the statement of profit or loss and other comprehensive income for Albany Ltd for the year ended 30 June 20X2.

(b) Draft the statement of changes in equity for Albany Ltd for the year ended 30 June 20X2.

(c) Draft the statement of financial position for Albany Ltd as at 30 June 20X2.

solution

(a) **Albany Ltd – Statement of profit or loss and other comprehensive income for the year ended 30 June 20X2**

	£000
Revenue	25,840
Cost of sales	−12,364
Gross profit	13,476
Distribution costs	−5,762
Administrative expenses	−3,081
Profit from operations	4,633
Finance costs	−200
Profit before tax	4,433
Tax	−1,475
Profit for the year from continuing operations	2,958
Other comprehensive income for the year	500
Total comprehensive income for the year	3,458

Workings

Cost of sales	£000
Opening inventories	4,285
Purchases	12,905
Closing inventories	−5,162
Depreciation	*276
Cost of sales =	12,364

* depreciation: buildings £5,500 x 2% x 40% = £44; plant and equipment (£5,800 − £2,900) x 20% x 40% = £232; total £276

Distribution costs	£000
Distribution costs	5,468
Accrual	18
Depreciation	*276
Distribution costs =	5,762

* depreciation as per cost of sales, at 40%

Administrative expenses	£000
Administrative expenses	2,933
Bad (irrecoverable) debt	10
Depreciation	*138
Administrative expenses =	3,081

* depreciation as per cost of sales, but at 20%

(b) Albany Ltd – Statement of changes in equity for the year ended 30 June 20X2

	Share capital	Other reserves	Retained earnings	Total equity
	£000	£000	£000	£000
Balance at 1 July 20X1	5,000	1,500	3,875	10,375
Changes in equity for 20X2				
Total comprehensive income		500	2,958	3,458
Dividends			−625	−625
Issue of share capital				
Balance at 30 June 20X2	5,000	2,000	6,208	13,208

(c)   Albany Ltd – Statement of financial position as at 30 June 20X2

	£000
Assets	
Non-current assets	
Property, plant and equipment	10,786
Current assets	
Inventories	5,162
Trade and other receivables	4,240
Cash and cash equivalents	385
	9,787
Total assets	20,573
EQUITY AND LIABILITIES	
Equity	
Share capital	5,000
Retained earnings	6,208
Revaluation reserve	500
Share premium	1,500
Total equity	13,208
Non-current liabilities	
Bank loan	4,000
	4,000
Current liabilities	
Trade and other payables	1,890
Tax liability	1,475
	3,365
Total liabilities	7,365
Total equity and liabilities	20,573

Workings

Property, plant and equipment	£000
Land and buildings – value	9,000
Accumulated depreciation – land and buildings	–534
Plant and equipment – cost	5,800
Accumulated depreciation – plant and equipment	–3,480
Property, plant and equipment =	10,786

Trade and other receivables	£000
Trade and other receivables	4,235
Bad (irrecoverable) debt	–10
Prepayment – trial balance	15
Trade and other receivables =	4,240

Trade and other payables	£000
Trade and other payables	1,872
Additional distribution costs accrued	18
Trade and other payables =	1,890

Retained earnings	£000
Retained earnings at start of year	3,875
Profit for year	2,958
Dividends paid	–625
Retained earnings =	6,208

Revaluation reserve	£000
Revaluation reserve at start of year	0
Other comprehensive income for year	500
Revaluation reserve =	500

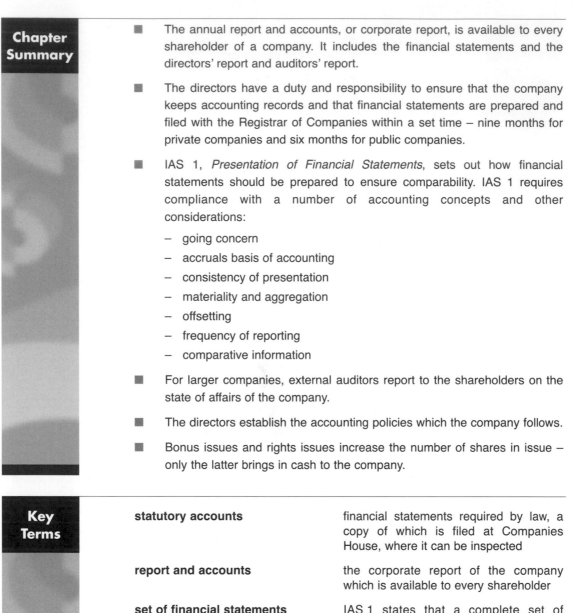

Chapter Summary

- The annual report and accounts, or corporate report, is available to every shareholder of a company. It includes the financial statements and the directors' report and auditors' report.

- The directors have a duty and responsibility to ensure that the company keeps accounting records and that financial statements are prepared and filed with the Registrar of Companies within a set time – nine months for private companies and six months for public companies.

- IAS 1, *Presentation of Financial Statements*, sets out how financial statements should be prepared to ensure comparability. IAS 1 requires compliance with a number of accounting concepts and other considerations:

  - going concern
  - accruals basis of accounting
  - consistency of presentation
  - materiality and aggregation
  - offsetting
  - frequency of reporting
  - comparative information

- For larger companies, external auditors report to the shareholders on the state of affairs of the company.

- The directors establish the accounting policies which the company follows.

- Bonus issues and rights issues increase the number of shares in issue – only the latter brings in cash to the company.

Key Terms

statutory accounts — financial statements required by law, a copy of which is filed at Companies House, where it can be inspected

report and accounts — the corporate report of the company which is available to every shareholder

set of financial statements — IAS 1 states that a complete set of financial statements comprises:

- statement of financial position
- statement of profit or loss and other comprehensive income
- statement of changes in equity
- statement of cash flows
- accounting policies and explanatory notes
- comparative information for the preceding period

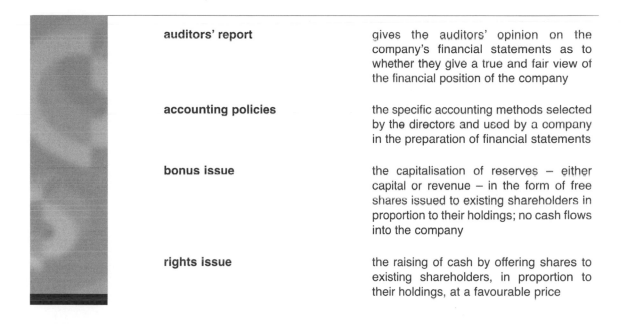

auditors' report	gives the auditors' opinion on the company's financial statements as to whether they give a true and fair view of the financial position of the company
accounting policies	the specific accounting methods selected by the directors and used by a company in the preparation of financial statements
bonus issue	the capitalisation of reserves – either capital or revenue – in the form of free shares issued to existing shareholders in proportion to their holdings; no cash flows into the company
rights issue	the raising of cash by offering shares to existing shareholders, in proportion to their holdings, at a favourable price

Activities

- Blank photocopiable pro-formas in the format used in AAT Assessments – of the statement of profit or loss and other comprehensive income, the statement of changes in equity, and the statement of financial position are included in the Appendix – it is advisable to enlarge them to full A4 size. Blank workings sheets are also included in the Appendix.

- Pro-formas and workings sheets are also available to download from www.osbornebooks.co.uk

3.1 Which of the following is included under the heading for 'Equity' in a statement of financial position?

1. retained earnings
2. share premium
3. bank loans
4. cash and cash equivalents

		✓
(a)	1 and 2	
(b)	3 and 4	
(c)	1, 2 and 4	
(d)	all of them	

3.2   Which of the following does not involve a cash flow?

1. a rights issue of shares

2. repayment of a bank loan

3. depreciation of non-current assets

4. a bonus issue of shares

	✓
(a) 1 and 2	
(b) 3 and 4	
(c) 2, 3 and 4	
(d) all of them	

3.3   Under IAS 1, *Presentation of Financial Statements*, which of the following is included in a complete set of financial statements?

1. profit or loss and other comprehensive income

2. statement of cash flows

3. statement of financial position

4. statement of changes in equity

	✓
(a) 1 and 2	
(b) 1, 2 and 3	
(c) 1, 2 and 4	
(d) all of them	

3.4   Under IAS 1, *Presentation of Financial Statements*, which of the following must be identified?

1. the name of the reporting entity

2. the currency of the financial statements

3. the period covered by the financial statements

4. the level of rounding used for money amounts

	✓
(a) none of them	
(b) 1, 2 and 3	
(c) 1, 2 and 4	
(d) all of them	

3.5 With which of the following accounting concepts and other considerations does IAS 1, *Presentation of Financial Statements* require compliance?

1. going concern
2. accrual basis of accounting
3. consistency of presentation
4. offsetting

		✓
(a)	all of them	
(b)	1 and 2	
(c)	1, 2 and 3	
(d)	1, 3 and 4	

3.6 A limited company has a large 'one-off' expense item this year. In accordance with IAS 1, *Presentation of Financial Statements*, how should this item be presented in the company's statement of profit or loss and other comprehensive income and/or the notes to the financial statements?

		✓
(a)	disclosed as an extraordinary item	
(b)	separate disclosure of the nature and amount	
(c)	not disclosed but added in to either distribution costs or administrative expenses	
(d)	not disclosed but deducted from revenue	

3.7 At the beginning of its financial year on 1 July 20-7, Chapelporth Ltd has issued ordinary share capital of £500,000 and retained earnings of £185,000.

The company has made a profit from operations of £135,000 for the year ended 30 June 20-8. The following payments have been made during the year ended 30 June 20-8:

		£
•	debenture interest	12,500
•	final ordinary dividend for the year ended 30 June 20-7	30,500
•	interim ordinary dividend for the half-year ended 31 December 20-7	18,000

Corporation tax to be paid for the year ended 30 June 20-8 is £48,000.

Required:

(a) Complete the statement of profit or loss and other comprehensive income from the profit from operations of £135,000 for the year ended 30 June 20-8.

(b) Prepare the statement of changes in equity for the year ended 30 June 20-8.

3.8 Mason Motors Limited is a car dealership with a share capital of £300,000.

The following information is available for the year ended 31 December 20-1:

- retained earnings at 1 January 20-1 is £100,000
- profit from operations for the year was £75,000
- loan interest of £5,500 was paid
- a transfer to general reserve of £20,000 was made
- corporation tax of £20,500 is to be paid on the year's profit
- an interim dividend of 10% was paid on the issued ordinary share capital of £300,000

Required:

(a) Complete the statement of profit or loss and other comprehensive income from the profit from operations of £75,000 for the year ended 31 December 20-1.

(b) Prepare the statement of changes in equity for the year ended 31 December 20-1.

3.9 At the beginning of its financial year the equity of Brayford Ltd consisted of 600,000 ordinary shares of 50p each and retained earnings of £150,000.

During the financial year a rights issue of shares was made. The shares were issued on the basis of two new shares for every five existing shares at the issue price of 70p per share. The issue was fully subscribed.

What will be the cash flow from the rights issue?

	✓
(a) £120,000	
(b) £168,000	
(c) £300,000	
(d) £450,000	

3.10 At the beginning of its financial year the equity of Carholme Ltd consisted of 800,000 ordinary shares of 25p each and retained earnings of £125,000.

During the financial year a bonus issue of shares was made. The shares were issued on the basis of one new share for every four shares held.

What will be the amounts of (1) share capital and (2) retained earnings after the bonus issue?

		✓
(a) (1) £250,000	(2) £75,000	
(b) (1) £250,000	(2) £125,000	
(c) (1) £200,000	(2) £75,000	
(d) (1) £250,000	(2) £175,000	

3.11 The equity section of the statement of financial position of Doddington Ltd at 1 January 20X2 is shown below:

Equity	£
Ordinary shares of 50p each fully paid	220,000
Retained earnings	118,000
	338,000

On 1 November 20X2, a rights issue of shares was made. The shares were issued on the basis of one new share for every two shares held at a price of 80p per share. The issue was fully subscribed.

During the year ended 31 December 20X2, dividends paid totalled £45,000.

The profit for the year ended 31 December 20X2 from continuing operations was £79,000.

Required:

Prepare the statement of changes in equity of Doddington Ltd for the year ended 31 December 20X2. Use the table provided.

Doddington Ltd – Statement of changes in equity for the year ended 31 December 20X2

	Share capital £	Other reserves £	Retained earnings £	Total equity £
Balance at 1 January 20X2				
Changes in equity for 20X2				
Profit for the year				
Dividends				
Issue of share capital				
Balance at 31 December 20X2				

3.12 The equity section of the statement of financial position of Martin Ltd at 30 June 20X4 is shown below:

Equity	£
Share capital	600,000
Share premium	90,000
Retained earnings	330,000
	1,020,000

The ordinary shares have a nominal value of 25p each.

On 1 January 20X5, a rights issue of shares was made. The shares were issued on the basis of one new share for every four existing shares at the issue price of 40p per share. The issue was fully subscribed.

During the year ended 30 June 20X5, dividends paid totalled £220,000.

The profit for the year ended 30 June 20X5 from continuing operations was £365,000.

Required:

Prepare the statement of changes in equity of Martin Ltd for the year ended 30 June 20X5. Use the table provided.

Martin Ltd – Statement of changes in equity for the year ended 30 June 20X5

	Share capital £	Other reserves £	Retained earnings £	Total equity £
Balance at 1 July 20X4				
Changes in equity for 20X5				
Profit for the year				
Dividends				
Issue of share capital				
Balance at 30 June 20X5				

3.13 The following figures are taken from the accounting records of Bourne Ltd at the end of the financial year on 31 December 20-6:

	£
Share capital	75,000
Land and buildings at cost	175,000
Accumulated depreciation of land and buildings to date	10,500
Plant and equipment at cost	25,000
Accumulated depreciation of plant and equipment to date	5,000
Inventories	10,750
Trade and other receivables	42,500
Trade and other payables	17,250
Cash and cash equivalents	1,950
Bank loan (repayable in 20-9)	55,000
Profit for the year from continuing operations	68,200
Corporation tax charge for the year	14,850
Dividends paid	10,000
Retained earnings at 1 January 20-6	19,400
Other comprehensive income for the year	0

Required:

Draft the statement of changes in equity for Bourne Ltd for the year ended 31 December 20-6, together with a statement of financial position.

3.14 You have been asked to help prepare the financial statements of Dudley Ltd for the year ended 31 March 20X1. The company's trial balance as at 31 March 20X1 and further information is shown below.

Dudley Ltd

Trial balance as at 31 March 20X1

	Debit	Credit
	£000	*£000*
Share capital		60,000
Revaluation reserve at 1 April 20X0		10,000
Trade and other payables		2,140
Land and buildings – value/cost	95,000	
– accumulated depreciation at 1 April 20X0		4,000
Plant and equipment – cost	32,000	
– accumulated depreciation at 1 April 20X0		14,000
Trade and other receivables	3,520	
Accruals		110
6% bank loan repayable 20X8		5,000
Cash and cash equivalents	1,742	
Retained earnings at 1 April 20X0		33,021
Interest paid	300	
Revenue		75,216
Purchases	45,834	
Distribution costs	10,272	
Administrative expenses	8,636	
Inventories at 1 April 20X0	4,683	
Dividends paid	1,500	
	203,487	203,487

Further information:

- The inventories at the close of business on 31 March 20X1 cost £5,129,000.

- Land, which is not depreciated, is included in the trial balance at a value of £45,000,000. It is to be revalued at £50,000,000 and this revaluation is to be included in the financial statements for the year ended 31 March 20X1.

- Depreciation is to be provided for the year to 31 March 20X1 as follows:

Buildings	2% per annum	Straight line basis
Plant and equipment	25% per annum	Reducing balance basis

Depreciation is to be apportioned as follows:

	%
Cost of sales	60
Distribution costs	30
Administrative expenses	10

- Trade receivables include a debt of £8,000 which is to be written off. Bad (irrecoverable) debts are to be classified as administrative expenses.

- Distribution costs of £10,000 owing at 31 March 20X1 are to be provided for.

- The corporation tax charge for the year has been calculated as £1,100,000.

- All of the operations are continuing operations.

Required:

(a) Draft the statement of profit or loss and other comprehensive income for Dudley Ltd for the year ended 31 March 20X1.

(b) Draft the statement of changes in equity for Dudley Ltd for the year ended 31 March 20X1.

(c) Draft the statement of financial position for Dudley Ltd as at 31 March 20X1.

3.15 You have been asked to help prepare the financial statements of Avanzi Ltd for the year ended 31 March 20X1. The company's trial balance as at 31 March 20X1 and further information is shown below.

Avanzi Ltd

Trial balance as at 31 March 20X1

	Debit	Credit
	£000	£000
Share capital		5,000
Share premium		1,500
Retained earnings at 1 April 20X0		2,050
Land and buildings – cost	7,000	
– accumulated depreciation at 1 April 20X0		1,000
Plant and equipment – cost	9,000	
– accumulated depreciation at 1 April 20X0		4,000
Trade and other receivables	3,400	
Trade and other payables		2,400
5% bank loan repayable 20X8		800
Cash and cash equivalents	600	
Accruals		190
Interest paid	40	
Revenue		22,400
Purchases	11,500	
Distribution costs	3,000	
Administrative expenses	2,550	
Inventories at 1 April 20X0	1,200	
Dividends paid	1,050	
	39,340	39,340

Further information:

- The share capital of the company consists of ordinary shares with a nominal value of £1.

- The company issued 1,000,000 new ordinary shares during the year. They had a nominal value of £1 but were sold for £1.50 per share. This transaction is included in the balances in the trial balance above.

- Land, which is not depreciated, is included in the trial balance at a value of £2,000,000.

- The inventories at the close of business on 31 March 20X1 cost £1,315,000.

- Depreciation is to be provided for the year to 31 March 20X1 as follows:

Buildings	2% per annum	Straight line basis
Plant and equipment	20% per annum	Reducing balance basis

Depreciation is to be apportioned as follows:

	%
Cost of sales	50
Distribution costs	30
Administrative expenses	20

- Trade receivables include a debt of £10,000 which is to be written off. Bad (irrecoverable) debts are to be classified as administrative expenses.

- Distribution costs of £20,000 owing at 31 March 20X1 are to be provided for.

- The corporation tax charge for the year has been calculated as £830,000.

- All of the operations are continuing operations.

Required:

(a) Draft the statement of profit or loss and other comprehensive income for Avanzi Ltd for the year ended 31 March 20X1.

(b) Draft the statement of changes in equity for Avanzi Ltd for the year ended 31 March 20X1.

(c) Draft the statement of financial position for Avanzi Ltd as at 31 March 20X1.

3.16 You have been asked to help prepare the financial statements of Sutar Ltd for the year ended 31 March 20X3. The company's trial balance as at 31 March 20X3 and further information is shown below.

Sutar Ltd

Trial balance as at 31 March 20X3

	Debit	Credit
	£000	£000
Share capital		5,000
Revaluation reserve at 1 April 20X2		1,000
Dividends paid	400	
Land and buildings – value/cost	8,500	
– accumulated depreciation at 1 April 20X2		564
Plant and equipment – cost	7,800	
– accumulated depreciation at 1 April 20X2		2,400
Trade and other receivables	5,455	
Trade and other payables		2,350
Retained earnings at 1 April 20X2		6,178
Cash and cash equivalents	304	
8% bank loan repayable 20X9		6,000
Interest paid	480	
Revenue		31,710
Purchases	15,525	
Distribution costs	6,842	
Administrative expenses	3,378	
Inventories at 1 April 20X2	6,531	
Accruals		13
	55,215	55,215

Further information:

- The share capital of the company consists of ordinary shares with a nominal value of £1.

- The inventories at the close of business on 31 March 20X3 cost £7,878,000.

- Land, which is not depreciated, is included in the trial balance at a value of £4,000,000. It is to be revalued at £4,500,000 and this revaluation is to be included in the financial statements for the year ended 31 March 20X3.

- Depreciation is to be provided for the year to 31 March 20X3 as follows:

Buildings	2% per annum	Straight line basis
Plant and equipment	20% per annum	Reducing balance basis

  Depreciation is to be apportioned as follows:

	%
Cost of sales	70
Distribution costs	20
Administrative expenses	10

- Trade receivables include a debt of £25,000 which is to be written off. Bad (irrecoverable) debts are to be classified as administrative expenses.

- Sutar Ltd owes £18,000 for hire of delivery vehicles during January to March 20X3.

- The corporation tax charge for the year has been calculated as £975,000.

- All of the operations are continuing operations.

Required:

(a)   Draft the statement of profit or loss and other comprehensive income for Sutar Ltd for the year ended 31 March 20X3.

(b)   Draft the statement of changes in equity for Sutar Ltd for the year ended 31 March 20X3.

(c)   Draft the statement of financial position for Sutar Ltd as at 31 March 20X3.

4 Accounting for assets

this chapter covers...

In this chapter we focus on the international financial reporting standards that impact on the way in which assets are accounted for in both the statement of profit or loss and other comprehensive income and the statement of financial position. We focus on assets, to cover:

- *property, plant and equipment (IAS 16)*

- *intangible assets (IAS 38)*

- *impairment of assets (IAS 36)*

- *leases (IAS 17)*

- *inventories (IAS 2)*

HOW TO STUDY THE ACCOUNTING STANDARDS

As we have seen in earlier chapters, international financial reporting standards – in the form of International Accounting Standards (IASs) and International Financial Reporting Standards (IFRSs) – play a major role in the presentation and detail of financial statements. A study of limited company accounts requires knowledge of a number of standards – in this book we have attempted, as far as possible, to group standards together where they relate to particular topics. Accordingly, this chapter focuses on those standards that relate to assets. The next chapter looks at the standards covering liabilities and the statement of profit or loss and other comprehensive income; Chapter 8 deals with consolidated financial statements, so the standards which cover group financial statements (and also associated companies) are covered there. The statement of cash flows is detailed in an accounting standard (IAS 7) and this is covered in Chapter 6. A few standards do not fit readily to such groupings and so these have been included at what seems to be the most logical place. We believe that this 'grouping' approach is preferable to explaining the standards in their numerical order, which results in a long 'list' where often unrelated topics follow one another.

the international financial reporting standards

The table on the next page shows the international financial reporting standards that are required for AAT's *Financial Statements* Assessment. (A full list of the reporting standards is available at www.ifrs.org.)

organising your study of accounting standards

In this textbook we cover the aspects of each international financial reporting standard that are required for AAT's *Financial Statements* Assessment. Note, however, that some standards cover more detailed issues that are not assessable. The texts of all current standards are available from the International Accounting Standards Board (www.ifrs.org).

For learning the key points of accounting standards, it is strongly recommended that you use a system of index cards (or an electronic version of index cards on your tablet or computer): put the number and name of each standard on the top of an index card and then outline the key points of the standards, using bullet point format, together with a cross-reference to the relevant pages of this textbook. This then forms a useful learning and revision aid which can be easily referred to at almost any time.

It is also important to keep up-to-date with any changes to accounting standards – on a monthly basis use accountancy magazines and web sites (see the web directory at the beginning of this book).

International Financial Reporting Standards (IFRSs)

International Accounting Standards (IASs)

ACCOUNTING FOR ASSETS

This chapter explains the accounting treatment of assets – non-current and current – as specified by the relevant international accounting standards. The diagram which follows shows the questions to be asked when dealing with assets:

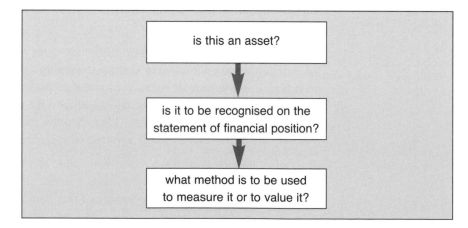

It is worth going back to the *Conceptual Framework for Financial Reporting* document for the definition of an asset (page 10): '*a resource controlled by the entity as a result of past events and from which future economic benefits are expected to flow to the entity.*'

The definition refers to a resource being *controlled* (and not necessarily owned). Thus a company which leases an asset – such as a machine – from a leasing company may well recognise the asset on its statement of financial position, even though it is not the legal owner. Note that there is also the requirement for the asset to generate future economic benefits for the entity.

In order to be recognised on the statement of financial position, assets must be capable of being reliably measured at either their cost or their value.

Once an asset is recognised on the statement of financial position, there is then the question of how it is to be subsequently measured – for example, at cost less depreciation/amortisation, or revaluation. The international financial reporting standards which follow in the chapter set out the recognition and measurement criteria of different classes of assets: *Property, Plant and Equipment* (IAS 16), *Intangible Assets* (IAS 38), and *Inventories* (IAS 2), together with *Impairment of Assets* (IAS 36) and *Leases* (IAS 17).

IAS 16 – PROPERTY, PLANT AND EQUIPMENT

This standard sets out the accounting treatment for property, plant and equipment (PPE). These are non-current tangible assets such as land and buildings, machinery, office equipment, shop fittings and vehicles.

The principal issues covered by the standard are the recognition of the assets, the determination of their carrying amounts (see below), and the depreciation charges and impairment losses (see IAS 36, *Impairment of Assets*, page 110) to be recognised in relation to them.

definitions

Property, plant and equipment are tangible assets held for use in the production or supply of goods and services, which are expected to be used for more than one period.

Depreciation is the systematic allocation of the depreciable amount of an asset over its useful life.

Depreciable amount is the cost or valuation of the asset, less any residual value.

Useful life is the length of time, or the number of units of production, for which an asset is expected to be used.

Fair value is the price that would be received to sell an asset or paid to transfer a liability in an orderly transaction between market participants at the measurement date (the date of the valuation).

Impairment loss is the amount by which the carrying amount of an asset exceeds its recoverable amount.

Recoverable amount is the higher of the asset's fair value less costs to sell, and its value in use.

Carrying amount is the amount at which an asset is recognised on the statement of financial position, after deducting any accumulated depreciation and impairment losses.

recognition

An item of property, plant and equipment (PPE) is to be recognised as an asset when

–   it is probable that **future economic benefits** will flow to the entity; and

–   the cost of the asset can be **measured reliably**

IAS 16 acknowledges that, after the initial purchase cost, there will often be further costs spent on PPE – the standard sets out the following guidelines for such subsequent expenditure:

■   the costs of day-to-day servicing of the asset, including the cost of small parts, are to be recognised in the statement of profit or loss and other comprehensive income

■   where parts of the asset require replacement at regular intervals – eg the seats of a bus or a train – the costs incurred can be recognised in the carrying amount of the PPE (subject to the recognition criteria – see above – of future economic benefits and reliable measurement)

■   where regular inspections have to be carried out to continue operating an asset – for example, an aircraft – the costs of the inspection can be recognised in the carrying amount (subject to the recognition criteria – see above)

Derecognition (which occurs when assets are disposed of) is explained on page 99.

measurement of property, plant and equipment

Initially PPE are measured at cost on the statement of financial position.

Cost is the purchase price, including any import duties and other taxes, plus any costs directly attributable (see below) to bring the asset to the location and condition for its intended use, plus the estimated costs of dismantling and removing the asset at the end of its useful life.

Attributable costs which **can be included** in the cost of the asset include:

- costs of site preparation
- initial delivery and handling costs
- installation and assembly costs
- costs of testing the asset
- professional fees, eg engineers, architects

Costs which **cannot be included** in the cost of the asset include administration and other general overhead costs, start-up costs of a new business or section of the business, start-up costs for introducing a new product or service – such as advertising and promotional costs.

After acquisition of PPE an entity must choose either the cost model or the revaluation model as its accounting policy – which is then applied to an entire class of PPE. The two models are defined as follows:

- **Cost model** – the asset is carried at cost less accumulated depreciation and impairment losses

- **Revaluation model** – the asset is carried on the statement of financial position at a revalued amount, being its fair value* less any subsequent depreciation and impairment losses (see IAS 36, *Impairment of Assets*, page 110); revaluations are to be made regularly to ensure that the carrying amount does not differ materially from its fair value at the date of the statement of financial position

    The frequency of revaluations depends upon changes in the fair values – when changes are frequent, annual revaluations are required; where changes are insignificant, revaluations can be made every three to five years.

    * fair value is defined on page 96; its use is subject to the fair value being able to be measured reliably

When an item of PPE is revalued, the entire class of assets to which it belongs must be revalued. Note that classes are groups of similar assets, for example land, buildings, machinery, vehicles, furniture and fixtures, office equipment, etc. Revaluations are dealt with as follows:

- any increase in value is recognised in other comprehensive income and is credited within equity to a **revaluation surplus** (although an increase which reverses part or all of a previous decrease for the same asset is recognised as income in the statement of profit or loss and other comprehensive income)

- any reduction in value is recognised as an expense in the statement of profit or loss and other comprehensive income (although a decrease which reverses part or all of a previous increase for the same asset is recognised in other comprehensive income and is debited to the revaluation surplus) – see also Step 3 of the impairment review on page 112

depreciation

The depreciable amount (cost less residual value) of an asset is to be allocated on a systematic basis over its useful life.

Note the following points:

- the residual value and the useful life of an asset are to be reviewed at least annually and, if they differ from previous estimates, any change is to be accounted for as a change in an estimate (the Case Study on page 105 shows how depreciation is recalculated following a change in useful life from a previous estimate)

- depreciation continues to be recognised even if the fair value of an asset exceeds its carrying amount (but there is no need for depreciation when the residual value is greater than the carrying amount)

- spending money on repair and maintenance of an asset does not remove the need for depreciation

- depreciation can be applied to separate parts of an asset where each part is a significant cost – for example, the engines of an aircraft are often depreciated separately from the body of the aircraft

- depreciation for the period is recognised in the statement of profit or loss and other comprehensive income (unless it is included in the carrying amount of another asset)

- when determining the useful life of an asset, the following factors need to be considered (even if the asset is not being used):

  - expected usage of the asset, ie the expected capacity or output

  - expected physical wear and tear, which depends on operational factors and the repair and maintenance programme

  - technical or commercial obsolescence, eg the introduction of new technology, changes in demand for the product or service

  - legal or similar limits on the use of the asset, eg the period for which an asset is leased

Freehold land is shown at cost and is not depreciated because it has an unlimited useful life (unless it is a mine or a quarry); note that leasehold land will be depreciated.

Land and buildings are separated out and accounted for separately – the land is not depreciated, but buildings have a limited useful life and are depreciated. An increase in the value of the land on which a building stands does not affect the depreciable amount of the building.

Depreciation methods include the straight-line method, the diminishing (reducing) balance method, and the units of production (output) method – you will be familiar with some of these from your previous studies. Key features of each of these are:

- straight-line depreciation results in a constant depreciation charge over the asset's useful life
- diminishing (reducing) balance depreciation results in a decreasing depreciation charge over the useful life (ic the depreciation in the early years is greater than in later years) – see also sum of the digits depreciation in the Case Study which follows
- units of production (or service) depreciation results in a depreciation charge based on the expected use or output

An entity chooses the depreciation method which best reflects the pattern in which the asset's economic benefits are consumed. The depreciation method is to be reviewed at least annually and, if there has been a change in the pattern of consumption of benefits, the method should be changed (this would be a change in an accounting estimate).

Derecognition occurs when an item of PPE is disposed of, or when no future economic benefits are expected from its use or disposal. Any gain or loss on disposal (ie the difference between the net disposal proceeds and the carrying amount) is recognised as income or expense in the statement of profit or loss and other comprehensive income.

For example, an item of PPE has a carrying amount (cost/revaluation less accumulated depreciation) of £1,500 and is now sold for £800: the loss on disposal of £700 is recognised as an expense in the statement of profit or loss and other comprehensive income.

A revaluation surplus relating to PPE may be transferred directly to retained earnings (and not through profit or loss) when the item is derecognised. Note also that IAS 16 allows for part of a revaluation surplus to be transferred to retained earnings during the asset's life – the amount being the difference between depreciation based on the revalued carrying amount and depreciation based on the asset's original cost.

disclosure in the financial statements

For each class of property, plant and equipment the financial statements are to show:
- the basis for determining the carrying amount
- the depreciation method(s) used
- the useful lives or depreciation rates
- the gross carrying amount (eg cost of the asset) and the accumulated depreciation and impairment losses at the beginning and end of the period
- a reconciliation of the carrying amount at the beginning and end of the period showing:
  - additions
  - disposals

- acquisitions through business combinations (see Chapter 8)
- revaluation increases
- impairment losses
- reversal of impairment losses
- depreciation
- other changes

As depreciation methods and the estimation of useful lives are matters of judgement, it is important to provide users of financial statements with information that enables them to review the policies selected by management and to enable comparison to be made with other companies. To this end it is necessary to disclose in the financial statements:

■ the depreciation for the period
■ the accumulated depreciation at the end of the period

Case Study

BROCKEN LIMITED: CALCULATING DEPRECIATION

situation

You are an accounts assistant at Brocken Limited, an engineering company. The company has recently bought a new computer-controlled cutting machine for use in the factory. You have been asked by the finance director to prepare depreciation calculations, based on the following information:

CUTTING MACHINE	
Cost price on 1 January 20-6	£20,000 (net of VAT)
Estimated life	4 years
Estimated production:	
20-6	60,000 units
20-7	50,000 units
20-8	25,000 units
20-9	25,000 units
total	160,000 units
Estimated residual value at end of four years	£4,000

The finance director wants to know which methods of depreciation are available to the company, and for you to prepare a table for each method showing the amount of depreciation expense per year recognised in the statement of profit or loss, and the carrying amount of the asset for the statement of financial position.

solution

You decide to calculate figures for four depreciation methods:

- straight-line depreciation
- diminishing (reducing) balance depreciation
- units of production depreciation
- sum of the digits depreciation

straight-line depreciation

With this method, a fixed percentage is written off the original cost of the asset each year. For this machine, twenty-five per cent of the depreciable amount will be written off each year by the straight-line method.

The method of calculating straight-line depreciation, taking into account the asset's estimated residual value at the end of its useful life, is:

$$\frac{\text{cost of asset} - \text{estimated residual (scrap or salvage) value}}{\text{number of years' expected use of asset}}$$

The machine is expected to have a residual value of £4,000, so the depreciation amount will be:

$$\frac{£20,000 - £4,000}{4 \text{ years}} = £4,000 \text{ per year}$$

diminishing (reducing) balance depreciation

With this method, a fixed percentage is written off the diminished balance each year. The diminished (reduced) balance is cost of the asset less depreciation to date. The machine is to be depreciated by 33.3% (one-third) each year, using the diminishing balance method (see calculations below). The depreciation amounts for the four years of ownership are:

	£
Original cost of machine	20,000
20-6 depreciation: 33.3% of £20,000	6,667
Carrying amount at end of 20-6	13,333
20-7 depreciation: 33.3% of £13,333	4,444
Carrying amount at end of 20-7	8,889
20-8 depreciation: 33.3% of £8,889	2,963
Carrying amount at end of 20-8	5,926
20-9 depreciation: 33.3% of £5,926	1,926
Residual value at end of 20-9	4,000

Note that the figures have been rounded to the nearest £, and depreciation for 20-9 has been adjusted by approximately £50 to leave a residual value of £4,000.

The formula to calculate the percentage of reducing balance depreciation is:

$$r = 1 - \sqrt[n]{\frac{s}{c}}$$

In this formula:

r	=	percentage rate of depreciation
n	=	number of years
s	=	residual value
c	=	cost of asset

For the machine above, the 33.3% is calculated as:

$$r = 1 - \sqrt[4]{\frac{4{,}000}{20{,}000}}$$

$$r = 1 - \sqrt[4]{0.2}$$ (to find the fourth root press the square root key on the calculator twice)

$$r = 1 - 0.669$$

$$r = 0.331 \text{ or } 33.1\% \text{ (which is close to the 33.3\% used above)}$$

units of production depreciation

This method uses the estimated number of units to be produced by the machine over its useful life. (In other circumstances it can be based on the number of hours' operation of a machine, or the number of miles/kilometres of a vehicle.)

Depreciation for a given year is calculated by reference to the number of units for that year.

The machine is to be depreciated by £16,000 (ie £20,000 – £4,000 residual value). As the total number of units to be produced by the machine is expected to be 160,000, then each year's depreciation will be calculated at £1,000 for every 10,000 units produced (£16,000 ÷ 160,000 units).

Depreciation amounts will be:

20-6	£6,000	depreciation for year
20-7	£5,000	depreciation for year
20-8	£2,500	depreciation for year
20-9	£2,500	depreciation for year
	£16,000	total depreciation

This method has the benefit of linking usage (ie units) to the depreciation amount. In years of high usage, depreciation is higher than in years of low usage. As the asset gets older, so the usage may be lower, but repair costs may be increasing: in this way the total expense (depreciation + repair costs) will probably be a similar amount from year-to-year.

sum of the digits depreciation

This method is often used as an approximation of diminishing (reducing) balance. Here the depreciation amount each year is calculated on the sum of the number of years of useful life. As the machine is expected to last for four years: the sum of the digits is 1 + 2 + 3 + 4 = 10. Depreciation is applied to the depreciable amount, £16,000 (ie £20,000 – £4,000 residual value) as follows:

20-6	4/10 x £16,000	=	£6,400	depreciation for year
20-7	3/10 x £16,000	=	£4,800	depreciation for year
20-8	2/10 x £16,000	=	£3,200	depreciation for year
20-9	1/10 x £16,000	=	£1,600	depreciation for year
			£16,000	total depreciation

In using this method, the digits count down from the number of years of useful life, ie the depreciation for year 1 is higher than that for year 2, etc. In this way, sum of the digits depreciation is similar to the diminishing (reducing) balance method.

depreciation methods compared
The following tables use the depreciation amounts calculated above.

	straight-line depreciation			
Year	1 Original cost	2 Depreciation for year	3 Depreciation to date	4 Carrying amount (ie column 1-3)
	£	£	£	£
20-6	20,000	4,000	4,000	16,000
20-7	20,000	4,000	8,000	12,000
20-8	20,000	4,000	12,000	8,000
20-9	20,000	4,000	16,000	4,000

These calculations will be used in the financial statements as follows: taking 20-7 as an example, the statement of profit or loss will recognise £4,000 (column 2) as an expense, while the statement of financial position will recognise £12,000 (column 4) as the carrying amount.

	diminishing balance depreciation			
Year	1 Original cost	2 Depreciation for year	3 Depreciation to date	4 Carrying amount (ie column 1-3)
	£	£	£	£
20-6	20,000	6,667	6,667	13,333
20-7	20,000	4,444	11,111	8,889
20-8	20,000	2,963	14,074	5,926
20-9	20,000	1,926	16,000	4,000

	units of production depreciation			
Year	1 Original cost	2 Depreciation for year	3 Depreciation to date	4 Carrying amount (ie column 1-3)
	£	£	£	£
20-6	20,000	6,000	6,000	14,000
20-7	20,000	5,000	11,000	9,000
20-8	20,000	2,500	13,500	6,500
20-9	20,000	2,500	16,000	4,000

sum of the digits depreciation				
	1	**2**	**3**	**4**
Year	**Original cost**	**Depreciation for year**	**Depreciation to date**	**Carrying amount (ie column 1-3)**
	£	£	£	£
20-6	20,000	6,400	6,400	13,600
20-7	20,000	4,800	11,200	8,800
20-8	20,000	3,200	14,400	5,600
20-9	20,000	1,600	16,000	4,000

COMPARISON OF DEPRECIATION METHODS

METHOD	depreciation amount	depreciation rate	suitability
straight-line	same money amount each year	lower depreciation percentage required to achieve same residual value	best used for non-current assets likely to be kept for the whole of their useful lives, eg machines, office equipment
diminishing balance	different money amounts each year: more than straight-line in early years, less in later years	higher depreciation percentage required to achieve same residual value – but can never reach nil value	best used for non-current assets which depreciate more in early years and which are not kept for whole of useful lives, eg vehicles
units of production	invariably different money amounts each year	depreciation is linked to production	allocates depreciation on a systematic basis over asset's useful life – suitable for non-current assets where units can be ascertained reliably, eg machinery, vehicles
sum of the digits	similar to diminishing balance	depreciation is linked to number of years of useful life, eg, for a four-year life, 1 year + 2 + 3 + 4 = 10 digits	often used as an approximation of diminishing balance depreciation

Note: Whichever depreciation method is selected, the total profits of the company over the life of the asset will be the same. The various methods will cause the profit for individual years to be different but, overall, the same total depreciation is recognised as an expense in the statement of profit or loss. IAS 16 requires that the depreciable amount (cost less residual value) of an asset is to be allocated on a systematic basis over its useful life. As depreciation is 'non-cash' there is no effect on the bank balance.

**Case
Study**

CHANGE IN USEFUL LIFE

This Case Study shows how to calculate depreciation amounts when there is a change in useful life from previous estimates.

situation

Newland Ltd has a financial year end of 31 December. On 1 January 20-1 Newland Ltd purchased an item of equipment for £500,000. The useful life of the equipment was anticipated as being six years and the residual value was estimated as £140,000. Newland Ltd depreciates its equipment on a straight-line basis.

On 1 January 20-4 the residual value was still estimated as £140,000, but the remaining useful life was re-assessed as five years.

What will be the depreciation charges over the life of the asset?

solution

The depreciation charges, using the straight-line method, calculated on the purchase of the equipment will be:

$$\frac{£500,000 - £140,000}{6 \text{ years}} = £60,000 \text{ per year}$$

Therefore the depreciation charges for 20-1 to 20-3 will be:

20-1	£60,000
20-2	£60,000
20-3	£60,000

On 1 January 20-4, when the useful life of the equipment is re-assessed, the carrying amount of the asset is:

original cost	£500,000
less depreciation to date	£180,000
carrying amount	£320,000

At this date the remaining useful life is expected to be five years, with the residual value still expected to be £140,000.
The revised depreciation calculation will be:

$$\frac{£320,000 - £140,000}{5 \text{ years}} = £36,000 \text{ per year}$$

Therefore the depreciation charges for 20-4 to 20-8 will be:

20-4	£36,000
20-5	£36,000
20-6	£36,000
20-7	£36,000
20-8	£36,000

By 31 December 20-8 the carrying amount of the equipment will be £140,000. If the amount received from the disposal of the asset differs from this then the gain or loss will be recognised as income or expense in the statement of profit or loss and other comprehensive income.

IAS 38 – INTANGIBLE ASSETS

This standard sets out the accounting treatment of expenditure on acquiring, developing, maintaining or enhancing intangible assets such as scientific or technical knowledge, design and implementation of new processes, licences, intellectual property, market knowledge, and trademarks (including brand names). Note that goodwill is not covered – see IFRS 3, *Business Combinations* (page 239).

definition

An intangible asset is defined as '*an identifiable non-monetary asset without physical substance*'. An asset is a resource:

– controlled by an entity as a result of past events (eg a purchase transaction), and

– from which future economic benefits (eg cash inflows) are expected to flow to the entity

Thus examples of intangible assets include computer software, patents, copyrights, customer lists, licences and marketing rights.

The definitions, above, give the three key elements of an intangible asset as being:

■ **identifiability** – the asset is either separable from the entity and is capable of being sold or transferred, or it arises from contractual or other legal rights

■ **control** – the entity has the power to obtain future economic benefits from the asset

■ **future economic benefits** – include revenue from the sale of products or services, cost savings, or other benefits

recognition

Intangible assets come about from two main sources: either they are purchased, or they are internally generated (ie created within the business). In both cases the intangible asset is recognised initially in the financial statements at cost price when:

– it is probable that the expected future economic benefits that are attributable to the asset will flow to the entity; and

– the cost of the asset can be measured reliably

Note that neither internally generated goodwill nor internally generated brands can be recognised as assets. (For goodwill which may feature in consolidated financial statements, see IFRS 3, *Business Combinations*.)

research and development

Many companies are involved in the research and development of new products or processes. Such activities often lead to the creation of internally generated intangible assets. In financial statements, we must be careful to distinguish between the research phase and the development phase by noting the definitions given in IAS 38:

- **research** is original and planned investigation undertaken with the prospect of gaining new scientific or technical knowledge and understanding
- **development** is the application of research findings or other knowledge to a plan or design for the production of new or substantially improved materials, devices, products, processes, systems or services before the start of commercial production or use

Thus research is experimental or theoretical work undertaken to gain new knowledge for its own sake, while development takes new knowledge in order to create new or improved products, services and systems up to the point of commercial use.

Examples of research are:

- activities to obtain new knowledge
- searches for alternatives for materials, products, processes, etc
- formulation/design/evaluation of possible alternatives for materials, products, processes, etc

Examples of development are:

- design/construction/testing of pre-production prototypes
- design of new technology production equipment
- design/construction/operation of a pilot production plant
- design/construction/testing of chosen alternative for materials, products, processes, etc

IAS 38 requires that revenue expenditure on research is to be recognised as an expense in the statement of profit or loss and other comprehensive income of the year in which it is incurred. However, capital expenditure on non-current assets – such as a new research laboratory – is to be recorded as non-current assets and depreciated over the useful lives of the assets.

Development costs are either recognised as an expense in the statement of profit or loss and other comprehensive income when they are incurred, or they are to be capitalised (ie recognised on the statement of financial position) as an intangible asset if the entity can demonstrate all of the following:

- the technical feasibility of completing the intangible asset so that it will be available for use or sale

- its intention to complete the intangible asset and to use or sell it

- its ability to use or sell the intangible asset

- the way in which the intangible asset will generate probable future economic benefits

- the availability of resources to complete the development and to use or sell the intangible asset

- its ability to measure the development expenditure reliably

Note that if the business cannot distinguish between the research phase and the development phase of a project, then all expenditure is to be treated as though it was for research – see above.

measurement of intangible assets

Initially, intangible assets are measured at cost on the statement of financial position. However, an entity must classify the useful lives of intangible assets as either

- finite, ie having a limited useful life; or

- indefinite, ie having no foreseeable limit to the period over which the asset is expected to generate net cash inflows

An intangible asset with a **finite life** is to be amortised over its useful life:

- the method of amortisation should reflect the pattern of benefits expected by the entity (if the pattern cannot be determined reliably, then the straight-line method should be used)

- the amount of amortisation is to be recognised as an expense in the statement of profit or loss and other comprehensive income

- the residual value should be assumed to be zero (unless there is an agreement for a third party to buy it at the end of its useful life, or where a residual value can be determined by reference to a market in such assets)

- the amortisation period (and method) should be reviewed at least annually, with appropriate changes being made where necessary

An asset with an **indefinite life** is not amortised. Instead, it is to be tested for impairment annually in accordance with IAS 36 *Impairment of Assets* (see page 110), and whenever there is an indication that the asset may be impaired. The useful life is to be reviewed each accounting period to determine whether or not it is still indefinite. If necessary, a change from indefinite to finite should be made and accounted for as a change in an accounting estimate.

POMONA AGROCHEMICAL COMPANY:
RESEARCH AND DEVELOPMENT COSTS

situation

Pomona Agrochemical Company has the following account in its bookkeeping system:

Dr				Research and Development Expenditure Account		Cr
20-1		£		20-1		£
24 Mar	Bank (research)	24,000				
18 Nov	Bank (development)	40,000				

The development costs have been incurred in respect of a new agricultural chemical, WACL X123. This product has been on sale since 1 January 20-2; revenue in the first few weeks look very promising and the company is forecasting good profits from it.

It is now February 20-2 and you are preparing the company's financial statements for the year ended 31 December 20-1. How will you deal with the research and development expenditure?

solution

research

The research costs of £24,000 will be recognised as an expense in the statement of profit or loss and other comprehensive income for the year ended 31 December 20-1.

development

The development costs of £40,000 should be recognised as an expense in the statement of profit or loss and other comprehensive income unless they meet the criteria set out in IAS 38. Here, the development costs of the new chemical do appear to fit the definition of intangible asset, ie 'an identifiable non-monetary asset without physical substance' and so they can be capitalised.

The asset is a resource

– controlled by an entity as a result of past events

– from which future economic benefits are expected to flow to the entity

Provided that the company can demonstrate *all* of the points which follow, then the development costs are to be recognised on the statement of financial position:

• the technical feasibility of completing the intangible asset so that it will be available for use or sale

• its intention to complete the intangible asset and use or sell it

• its ability to use or sell the intangible asset

• the way in which the intangible asset will generate probable future economic benefits

• the availability of resources to complete the development and to use or sell the intangible asset

• its ability to measure the development expenditure reliably

As the new chemical is already on sale and the company is forecasting good profits,

it seems most likely that the development costs can be capitalised and recognised on Pomona's statement of financial position as an intangible non-current asset with a value of £40,000 at 31 December 20-1.

As the new chemical is now in production, the asset must now be amortised over its useful life, so the question for the following year's accounts (20-2) will be to decide how long revenue from the product will last – this will determine the amount of amortisation to be recognised in the statement of profit or loss and other comprehensive income for the year ended 31 December 20-2, and the reduced value of the intangible asset for the year end statement of financial position.

If the company believes that the asset has an indefinite life, it will not be amortised. Instead, it will be tested for impairment annually, and also whenever there is an indication that the asset may be impaired.

IAS 36 – IMPAIRMENT OF ASSETS

This standard sets out the accounting procedures to ensure that assets are carried on the statement of financial position at no more than their value, or recoverable amount. If the recoverable amount of an asset is less than its carrying amount, then the carrying value is to be reduced. This is an impairment loss, which is recognised as an expense in the statement of profit or loss and other comprehensive income.

definitions

Carrying amount is the amount at which an asset is recognised after deducting any accumulated depreciation (amortisation) and accumulated impairment losses.

Note: the term 'amortisation' is customarily used in relation to intangible non-current assets instead of 'depreciation' – however, the two terms have the same meaning

Impairment loss is the amount by which the carrying amount of an asset exceeds its recoverable amount.

Fair value is the price that would be received to sell an asset or paid to transfer a liability in an orderly transaction between market participants at the measurement date (the date of the valuation).

Recoverable amount of an asset is the higher of its fair value, less costs of disposal, and its value in use.

Value in use is the present value of the future cash flows expected to be derived from an asset.

scope of the standard

IAS 36 applies to most non-current assets, such as land and buildings, plant and machinery, vehicles, goodwill and other intangible assets. It does not apply to current assets such as inventories.

Impairment occurs when the recoverable amount is less than the asset's carrying amount. The principle of IAS 36 is that assets need to be reviewed for each year's statement of financial position to assess whether there is any indication of impairment. The standard provides a number of indications of impairment (see below). Certain assets have to be tested for impairment annually by comparing carrying value with recoverable amount – these assets include

- an intangible asset with an indefinite useful life
- an intangible asset not yet available for use
- goodwill acquired in a business combination (see Chapter 8)

indications of impairment

IAS 36 gives a number of external and internal indications of impairment, including:

External sources of information

- a significant fall in the asset's value
- adverse effects on the entity caused by technology, markets, the economy, laws
- increases in interest rates
- the market value of the entity is less than the carrying amount of net assets

Internal sources of information

- obsolescence or physical damage to the asset
- adverse effects on the asset of a significant reorganisation within the entity
- the economic performance of the asset is worse than expected

There may well be other indications – in particular, evidence from internal financial statements can indicate that an asset may be impaired. Examples include:

- a fall in the profit (or an increase in the loss) from operations
- a fall in the cash flows from operations, or a negative cash flow
- a fall in budgeted cash flows, or budgeted profit from operations

The normal expectation is that there will be no indication of impairment but, where there is, the entity must carry out an impairment review.

the impairment review

An impairment review involves comparing the asset's carrying amount with the recoverable amount. The three steps are as follows (see also the Case Study, on page 113):

STEP 1   What is the asset's carrying amount (ie cost/revaluation less depreciation/amortisation to date)?

STEP 2   What is the asset's recoverable amount? See diagram below.

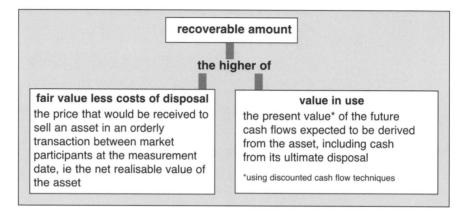

STEP 3   If carrying amount is greater than recoverable amount, then the asset is impaired and should be written down to its recoverable amount on the statement of financial position. The amount of the impairment loss is recognised as an expense in the statement of profit or loss and other comprehensive income unless it relates to a previously revalued asset, when it is recognised as a decrease in other comprehensive income and is debited to the revaluation surplus within equity (to the extent of the revaluation surplus for that particular asset).

recognition of impairment losses

An impairment loss is to be recognised when the recoverable amount is less than the carrying amount. The asset is reduced to its recoverable amount and the impairment loss is recognised immediately as an expense in the statement of profit of loss and other comprehensive income (unless it relates to a previously revalued asset when it is recognised as a decrease in other comprehensive income and is debited to the revaluation surplus within equity – to the extent of the revaluation surplus for that particular asset).

After recognition of an impairment loss, depreciation/amortisation will need to be adjusted for future financial periods.

disclosure in the financial statements

The financial statements must disclose the amount of impairment losses recognised in the statement of profit or loss and other comprehensive income, including impairment losses on revalued assets recognised in other comprehensive income.

INITIAL TRAINING PLC: THE IMPAIRMENT REVIEW

situation

Initial Training plc is a large training organisation providing 'return-to-work' courses.

You are helping to prepare the company's year end financial statements and have been asked by your boss, the company accountant, to carry out an impairment review of non-current assets held at the training centre at Rowcester. Today you have obtained details of the two photocopiers in the print room at Rowcester:

- **Machine 1** is six years old and is a relatively slow photocopier based on old technology. The cost of this machine was £8,000 and depreciation to date (the year end) is £4,800, giving it a carrying amount of £3,200. Since the arrival of the other photocopier, this machine has been relegated to 'standby' use.

- **Machine 2** is only a few months old. It is a digital copier incorporating the latest technology. It is very fast and versatile, and has the capacity to meet the needs of the entire training centre. It cost £15,000 and depreciation to the end of the financial year will be £1,500, giving it a carrying amount of £13,500. This machine is much preferred by the staff who use it as a first choice.

solution

The impairment review you carry out is as follows:

Machine 1

- Carrying amount: £3,200
- The company accountant has given you the following information to enable you to calculate the recoverable amount:

  the higher of

  – fair value: £1,000 resale value of machine on the secondhand market (there would be no selling costs on disposal)

  – value in use: £2,000 being the present value of the future benefits from continued use as a standby machine, including cash from its ultimate disposal

  Therefore the recoverable amount is £2,000.

- As carrying amount (£3,200) is greater than the machine's recoverable amount (£2,000), the asset is impaired. Accordingly, the amount of the impairment loss

(£1,200) is to be recognised as an expense in the statement of profit or loss and other comprehensive income, and the value of the machine will be recognised on the company's statement of financial position at the recoverable amount of £2,000.

Machine 2

- Carrying amount: £13,500
- You are given the following information to enable you to calculate the recoverable amount:

  the higher of

  - fair value: £10,000 resale value of machine on the secondhand market (there would be no selling costs on disposal)

  - value in use: £55,000 being the present value of the future benefits from continued use as the main machine, including cash from its ultimate disposal

  Therefore recoverable amount is £55,000.

- As carrying amount (£13,500) is less than the machine's recoverable amount (£55,000), the asset is not impaired. Accordingly, the machine will be recognised on the company's statement of financial position at cost price less depreciation to date.

IAS 17 – LEASES

Tutorial note:

IAS 17, *Leases,* is currently under review by the International Accounting Standards Board. It is likely that the distinction between finance leases and operating leases will be abandoned. Keep up-to-date with this and other IASB developments at www.ifrs.org

Leasing is the means by which companies obtain the right to use non-current assets, such as machinery or vehicles. The lessee makes agreed payments for a period of time to a lessor (often a finance company). There may be provision in a lease contract for legal title of the leased asset to pass to the lessee.

IAS 17 sets out the accounting treatment where assets are obtained for use by a business under:

- a **finance lease** (usually a longer term lease, under which substantially all the risks and rewards of ownership are transferred to the lessee)

- an **operating lease** (usually a shorter term lease, where there is no substantial transfer of the risks and rewards of ownership to the lessee)

A simple example illustrates the difference between these: hiring a van for the weekend to move some furniture is an operating lease; a business that leases a van under a four or five year contract does so under a finance lease.

Deciding whether a lease is a finance lease or an operating lease depends on the commercial substance of the transaction rather than the legal form of the contract. However, a finance lease is usually characterised by **one or more** of the following:

■ the lease transfers ownership of the asset to the lessee by the end of the lease term

■ the lessee has the option to purchase the asset at a price that is expected to be sufficiently lower than the fair value* at the date the option becomes exercisable for it to be reasonably certain, at the inception of the lease, that the option will be exercised

■ the lease term is for the major part of the economic life of the asset, even if the title is not transferred

■ at the inception of the lease, the present value of the minimum lease payments amounts to at least substantially all of the fair value* of the leased asset

■ the leased assets are of such a specialised nature that only the lessee can use them without major modifications

*   fair value: defined in IAS 17 as the amount for which an asset could be exchanged, or a liability settled, between knowledgeable, willing parties in an arm's length transaction

These characteristics can be summarised in the diagram shown on the next page, but do note that the judgement as to how a lease is classified is a matter of overall balance.

Other indications of a finance lease include one or more of the following:

■ if the lessee can cancel the lease, the lessor's losses associated with the cancellation are borne by the lessee

■ gains or losses from fluctuations in the fair value of the residual value accrue to the lessee (eg by means of a rebate of lease payments)

■ the lessee has the ability to continue the lease for a secondary period at substantially lower lease payments

Note that for leases of land and buildings the following apply:

■ the two elements – land and buildings – are normally considered separately

■ land is often classified as an operating lease (because land normally has an indefinite economic life, and a lease can only ever be for a short part of that life), unless title passes to the lessee by the end of the lease term

■ buildings can be either a finance lease or an operating lease, depending on the characteristics (see above) set out in IAS 17

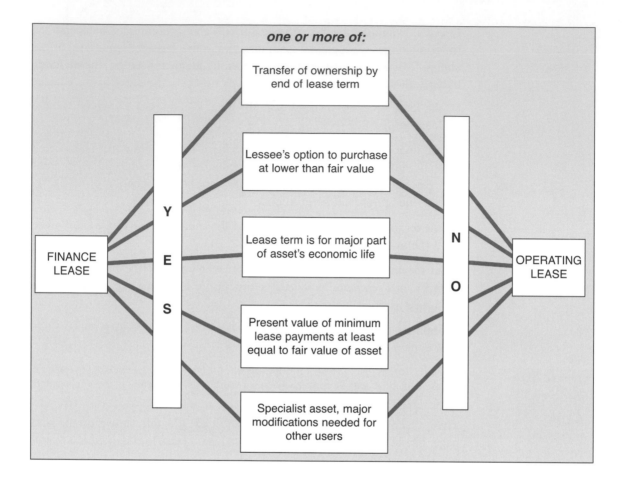

accounting for finance leases by lessees

A finance lease is initially recognised on the statement of financial position as an asset, together with a corresponding liability to the lessor. The amount shown will be the lower of the fair value of the asset and the present value of the minimum lease payments. Any initial direct costs of the lessee are added to the amount recognised as an asset.

Note the following points:

■ The minimum lease payments are the payments over the lease term that the lessee is, or can be, required to make.

■ To calculate the present value requires the minimum lease payments to be discounted at the interest rate implicit in the lease, if practicable, or to use the lessee's incremental borrowing rate. (The *interest rate implicit in the lease* is the discount rate at which the present value of the minimum lease payments plus the residual value are equal to the fair value of the leased asset. The *lessee's incremental borrowing rate of interest* is the rate of interest that the lessee would have to pay on a similar lease.)

Finance lease payments to the lessor are then apportioned between the finance charge – recognised as an expense in the statement of profit or loss and other comprehensive income – and a reduction of the outstanding liability on the statement of financial position. The finance charge is to be such that it gives a constant rate of interest on the remaining balance of the liability (although IAS 17 allows these calculations to be approximated).

The leased asset is depreciated on the same basis as assets which are owned – the amount of depreciation being recognised as an expense in the statement of profit or loss and other comprehensive income. If there is the possibility that the lessee will not obtain ownership at the end of the lease period, then the asset is to be depreciated over the shorter of the lease term or the useful life of the asset.

accounting for operating leases by lessees

With an operating lease, lease payments are recognised as an expense in the statement of profit or loss and other comprehensive income on a straight-line basis over the lease term (unless another basis is more representative of the time pattern of the user's benefit).

Case Study

WYVERN ENGINEERING LIMITED: ACCOUNTING FOR LEASING

situation

Wyvern Engineering Limited is leasing two machines for use in its business:

1 A **portable compressor** is leased from The Hire Shop as and when it is needed at a cost of £100 per week; usage was as follows:

20-1	5 weeks
20-2	3 weeks
20-3	6 weeks
20-4	10 weeks

When the machine is not being used, Wyvern Engineering returns it to The Hire Shop where it is available for hire by other customers. The estimated useful life of the machine is six years.

2 A **pressing machine** is leased from Mercia Finance plc from 1 January 20-1. The details are:

cost price of machine	£10,000
leasing period	4 years
estimated useful life	4 years
leasing payments	£3,500 per year (payable monthly on 1st of each month in advance)
Wyvern Engineering's borrowing rate	10%

Explain how these two leases will be recorded in the financial statements of the lessee. Show relevant extracts from the statement of profit or loss and other comprehensive income and the statement of financial position for the years ending 31 December 20-1, 20-2, 20-3 and 20-4.

solution

1 The **portable compressor** is being leased under an operating lease because
   - the lessee is leasing the machine for a period which is substantially less than its total useful life
   - the lessor retains the risks and rewards of ownership of the asset and is responsible for the costs of repairs and maintenance

   The only accounting entries will be an expense in the statement of profit or loss and other comprehensive income for the lease payments in each financial year. These are recognised at their actual cost each year (rather than on a straight-line basis) as this is more representative of the time pattern of the benefit to Wyvern Engineering.

2 The **pressing machine** is being leased under a finance lease because
   - the present value of the leasing payments amounts to substantially all of the asset's fair value, ie *£14,000 (£3,500 x 4 years), compared with £10,000
   - substantially all the risks and rewards of ownership are transferred to the lessee

   The accounting entries are shown below.

   * For simplicity, the £14,000 has not been discounted; at a 10% discount rate the present value would be approximately £12,000 – above the asset's fair value.

accounting entries: operating lease for the portable compressor

Debit statement of profit or loss and other comprehensive income with actual lease payments, ie

	£
20-1	500
20-2	300
20-3	600
20-4	1,000

accounting entries: finance lease for the pressing machine

The first step is to apportion the leasing payments between finance charges and capital payments. With total leasing payments of £14,000 and the cost price of the machine at £10,000, the finance charges and capital payments are as follows:

	leasing payment	finance charge	capital payment
	£	£	£
20-1	3,500	1,600	1,900
20-2	3,500	1,200	2,300
20-3	3,500	800	2,700
20-4	3,500	400	3,100
	14,000	4,000	10,000

The finance charge has been calculated here using the **sum-of-the-digits method** (see page 102). This is acceptable under IAS 17, being a form of approximation (a more accurate way is to use the **actuarial method**, described on the next page). The calculations are as follows:

20-1	4/(1 + 2 + 3 + 4) x £4,000	=	£1,600
20-2	3/(1 + 2 + 3 + 4) x £4,000	=	£1,200
20-3	2/(1 + 2 + 3 + 4) x £4,000	=	£800
20-4	1/(1 + 2 + 3 + 4) x £4,000	=	£400

Depreciation on the machine (using the straight-line method) is:

$$\frac{£10,000}{4 \text{ years}} = £2,500 \text{ per year}$$

statement of profit or loss and other comprehensive income: extracts

£

20-1

Operating lease	500
Finance charge under finance lease	1,600
Depreciation of machinery	2,500
	4,600

20-2

Operating lease	300
Finance charge under finance lease	1,200
Depreciation of machinery	2,500
	4,000

20-3

Operating lease	600
Finance charge under finance lease	800
Depreciation of machinery	2,500
	3,900

20-4

Operating lease	1,000
Finance charge under finance lease	400
Depreciation of machinery	2,500
	3,900

statement of financial position: extracts

Notes:

- only the finance lease is recognised on the statement of financial position
- the extracts from the statement of financial position do not balance until the last year (20-4) because of the expense of the finance charge in the statement of profit or loss and other comprehensive income

20-1	£
Non-current assets	
Machinery under finance lease at cost	10,000
Less depreciation to date	2,500
	7,500
Liabilities	
Current – obligation under finance lease	*2,300
Non-current – obligation under finance lease	5,800
£10,000 – £1,900 capital payment	= 8,100

* next year's payments are a current liability

20-2	£
Non-current assets	
Machinery under finance lease at cost	10,000
Less depreciation to date	5,000
	5,000
Liabilities	
Current – obligation under finance lease	2,700
Non-current – obligation under finance lease	3,100
£10,000 – (£1,900 + £2,300 capital payments)	= 5,800

20-3	£
Non-current assets	
Machinery under finance lease at cost	10,000
Less depreciation to date	7,500
	2,500
Liabilities	
Current – obligation under finance lease	
£10,000 – (£1,900 + £2,300 + £2,700 capital payments)	= 3,100

20-4 The statement of financial position will show neither asset nor liability, as the leasing contract will terminate on 31 December 20-4. The leasing payment of £3,500 made in this year will be split £400 to the finance charge and £3,100, so eliminating the liability for the lease.

actuarial method of calculating the finance charge

An alternative to the sum-of-the-digits method is to use the actuarial method. This is a more accurate method of apportioning finance charges over the period of the lease so as to give a constant rate of interest on the capital amount of the lease. Using this method the rate of interest for the lease of the pressing machine is found (either by using actuarial tables or by trial and error) to be approximately 11.5 per cent, as follows:

year	leasing payments due at start of year	leasing payments during year	leasing payments due at end of year	finance charge at 11.5%*	capital payment
	£	£	£	£	£
20-1	14,000	3,500	10,500	1,610	1,890
20-2	10,500	3,500	7,000	1,208	2,292
20-3	7,000	3,500	3,500	805	2,695
20-4	3,500	3,500	nil	**377	3,123
		14,000		4,000	10,000

* leasing payments due at start of year x 11.5%

** £403 – £26 adjustment (to make total finance charge £4,000) = £377

Note that the finance charge has been slightly approximated in the above calculation because the leasing payments due at the start of the year have been used instead of the **average amount** due during the year.

In the same way as with the sum-of-the digits calculations, the finance charge is debited in the statement of profit or loss and other comprehensive income, while the capital payments are used to calculate the liabilities under the finance lease to be shown in the statement of financial position.

IAS 2 – INVENTORIES

Inventories are assets **held for sale** in the ordinary course of business.

Companies often have inventories in various forms:

- raw materials, for use in a manufacturing process
- work-in-progress (partly manufactured goods)
- finished goods, made by the business and ready for resale to customers
- finished goods, which have been bought in by the business for resale

Note that IAS 2 applies to all types of inventories, except for the valuation of construction contracts, and certain other specialist assets.

The principle of inventory valuation, as set out in IAS 2, is that inventories should be valued at *'the lower of cost and net realisable value'*. This valuation is illustrated by the diagram on the next page:

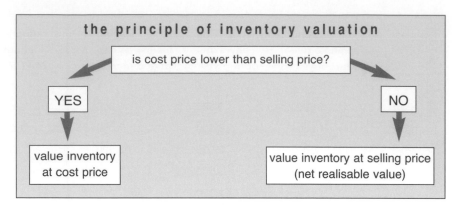

Thus two different inventory values are compared:

■ cost, including additional costs to bring the product or service to its present location and condition (eg import duties and other taxes, transport and handling costs directly attributable to the purchase)

■ net realisable value (the estimated selling price less the estimated costs of completion and the estimated costs necessary to make the sale)

The lower of these two values is taken, and different items or groups of inventory are compared separately. These principles are illustrated in the two Case Studies which follow.

Case Study

THE CLOTHING STORE: INVENTORY VALUATION

situation

The Clothing Store bought in a range of 'designer' beachwear in the Spring, with each item costing £15 and retailing for £30. Most of the goods sell well but, by Autumn, ten items remain unsold. These are put on the 'bargain rail' at £18 each. On 31 December, at the end of the store's financial year, five items remain unsold. At what price will they be included in the year end inventories valuation?

Twelve months later, three items still remain unsold and have been reduced further to £10 each. At what price will they now be valued in the year end inventories valuation?

solution

• At 31 December, the five items will be valued at a cost of £15 each,

  ie 5 x £15 = £75.

• Twelve months later, the three items remaining unsold will be valued at a net realisable value of £10 each, ie 3 x £10 = £30.

Important note: Inventories are never valued at selling prices when selling prices are above cost prices. The reason for this is that selling prices includes profit, and to value inventories in this way would recognise the profit in the financial statements before it has been realised.

Case Study

PAINT AND WALLPAPER SUPPLIES: INVENTORY VALUATION

situation

The year end valuations for the two main groups of inventory held by the business Paint and Wallpaper Supplies are found to be:

	Cost	Net Realisable Value
	£	£
Paints	2,500	2,300
Wallpapers	5,000	7,500
	7,500	9,800

Which of the following inventories valuations do you think is correct?

(a)   £7,500

(b)   £9,800

(c)   £7,300

(d)   £10,000

solution

Inventory valuation (c) is correct, because it has taken the 'lower of cost and net realisable value' for each group of inventory, ie

Paints (at net realisable value)	£2,300
Wallpapers (at cost)	£5,000
	£7,300

You will also note that this valuation is the lowest of the four possible choices.

inventory valuation methods

IAS 2 allows two different methods to be used to calculate the cost price of inventories.

■ **FIFO** (first in, first out) – this method assumes that the first items acquired are the first to be used, so that the valuation of inventory on hand at any time consists of the most recently acquired items.

■ **AVCO** (average cost), or **weighted average cost method** – here the average cost of items held at the beginning of the period is calculated; as new inventory is acquired a new average cost is calculated (usually based on a weighted average, using the number of units bought as the weighting).

The same inventory valuation is to be used for all inventories having a similar nature and use to the entity. Where there are inventories with a different nature or use, different valuations may be justified – for example, goods bought in especially for a specific project (and not interchangeable with other inventories) – are to be valued at their individual costs.

The use of a valuation method does not necessarily correspond with the method of physical distribution adopted in a firm's stores. For example, in a car factory, one car battery of type X is the same as another, and no-one will be concerned if the storekeeper issues one from the latest batch received, even if the FIFO method has been adopted. However, perishable goods are always physically handled on the basis of first in, first out, even if the inventory records use the AVCO method.

Having chosen a suitable inventory valuation method, a business would continue to use that method unless there were good reasons for making the change. This is in line with the consistency concept of accounting.

Note that LIFO (last in, first out) cannot be used under IAS 2.

net realisable value

Where the cost of inventories is not recoverable – eg goods have been damaged, or have become obsolete, or their selling prices have declined – they should be written down to their net realisable value. This is usually done on an item-by-item basis but can also be done on a group basis, eg where the inventory relates to the same product line.

closing inventory valuation for a manufacturer

The principles of IAS 2 are applied to a manufacturer, who may hold three types of inventories at the year-end:

- raw materials
- work-in-progress
- finished goods

For **raw materials,** the comparison is made between cost (which can be found using either FIFO or AVCO) and net realisable value.

For **work-in-progress** and **finished goods**, IAS 2 requires that the cost valuation includes expenditure not only on direct materials but also on the costs of conversion, that is direct labour, direct expenses and production overheads. Thus for work-in-progress and finished goods, 'cost' comprises:

- direct materials (the purchase price, including import duties, transport and handling costs, less trade discounts and rebates)
- direct labour
- direct expenses
- production overheads (to bring the product to its present location or condition)
- other overheads, if any, (to bring the product to its present location and condition)

Note that the inventory valuation cannot include abnormal waste (eg of materials and labour), storage costs, administrative overheads not related to production, selling costs, and the interest cost when inventories are purchased with deferred settlement terms.

The 'cost' is then compared with net realisable value, and the lower figure is taken as the inventory valuation.

Case Study

XYZ MANUFACTURING: INVENTORIES VALUATION

situation

XYZ Manufacturing started in business on 1 July 20-5 producing security devices for doors and windows. During the first year 2,000 units were sold and at the end of the year, on 30 June 20-6, there were 200 finished units in the warehouse and 20 units which were exactly half-finished as regards direct materials, direct labour and production overheads.

Costs for the first year were:	£
Direct materials used	18,785
Direct labour	13,260
Production overheads	8,840
Non-production overheads	4,420
TOTAL COST FOR YEAR	45,305

At 30 June 20-6 it was estimated that the net realisable value of each completed security device was £35. At the same date, the company holds raw materials as follows:

	cost	net realisable value
	£	£
Material X	1,400	1,480
Material Y	400	360
Material Z	260	280

Calculate the inventories valuation at 30 June 20-6 for:

• raw materials

• work-in-progress

• finished goods

solution

RAW MATERIALS

Using the IAS 2 rule of 'the lower of cost and net realisable value' the total value is:

	£	
Material X	1,400	(cost)
Material Y	360	(net realisable value)
Material Z	260	(cost)
	2,020	

WORK-IN-PROGRESS

To calculate the value of work-in-progress and finished goods we need to know the production cost, ie direct materials, direct labour and production overheads. This is:

	£
Direct materials used	18,785
Direct labour	13,260
Production overheads	8,840
PRODUCTION COST FOR YEAR	40,885

All these costs must be included because they have been incurred in bringing the product to its present location or condition. Non-production overheads are not included because they are not directly related to production. Thus, a production cost of £40,885 has produced:

Units sold	2,000
Closing inventory of completed units	200
Closing inventory of work-in-progress –	
20 units exactly half-finished equals	
10 completed units	10
PRODUCTION FOR YEAR	2,210

The **cost per unit** is: $\dfrac{£40,885}{2,210}$ = **£18.50 per unit**

The 20 half-finished units have a cost of (20 ÷ 2) x £18.50 = **£185**. They have a net realisable value of (20 ÷ 2) x £35 = £350. The value of work-in-progress will, therefore, be recognised in the financial statements as £185, which is the lower of cost and net realisable value.

FINISHED GOODS

The completed units held at the end of the year have a production cost of 200 x £18.50 = £3,700, compared with a net realisable value of 200 x £35 = £7,000. Applying the rule of lower of cost and net realisable value, finished goods inventory will be valued at **£3,700**.

Chapter Summary

- International financial reporting standards comprise IASs and IFRSs.

- IAS 16, *Property, Plant and Equipment,* sets out the principles of accounting for non-current assets such as land and buildings, machinery, office equipment, shop fittings and vehicles. It covers
  - recognition
  - initial measurement
  - cost and revaluation models
  - depreciation
  - derecognition

- IAS 38, *Intangible Assets,* sets out the accounting treatment of expenditure on acquiring, developing, maintaining or enhancing intangible assets. It covers
  - recognition
  - initial measurement
  - cost and revaluation models
  - amortisation of intangible assets with finite lives

- IAS 36, *Impairment of Assets,* sets out the accounting procedures to ensure that assets are carried on the statement of financial position at no more than their value, or recoverable amount. The standard requires an impairment review to be carried out when there is evidence that impairment has taken place. The standard gives a number of indicators of impairment.

- IAS 17, *Leases,* sets out the accounting treatment for
  - operating leases
  - finance leases

  Interest on finance leases may be calculated using either the sum-of-the-digits or the actuarial methods.

- IAS 2, *Inventories,* requires that inventories are valued at the lower of cost and net realisable value. Valuation methods include:
  - FIFO (first in, first out)
  - AVCO (average cost, based as a weighted average cost)

  LIFO (last in, first out) cannot be used under IAS 2.

Key Terms	**IAS**	International Accounting Standard (part of the rules of accounting)
	IFRS	International Financial Reporting Standard (part of the rules of accounting)
	asset	a resource controlled by the entity as a result of past events and from which future economic benefits are expected to flow to the entity
	property, plant and equipment	tangible assets held for use in the production or supply of goods and services, which are expected to be used for more than one period
	depreciable amount	the cost of the asset, less any residual value
	fair value	the price that would be received to sell an asset or paid to transfer a liability in an orderly transaction between market participants at the measurement date (note that IAS 17, *Leases*, uses a different definition – see page 114)
	carrying amount	the amount at which an asset is recognised on the statement of financial position, after deducting any accumulated depreciation or impairment losses
	cost model	asset is carried at cost less accumulated depreciation and impairment losses
	revaluation model	asset is carried at a revalued amount, being its fair value less any subsequent depreciation and impairment losses
	intangible asset	an identifiable non-monetary asset without physical substance
	research	original and planned investigation undertaken with the prospect of gaining new scientific or technical knowledge and understanding
	development	the application of research findings or other knowledge to a plan or design for the production of new or substantially improved materials, devices, products, processes, systems or services before the start of commercial production or use
	depreciation/amortisation	the systematic allocation of the depreciable amount of an asset over its useful life (note: the term 'amortisation' is customarily used in relation to intangible assets)

impairment loss	the amount by which the carrying amount of an asset exceeds its recoverable amount
recoverable amount	the higher of an asset's fair value, less costs of disposal, and its value in use
value in use	the present value of the future cash flows expected to be derived from the asset, including cash from its ultimate disposal
operating lease	a shorter-term lease, where there is no transfer of the risks and rewards of ownership to the lessee
finance lease	a longer-term lease, under which substantially all the risks and rewards of ownership are transferred to the lessee
lessee	the user of a leased asset
first in, first out (FIFO)	inventory valuation method which assumes that the first items acquired are the first to be used
average cost (AVCO)	inventory valuation method which calculates an average cost (based on a weighted average) whenever new inventory is acquired

Activities

4.1 A limited company has purchased a new machine with the following expenditure:

	£
Invoice price of the machine	30,500
Delivery costs	1,300
Installation and assembly costs	2,200
Cost of testing the machine	900
Total expenditure	34,900

Under IAS 16, *Property, Plant and Equipment*, what cost will the company include in property, plant and equipment?

		✓
(a)	£33,600	
(b)	£31,800	
(c)	£34,000	
(d)	£34,900	

4.2 Laceby Ltd purchased an item of plant for £350,000 on 1 January 20X2. The useful life was anticipated as being seven years and the residual value was estimated as £140,000.

Laceby Ltd depreciates plant on a straight-line basis.

The residual value was still considered to be £140,000 at 1 January 20X6 but the remaining useful life was re-assessed to be five years.

What is the depreciation charge for the item of plant for the year to 31 December 20X6?

		✓
(a)	£46,000	
(b)	£30,000	
(c)	£28,000	
(d)	£18,000	

4.3 Under IAS 38, *Intangible Assets:*

(a) define an intangible asset

(b) give two examples of intangible assets

(c) state and explain the three key elements of an intangible asset

4.4 Which **ONE** of the following is an intangible asset?

		✓
(a)	share premium	
(b)	trademarks	
(c)	trade receivables	
(d)	property	

4.5 IAS 38, *Intangible Assets,* requires certain items of expenditure to be written off to the statement of profit or loss and other comprehensive income in the year in which it is incurred. Which **ONE** of the following must be written off in this way?

		✓
(a)	research expenditure	
(b)	development expenditure	
(c)	internally generated goodwill	
(d)	internally generated brands	

4.6 Under IAS 38, *Intangible Assets:*

(a) what are the points, all of which must be demonstrated, before development costs can be recognised on the statement of financial position?

(b) which costs can be included in the development of internally generated intangible assets, and which costs are excluded?

4.7 During the financial year, a limited company has incurred development expenditure of £20,000 and research expenditure of £10,000. In compliance with IAS 38, *Intangible Assets,* which of the following statements is true?

	✓
(a) Expenditure of £30,000 may be recognised as an expense in this year's statement of profit or loss and other comprehensive income.	
(b) Expenditure of £10,000, subject to satisfying certain criteria, may be recognised as an intangible asset.	
(c) Expenditure of £20,000, subject to satisfying certain criteria, may be recognised as an intangible asset.	
(d) Expenditure of £30,000, subject to satisfying certain criteria, may be recognised as an intangible asset.	

4.8 Under IAS 36, *Impairment of Assets*:

(a) explain how an impairment review is carried out, and define the terms used.

(b) state how an impairment loss is recorded in the financial statements.

4.9 IAS 36, *Impairment of Assets*, gives a number of indications of impairment.

State four external sources of information and three internal sources of information that may indicate impairment.

4.10 A business has four assets which the directors wish to test for impairment:

Asset	Carrying amount	Fair value, less costs of disposal	Value in use
	£	£	£
1	10,000	9,000	11,000
2	15,000	15,000	14,000
3	30,000	27,000	28,000
4	40,000	39,000	38,000

Which of the above assets is impaired according to IAS 36, *Impairment of Assets*?

		✓
(a)	1	
(b)	2	
(c)	1 and 2	
(d)	3 and 4	

4.11 According to IAS 17, *Leases*, when should a lease be classified as a finance lease and when should it be classified as an operating lease?

Finance lease

Operating lease

4.12 According to IAS 17, *Leases*:

(a) How is a finance lease accounted for in the financial statements of the lessee at the commencement of the lease term?

(b) How is an operating lease accounted for in the financial statements of the lessee?

4.13 **(a)**   Explain how the following methods are used to apportion interest on a finance lease over the lease term:

- sum-of-the-digits
- actuarial method

Sum-of-the-digits

Actuarial method

(b)   JK Ltd is leasing an asset under a finance lease.

Complete the following table to show the finance charge for each year from 20-1 to 20-4 using the actuarial method at a rate of 12 per cent. Note that JK Ltd's policy is to calculate the finance charge on payments due at the start of the year.

Year	Leasing payments due at start of year £	Leasing payments during year £	Finance charge £
20-1	20,000	5,000	
20-2	15,000	5,000	
20-3	10,000	5,000	
20-4	5,000	5,000	

4.14   Which **ONE** of the following statements best describes the valuation of inventories under IAS 2, *Inventories*?

		✓
(a)	at the higher of the FIFO and AVCO methods	
(b)	at the higher of cost and net realisable value	
(c)	using the AVCO method	
(d)	at the lower of cost and net realisable value	

4.15 Par for the Course Ltd sells golf equipment from its website. At the end of the financial year the company has the following groups of inventories:

Inventory	Cost £	Net realisable value £
Golf balls	10,400	10,200
Clubs	44,900	62,100
Golf shoes	18,300	17,500
Golf bags	22,600	34,900
Total	96,200	124,700

In accordance with IAS 2, *Inventories*, what is the correct valuation for the company's financial statements?

		✓
(a)	£96,200	
(b)	£124,700	
(c)	£125,700	
(d)	£95,200	

Accounting for liabilities and the statement of profit or loss

this chapter covers...

This chapter focuses on the international financial reporting standards that impact mainly on the way in which liabilities are accounted for in both the statement of profit or loss and other comprehensive income and the statement of financial position. We then turn our attention to those standards that affect principally the statement of profit or loss and other comprehensive income.

For the liabilities side of the statement of financial position we consider standards that cover:

■ *income taxes (IAS 12)*

■ *leases (IAS 17)*

■ *provisions, contingent liabilities and contingent assets (IAS 37)*

■ *events after the reporting period (IAS 10)*

Accounting standards which affect mainly the statement of profit or loss and other comprehensive income include:

■ *property, plant and equipment (IAS 16)*

■ *revenue (IAS 18)*

ACCOUNTING FOR LIABILITIES

The first part of this chapter explains the accounting treatment of liabilities – non-current and current – as specified by the relevant international financial reporting standards. It is well worth going back to the *Conceptual Framework for Financial Reporting* for the definition of a liability (page 10): '*a present obligation of the entity arising from past events, the settlement of which is expected to result in an outflow from the entity of resources embodying economic benefits.*'

Note the three key parts of the definition:
- a present obligation of the entity
- arising from past events
- the settlement of which is expected to result in an outflow from the entity

Thus a company which has bought goods or services on credit has a present obligation in the form of an amount owed to trade payables, which arises from past events such as a purchase order made last month, and which will result in settlement in the form of resources embodying economic benefits, ie payment will be made from the company's bank account.

In order to be recognised on the statement of financial position, liabilities must be capable of being reliably measured. If the liability cannot be reliably measured then it will often be disclosed in the notes to the accounts, eg a contingent liability.

The international financial reporting standards which follow set out the recognition and measurement criteria of different liabilities. *Income Taxes* (IAS 12), *Leases* (IAS 17), *Provisions, Contingent Liabilities and Contingent Assets* (IAS 37) and *Events after the Reporting Period* (IAS 10).

IAS 12 – INCOME TAXES

This standard sets out the accounting treatment for taxes on income – such as the corporation tax which is paid by UK companies and is based on their profits. In the UK, the Chancellor of the Exchequer sets out, in budget announcements, the various rates of corporation tax. Most larger companies in the UK pay part of their tax due every three months, with some amounts due to be paid in the current accounting period and other amounts due in the following accounting period.

current tax

This is the amount of income taxes payable in respect of the taxable profit for the year. Note that taxable profit may well differ from the accounting profit shown by the statement of profit or loss and other comprehensive income – this is because the tax authorities (in the UK, HM Revenue & Customs) determine the rules as to which expenses are allowable for tax purposes.

The tax expense for the year, from the ordinary activities of the entity, is recognised on the face of the statement of profit or loss and other comprehensive income. The amount of unpaid current tax is recognised as a liability on the statement of financial position, under the heading of current liabilities. When an entity has overpaid tax, then the excess amount is recognised as an asset, under the heading of current assets.

The amount of current tax is to be measured in the financial statements using the tax rates applicable at the date of the statement of financial position.

estimates of tax

A business often has to estimate the amount of tax due on its profits, and records the amount of the estimate in its financial statements. The reason for making an estimate is because the tax authorities will not be able to confirm the amount payable until after they have received the statement of profit or loss and other comprehensive income and have agreed the expenses that are allowable for tax purposes.

When the business makes an estimate of tax it is likely that the estimate will differ from the actual liability. As a consequence, an adjustment will need to be made in the financial statements of the next accounting period.

example 1

20X1   Estimated corporation tax charge £40,000

20X1   Actual corporation tax charge £35,000

20X2   Estimated corporation tax charge £25,000

As the company has over-estimated its corporation tax liability for 20X1 by £5,000, its financial statements for 20X2 will adjust for this prior period and show:
- statement of profit or loss and other comprehensive income:
  tax £20,000 (ie £25,000 estimated, less £5,000 over-estimated in 20X1)
- statement of financial position: tax liability £25,000 (ie the estimated tax payable for 20X2)

example 2

20X4   Estimated corporation tax charge £20,000

20X4   Actual corporation tax charge £22,000

20X5   Estimated corporation tax charge £30,000

Here the company has under-estimated its corporation tax liability for 20X4 by £2,000, its financial statements for 20X5 will adjust for this prior period and show:

- statement of profit or loss and other comprehensive income:

  tax £32,000 (ie £30,000 estimated, plus £2,000 under-estimated in 20X4)

- statement of financial position: tax liability £30,000 (ie the estimated tax payable for 20X5)

Case Study

SANTA PLC: SHOWING THE TAX LIABILITIES

situation

The following balances are taken from the accounting system of Santa plc as at 31 December 20-3:

	£	£
Inventories	51,200	
Property, plant and equipment at cost or revaluation	250,000	
Cash and cash equivalents	4,500	
Share capital		100,000
Share premium account		25,000
Trade payables		75,400
Trade receivables	92,800	
Revaluation reserve		50,000
Loan (repayable in 20-8)		40,000
Profit before tax		68,300
Retained earnings at start of year		69,800
Dividends paid	30,000	
	428,500	428,500

The tax liability on the profits for the year is estimated to be £25,400

You are helping with the year end financial statements and are asked to prepare:

- statement of profit or loss, starting with profit before tax
- statement of financial position

for the year ended 31 December 20-3.

solution

SANTA PLC
Statement of profit or loss (extract)
for the year ended 31 December 20-3

	£
Profit before tax	68,300
Tax	–25,400
Profit for the year	42,900

Statement of financial position as at 31 December 20-3

ASSETS	£
Non-current assets	
Property, plant and equipment at cost or revaluation	250,000
Current assets	
Inventories	51,200
Trade receivables	92,800
Cash and cash equivalents	4,500
	148,500
Total assets	398,500

EQUITY AND LIABILITIES	
Equity	£
Share capital	100,000
Share premium	25,000
Revaluation reserve	50,000
Retained earnings	*82,700
Total equity	257,700
Non-current liabilities	
Loan	40,000
	40,000
Current liabilities	
Trade payables	75,400
Tax payable	25,400
	100,800
Total liabilities	140,800
Total equity and liabilities	398,500

* £69,800 at start + £42,900 profit for year – £30,000 dividends paid

LIABILITIES SIDE OF STATEMENT OF FINANCIAL POSITION

Three further accounting standards impact mainly on the liabilities side of the statement of financial position:

IAS 17 – *Leases*

IAS 37 – *Provisions, contingent liabilities and contingent assets*

IAS 10 – *Events after the reporting period*

Note that these standards often also have an effect on both the statement of profit or loss and other comprehensive income and on the assets side of the statement of financial position.

IAS 17 – Leases

This standard has already been looked at in detail in Chapter 4 (pages 114-121).

On the lessee's statement of financial position, finance leases are recognised as liabilities at the lower of the fair value of the asset being leased and the present value of the minimum lease payments. The amount is to be split between non-current and current liabilities, as appropriate.

IAS 37 – Provisions, contingent liabilities and contingent assets

These three items – provisions, contingent liabilities, contingent assets – represent uncertainties that may have an effect on future financial statements. They need to be accounted for consistently so that users can have a fuller understanding of their effect on financial statements.

The objective of IAS 37 is to ensure that appropriate recognition criteria and measurement bases are applied to provisions, contingent liabilities and contingent assets and that sufficient information is disclosed in the notes to the financial statements to enable users to understand their nature, timing and amount.

provisions

A **provision** is a liability of uncertain timing or amount.

A **liability** is

- a present obligation as a result of past events
- where settlement is expected to result in an outflow of economic benefits (eg payment will be made)

An **obligating event** is an event that creates a legal or constructive obligation resulting in an entity having no realistic alternative to settling the obligation.

A **legal obligation** derives from a contract, legislation, or other operation of law.

A **constructive obligation** derives from an entity's actions such as an established pattern of past practice (eg to refund the difference if another local shop is currently selling the same goods at a lower price), or where the entity has created a valid expectation (eg to refund cash against returned goods without insisting on seeing the receipt).

A provision is to be recognised as a liability in the financial statements when:

- an entity has a present obligation as a result of a past event
- it is probable that an outflow of economic benefits will be required to settle the obligation
- a reliable estimate can be made of the amount of the obligation

Unless all of these conditions are met, no provision should be recognised (in which case the liability may be contingent – see next page).

IAS 37 uses the word 'probable', in connection with the outflow of economic benefits, as being more likely to occur than not, ie a more than 50% likelihood of its occurrence.

The 'reliable estimate' of the amount of the obligation should be the best estimate of the expenditure required to settle the present obligation, or to transfer it to a third party, at the date of the statement of financial position.

Notes:

■ Provisions are different from other liabilities such as trade payables and accruals. This is because, with provisions, there is uncertainty as to the timing or amount of the future expenditure required to settle. Contrast this with trade payables where the goods or services have been received or supplied and the amount due has either been invoiced or agreed with the supplier. Similarly, with accruals there is a liability to pay and, even if the amount may have to be estimated, the uncertainty is usually much less than for provisions.

■ All provisions are contingent (because they are uncertain in timing or amount) but the word 'contingent' is used for assets and liabilities that are not recognised in the financial statements because their existence will be confirmed only by uncertain future events, which may or may not occur.

The amount of the change in the provision is recognised as an expense in the statement of profit or loss and other comprehensive income, and the total amount of the provision is shown as a liability on the statement of financial position (under the heading long-term provisions). For each statement of financial position, the amount of provisions is to be reviewed and adjusted to reflect the current best estimate. If a provision is no longer required, it is to be reversed and shown as income in the statement of profit or loss and other comprehensive income. Provisions are only to be used for the expenditure for which the provision was originally recognised – to do otherwise would be to conceal the impact of different events on the financial statements. Provisions should not be recognised for future operating losses – they do not meet the definition of a liability nor the recognition criteria for provisions.

Disclosure in the notes to the financial statements requires:

- details of changes in the amount of provisions between the beginning and end of the year
- a description of the provision(s) and expected timings of any resulting transfers
- an indication of the uncertainties regarding the amount or timing of any resulting transfers

contingent liabilities

A **contingent liability** is:

- **either** a possible obligation arising from past events whose existence will be confirmed only by the occurrence or non-occurrence of one or more uncertain future events not wholly within the entity's control
- **or** a present obligation that arises from past events but is not recognised because:
    (a) **either** it is not probable that an outflow of economic benefits will be required to settle the obligation
    (b) **or** the obligation cannot be measured with sufficient reliability

Note that a contingent liability is a **possible** obligation, ie less than 50% likelihood of its occurrence (contrast this with the **probable** obligation of a provision, ie more than 50% likelihood of its occurrence).

A contingent liability is not recognised in the financial statements; however, it should be disclosed as a note to the statements which includes:

- a brief description of the nature of the contingent liability
- an estimate of its financial effect
- an indication of the uncertainties relating to the amount or timing of any outflow
- the possibility of any re-imbursement

Note that where a contingent liability is considered to be remote (contrast with possible), then no disclosure is required in the notes to the statements.

contingent assets

A **contingent asset** is a possible asset arising from past events whose existence will be confirmed only by the occurrence or non-occurrence of one or more uncertain future events not wholly within the entity's control.

A business should not recognise a contingent asset in its financial statements (because it could result in the recognition of income that may never be realised). However, when the realisation of the profit is virtually certain, then the asset is no longer contingent and its recognition in the statements is appropriate.

A contingent asset is disclosed only where an inflow of economic benefits is probable; disclosure in the notes to the financial statements should include:

– a brief description of the nature of the contingent asset

– an estimate of its financial effect

Note that, where the asset is considered to be either possible or remote, then no disclosure is required in the notes to the statements.

summary

The following diagram summarises the ways in which provisions, contingent liabilities and contingent assets are to be handled in the financial statements.

PROVISIONS (more than 50% likelihood of occurrence)	**CONTINGENT LIABILITIES** (less than 50% likelihood of occurrence)	
Probable • provision recognised in financial statements as a liability • disclosure of provision in notes, giving details of the figure shown in the statements	*Possible* • no liability recognised in financial statements • disclosure of contingent liability in notes	*Remote* • no liability recognised in financial statements • no disclosure of contingent liability in notes
CONTINGENT ASSETS		
Probable • no asset recognised in financial statements • disclosure of contingent asset in notes	*Possible* • no asset recognised in financial statements • no disclosure of contingent asset in notes	*Remote* • no asset recognised in financial statements • no disclosure of contingent asset in notes

Case Study

WYVERN WATER: WHAT SHOULD BE SHOWN IN THE FINANCIAL STATEMENTS?

situation

Wyvern Water Limited is a producer of spa water which is bottled at source high in the Wyvern Hills. The company also produces a very successful high energy drink – with a secret mix of Wyvern Water, glucose, and vitamins – marketed under the 'Dr Wyvern' label to sports enthusiasts.

You are helping to prepare the year end financial statements and have been asked to decide how the following should be reported in the year to 31 December 20-1.

1   Earlier in the year, a small batch of bottles of spa water was contaminated with oil from the bottling machinery. Although the problem was spotted by quality control checks, and most bottles were withdrawn from sale, some were sold to the public. In a few instances consumers of the water suffered severe stomach upsets and had to spend a night in hospital. These consumers are currently suing Wyvern Water for damages. The company's legal representatives consider that it is probable that the company will lose the case and that damages of £50,000 will be awarded against the company.

2   Wyvern Water holds worldwide patents and trademarks for the 'Dr Wyvern' energy drink. However, it has recently had letters from somebody claiming to be a Dr Wyvern who says that he devised the secret formula for the drink over fifty years ago. The mysterious Dr Wyvern is claiming royalties on sales of the drink for the past fifty years and says he will sue the company for £10m if he is not paid. Wyvern Water has checked carefully and found that the formula for the high energy drink was devised ten years ago by its own development team and that all applicable patents and trademarks are held. The company has sought legal advice and been advised that it is extremely unlikely that the claimant's case, if it gets to court, will be successful.

3   During the year Wyvern Water Limited has formed a separate company, Wyvern Foods Limited, to manufacture 'homestyle' pies and cakes. Wyvern Water has given a guarantee to Mercia Bank plc in respect of bank overdraft facilities provided to Wyvern Foods. At 31 December 20-1 it is considered possible (but not probable) that Wyvern Water will have to make payment under the guarantee.

solution

1   Court case for damages

* The present obligation is the potential liability to pay damages from a past event, ie the sale of contaminated bottled water.
* It is probable that the company will lose the case and have to pay damages.
* The amount of damages is reliably estimated at £50,000.
* The company will record a provision as an expense in its statement of profit or loss and other comprehensive income and will record a liability on its statement of financial position (under the heading long-term provisions).
* Details of the provision will be disclosed in the notes to the financial statements.

2   Claim for past royalties

- This is a possible obligation arising from past events, ie the sale of 'Dr Wyvern' energy drink.

- However, the possible obligation will be confirmed only by a future event – a court case.

- Legal advice considers the claimant's chances of success in a court case to be remote.

- This is a contingent liability, which will not be recognised in the accounts.

- Because the likelihood of losing the case is remote, there will be no disclosure of the contingent liability in the notes to the financial statements.

3   Bank guarantee

- The guarantee is a present obligation arising from a past event, ie the giving of the bank guarantee.

- However, at 31 December 20-1, no transfer of economic benefits is probable to settle the obligation.

- This is a contingent liability, which will not be recognised in the accounts.

- Because the likelihood of having to meet the terms of the guarantee is possible (but not probable), details of the contingent liability will be disclosed in the notes to the financial statements.

IAS 10 – Events after the reporting period

Events after the reporting period are favourable or unfavourable events that take place after the financial statements have been prepared at the year end and before the time when the statements are authorised for issue to interested parties.

This standard recognises that there may be events which occur, or information that becomes available after the end of the financial year, that need to be reflected in the financial statements. For example, if a customer becomes insolvent after the year end and the amount of the trade receivable is material, it may be necessary to make changes in the financial statements for the year to reflect this.

Any such changes can only be made in the period
- after the end of the financial year, and
- before the financial statements are authorised for issue (usually by the board of directors)

Once the financial statements have been authorised for issue, they cannot be altered.

IAS 10 distinguishes between
- adjusting events, and
- non-adjusting events

Adjusting events provide evidence of conditions that existed at the end of the reporting period. If material, adjustments should be made to the amounts shown in the financial statements. Examples of adjusting events include:

– the settlement after the end of the reporting period of a court case which confirms that a present obligation existed at the year end

– non-current assets, the determination after the reporting period of the purchase price, or sale price, of assets bought or sold before the year end

– assets, where a valuation shows impairment

– inventories, where net realisable value falls below cost price

– trade receivables, where a customer has become insolvent

– the determination after the reporting period of the amount of profit-sharing or bonus payments

– the discovery of fraud or errors that show that the financial statements are incorrect

Non-adjusting events are indicative of conditions that arose after the end of the reporting period. No adjustment is made to the financial statements; instead, if material, they are disclosed by way of notes which explain the nature of the event and, where possible, give an estimate of its financial effect. Examples of non-adjusting events include:

– business combinations (see Chapter 8)

– discontinuing a significant part of the business

– major purchase of assets

– losses of production capacity, eg caused by fire, flood or strikes

– announcing or commencing a major restructuring

– major share transactions

– large changes in asset prices or foreign exchange rates

– changes in tax rates

– entering into significant commitments or contingent liabilities

– commencing litigation based on events arising after the reporting period

Dividends declared or proposed on ordinary shares after the reporting period are not to be recognised as a liability on the statement of financial position. Instead, they are non-adjusting events which are disclosed by way of a note – see also page 65 for more on the treatment of dividends in financial statements.

Going concern – an entity cannot prepare its financial statements on a going concern basis if, after the reporting period, management determines either that it intends to liquidate the business or to cease trading, or that there is no realistic alternative to these courses of action.

Date of authorisation for issue – entities must disclose the date when the financial statements were authorised for issue and who gave that authorisation. (If anyone has the power to amend the financial statements after issue, this fact must be disclosed.)

STATEMENT OF PROFIT OR LOSS

In this section we look at accounting standards that affect mainly the statement of profit or loss and other comprehensive income:

IAS 16   – *Property, plant and equipment*

IAS 18   – *Revenue*

Note that these standards often also have an effect on the statement of financial position – affecting either assets or liabilities.

IAS 16 – Property, plant and equipment

We have already seen – in Chapter 4 – how this standard sets out the principles of accounting for tangible non-current assets. This standard affects both the statement of financial position and the statement of profit or loss and other comprehensive income.

The statement of profit or loss and other comprehensive income is mainly affected by the depreciation expense, where the objective of depreciation is to allocate systematically the depreciable amount of an asset over its useful life.

All tangible non-current assets having a known useful life are to be depreciated (the usual exception is land).

Further details of IAS 16 are given on pages 95-105.

IAS 18 – Revenue

This standard sets out the accounting treatment to ensure that the revenue shown in the statement of profit or loss and other comprehensive income is correctly stated.

Revenue is the gross inflow of economic benefits during the period arising in the course of the ordinary activities of an entity when those inflows result in increases in equity, other than increases relating to contributions from equity participants. Examples of revenue include sales of goods, rendering of services, interest, royalties and dividends.

> **Tutorial note:** the term 'income' – which is defined in the *Conceptual Framework for Financial Reporting* (see page 10) – is a wider definition that includes both revenue from ordinary activities and other comprehensive income (such as the revaluation of assets).

Fair value is the price that would be received to sell an asset or paid to transfer a liability in an orderly transaction between market participants at the measurement date.

IAS 18 states that revenue is to be measured at the fair value of the consideration received or receivable. The standard then sets out the rules for the recognition of the three types of revenue:

- sale of goods
- rendering of services
- interest, royalties and dividends

Note that taxes, eg Value Added Tax, are excluded from revenue.

sale of goods

Revenue from the sale of goods is to be recognised when all of the following criteria have been met:

- the seller of the goods has transferred to the buyer the significant risks and rewards of ownership
- the seller retains no continuing managerial involvement in the goods and no effective control over the goods
- the amount of revenue can be measured reliably
- it is probable that the economic benefits will flow to the seller
- the costs incurred, or to be incurred, in respect of the transaction can be measured reliably

rendering of services

For the sale of services, revenue is to be recognised by reference to the stage of completion (eg the percentage of completeness) of the transaction at the date of the statement of financial position. All of the following criteria must be met:

- the amount of revenue can be measured reliably
- it is probable that the economic benefits will flow to the seller of the service
- at the date of the statement of financial position, the stage of completion can be measured reliably
- the costs incurred, and the costs to complete, in respect of the transaction can be measured reliably

interest, royalties and dividends

Revenue for these items, provided that it is probable that the economic benefits will flow to the entity and that the amount of revenue can be measured reliably, is to be recognised in the following way:

- for interest – using a time basis to calculate the interest
- for royalties – on an accrual basis in accordance with the royalty agreement
- for dividends – when the shareholder's right to receive payment is established

Chapter Summary

- IAS 12, *Income Taxes*, requires that current tax is to be recognised on the face of the statement of profit or loss and other comprehensive income. The amount of unpaid current tax is recognised as a liability on the statement of financial position.

- IAS 17, *Leases*, requires that, on the lessee's statement of financial position, finance leases are to be recognised as liabilities at the lower of the fair value of the asset being leased and the present value of the minimum lease payments. The amount is to be split between non-current and current liabilities, as appropriate. See also pages 114-121.

- IAS 37, *Provisions, Contingent Liabilities and Contingent Assets*, ensures that appropriate recognition criteria and measurement bases are applied to these three types of uncertainties. It requires that sufficient information is disclosed in the notes to the financial statements to enable users to understand their nature, timing and amount.

- IAS 10, *Events after the Reporting Period*, allows for events which may occur, or information that becomes available, in the period between the end of the financial year and the date the financial statements are authorised for issue to be reflected in the financial statements. The standard distinguishes between adjusting events and non-adjusting events.

- IAS 16, *Property, Plant and Equipment*, requires that all tangible non-current assets having a known useful life are to be depreciated (the usual exception is land). See also pages 95-105.

- IAS 18, *Revenue*, sets out the accounting treatment to ensure that the revenue shown in the statement of profit or loss and other comprehensive income is correctly stated. It covers the rules for the recognition of three types of revenue:

  - sale of goods

  - rendering of services

  - interest, royalties and dividends

current tax	the amount of income taxes payable in respect of the taxable profit for the year
provision	a liability of uncertain timing or amount
contingent liability	**either** a possible obligation arising from past events whose existence will be confirmed only by the occurrence or non-occurrence of one or more uncertain future events not wholly within the entity's control; **or** a present obligation that arises from past events but is not recognised because: – it is not probable that an outflow of economic benefits will be required to settle the obligation; or – the obligation cannot be measured with sufficient reliability
contingent asset	a possible asset arising from past events whose existence will be confirmed only by the occurrence or non-occurrence of one or more uncertain future events not wholly within the entity's control
adjusting event	an event that provides evidence of conditions in existence at the end of the reporting period; if material, changes should be made to the amounts shown in the financial statements
non-adjusting event	an event that is indicative of conditions that arose after the end of the reporting period. No adjustment is made to the financial statements; instead, if material, it is disclosed by way of a note which explains the nature of the event and, where possible, gives an estimate of its financial effect
revenue	the gross inflow of economic benefits during the period arising in the course of the ordinary activities of an entity when those inflows result in increases in equity, other than increases relating to contributions from equity participants

Activities

5.1   **(a)**   How does the *Conceptual Framework for Financial Reporting* define a liability?

(b)   Demonstrate how the definition of a liability relates to an amount owed to trade payables.

5.2   Indicate whether the following statements are true or false.

	True	False
(a) In order to be recognised on the statement of financial position, liabilities must be capable of being reliably measured.		
(b) Where a liability cannot be reliably measured, an estimate can be made and the amount of the estimate is recognised on the statement of financial position.		

5.3   Chen Limited has a corporation tax charge of £50,000 based on its profits for the current year. Where is this recognised in the year end financial statements?

(a) in the statement of profit or loss and other comprehensive income and as a current liability in the statement of financial position	
(b) in the statement of profit or loss and other comprehensive income and as a current asset in the statement of financial position	
(c) in the statement of profit or loss and other comprehensive income and as a non-current liability in the statement of financial position	
(d) as a current liability in the statement of financial position only	

5.4   The corporation tax charge of Marchant Ltd based on its current year profits is £30,000. The company had over-estimated its corporation tax liability for the previous year by £5,000.

What will be the corporation tax charge and the corporation tax liability recognised in the financial statements of Marchant Ltd at the end of the current accounting period?

Corporation tax charge	Corporation tax liability	✓
£	£	
25,000	30,000	
30,000	25,000	
35,000	35,000	
30,000	30,000	

5.5   The following balances are taken from the accounting system of Rathod Ltd as at 31 March 20X4.

	£	£
Inventories	15,500	
Property, plant and equipment	125,000	
Cash and cash equivalents	4,000	
Share capital		100,000
Trade payables		19,500
Trade receivables	22,400	
Profit before tax		40,700
Retained earnings at start of year		29,200
Dividends paid	22,500	
	189,400	189,400

Notes:

·   Corporation tax liability on the profits for the year is £9,500

You are to prepare:

·   statement of profit or loss, starting with profit before tax

·   statement of financial position

for the year ended 31 March 20X4.

(Note: a statement of changes in equity is not required)

5.6 Under IAS 17, *Leases*, how should finance leases be recognised as liabilities on a lessee's statement of financial position?

✓

(a) at the higher of fair value less costs to sell and value in use of the asset being leased	
(b) at the higher of the fair value of the asset being leased and the present value of the minimum lease payments	
(c) at the lower of the fair value of the asset being leased and the present value of the minimum lease payments	
(d) at the value in use of the asset being leased	

5.7 **(a)** Define a provision and explain how it differs from a liability such as trade payables.

(b) Define a contingent liability and explain how it differs from a provision.

(c) Explain how provisions and contingent liabilities are handled in year end financial statements.

5.8 Aslam Ltd is being sued by a former employee following an accident at work. The company will have to pay substantial damages if it loses the case. At the end of its financial year, the company's lawyers advise that it is probable (ie more than 50% likelihood) that it may lose the case.

In accordance with IAS 37, *Provisions, Contingent Liabilities and Contingent Assets* the probable future outflow should be:

✓

(a) recognised in the financial statements as a contingent liability	
(b) only disclosed as a note to the financial statements	
(c) neither recognised in the financial statements nor disclosed as a note	
(d) recognised in the financial statements as a provision	

5.9 A contingent asset should be disclosed in the notes to the financial statements only where the inflow of economic benefits is probable.

Is this statement true or false?

True / False

5.10 With reference to IAS 10, *Events after the Reporting Period*:

(a) Define adjusting events.

(b) Define non-adjusting events.

(c) Explain how adjusting events and non-adjusting events are handled in the year end financial statements to which they relate.

5.11 Zhang Ltd prepares its financial statements to 31 March each year. The following events took place after 31 March but before the date on which the financial statements were authorised for issue:

1. non-current assets held at the end of the financial year are found to have a valuation materially below their carrying amount

2. evidence of a material error is found which shows that the financial statements are incorrect

Which of the above is likely to be classified as an adjusting event under IAS 10, *Events after the Reporting Period*?

✓

(a) 1 only	
(b) 2 only	
(c) 1 and 2	
(d) neither 1 nor 2	

5.12 A major customer who owes money to a company at the end of the financial year is declared bankrupt before the date of authorising the financial statements for issue. Under IAS 10, *Events after the Reporting Period*, this should be classified as a non-adjusting event.

Is this statement true or false?

True / False

5.13 With reference to IAS 18, *Revenue*:

(a) define the term 'revenue'

(b) define the term 'fair value'

(c) state the three types of revenue to which the IAS applies

5.14 According to IAS 18, *Revenue*, how is revenue to be measured?

✓

(a) at the fair value of the consideration received or receivable	
(b) at the lower of cost and net realisable value	
(c) at cost or revaluation, less impairment losses	
(d) at the amount of cash and cash equivalents received	

5.15 In the rules for the recognition of revenue given in IAS 18, *Revenue*, which of the following are set out in detail?

1. interest

2. royalties

3. sale of goods

4. rendering of services

5. dividends

	✓
(a) 3 and 4	
(b) 2, 3 and 4	
(c) 1, 2, 3 and 4	
(d) all of them	

5.16 According to IAS 18, *Revenue*, which of the following criteria must be met before revenue from the sale of goods can be recognised in financial statements?

1. the seller of the goods has transferred to the buyer the significant risks and rewards of ownership

2. the seller retains no continuing managerial involvement in the goods and no effective control over the goods

3. the amount of revenue can be measured reliably

4. it is probable that the economic benefits will flow to the seller

5. the costs incurred, or to be incurred, in respect of the transaction can be measured reliably

	✓
(a) all of them	
(b) 1, 2 and 3	
(c) 1, 2, 3 and 4	
(d) 2, 3, 4 and 5	

5.17 Answer the following questions which the directors of Gernroder Limited have asked concerning the financial statements for the year ended 30 September 20-6. Where appropriate, make reference to international financial reporting standards to justify your answers.

(a) The auditors have asked us to reduce the value of some of our inventory – from the cost of £156,590 to £101,640, which is the amount at which we sold the inventory after the year end. Why should something which happened after the year end be at all relevant to the balances at the year end?

(b) Our accountant knows that, in early October, we announced our proposal to pay a final dividend of £75,000 for the year but she hasn't shown a liability for it in the financial statements.

(c) We had to dismiss an employee in early October. The former employee has now started legal proceedings for unfair dismissal. Our lawyers tell us that the company will probably lose the case and think that a reliable estimate of damages awarded against us is £20,000. As we employed this person at the financial year end we feel that we ought to show the estimated amount of damages as an expense in the statement of profit or loss and other comprehensive income and as a liability on the statement of financial position.

6 Statement of cash flows

this chapter covers...

In this chapter we study the statement of cash flows, which links profit from the statement of profit or loss and other comprehensive income with changes in assets and liabilities in the statement of financial position, and the effect on the cash of the company. We will cover:

- *an appreciation of the need for a statement of cash flows*

- *the cash flows for the sections of the statement*

- *how the cash flows relate to the areas of business activity*

- *the interpretation of a statement of cash flows*

The international financial reporting standard that sets out the layouts and gives detailed guidance on the preparation of statements of cash flows is IAS 7.

There are two ways of setting out statements of cash flows: the direct method and the indirect method. The main part of the chapter focuses on the indirect method and then, on page 175, we see how the direct method is used and we note that it is only the first section of the statement of cash flows that varies between the two methods. (Note that AAT's Assessment for Financial Statements requires the statement of cash flows to be drafted using only the indirect method. For the direct method, a knowledge of examples of cash flows from operating activities – see page 175 – is required.)

INTRODUCTION

The statement of profit or loss and other comprehensive income shows profitability, and the statement of financial position shows asset strength. While these two financial statements give us a great deal of information on the progress of a company during an accounting period, profit does not equal cash, and strength in assets does not necessarily mean a large bank balance.

The **statement of cash flows** links profit with changes in assets and liabilities, and the effect on the cash of the company.

A statement of cash flows uses information from the accounting records (including statements of profit or loss and other comprehensive income and financial position) to show an overall view of money flowing in and out of a company during an accounting period.

Such a statement explains to the shareholders why, after a year of good profits for example, there is a reduced balance at the bank or a larger bank overdraft at the year-end than there was at the beginning of the year. The statement of cash flows concentrates on the liquidity of the business: it is often a lack of cash (a lack of liquidity) that causes most businesses to fail.

Such is the importance of cash flows that companies preparing and presenting accounts in accordance with international financial reporting standards are required to include a statement of cash flows as an integral part of their financial statements.

FORMAT OF THE STATEMENT OF CASH FLOWS

IAS 7, *Statement of Cash Flows*, provides the guidelines for a format, divided into three sections:

- **Operating activities** – the main revenue-producing activities of the business, together with the payment of interest and tax
- **Investing activities** – the acquisition and disposal of non-current assets, and other investments, together with interest and dividends received
- **Financing activities** – receipts from the issue of new shares, payments to repay shares, changes in long-term borrowings, payment of dividends

The cash flows for the year affecting each of these three areas of business activity are shown in the statement.

At the bottom of the statement of cash flows is shown the net increase in cash and cash equivalents for the period, together with the cash and cash equivalents, both at the beginning and at the end of the period.

Note the following terms:

- **cash**, which comprises cash on hand and demand deposits
- **cash equivalents**, which are short-term, highly liquid investments that can easily be converted into cash (an example of a cash equivalent is money held in a term account, provided that the money can be withdrawn within three months from the date of deposit)

Bank overdrafts which are payable on demand are included as a part of cash and cash equivalents.

The diagram on the next page shows the main cash flows (inflows and outflows of cash and cash equivalents) under each heading, and indicates the content of the statement of cash flows. The first section – operating activities – needs a word of further explanation, particularly as it is the main source of cash flow for most companies.

operating activities (indirect method)

The cash flow from operating activities is calculated by using figures from the statements of profit or loss and other comprehensive income and financial position as follows:

	profit from operations* (profit, before deduction of tax & interest)
add	depreciation charge for the year
add	loss on sale of non-current assets, or *deduct* gain on sale of non-current assets – see page 166
deduct	dividends received (shown in investing activities)
add	decrease in inventories, or *deduct* increase in inventories
add	decrease in trade and other receivables, or *deduct* increase in trade and other receivables
add	increase in trade and other payables, or *deduct* decrease in trade and other payables
equals	**cash used in/from operations**
deduct	interest paid in period
deduct	tax paid on income in period (eg corporation tax)
equals	**net cash used in/from operating activities**

* 'Profit from operations' is always the starting point in AAT Assessments where a task requires you to reconcile profit or loss to the net cash from operating activities. An example of such a reconciliation is shown on page 162.

Notes:

- Depreciation is added to profit because depreciation is a non-cash expense, that is, no money is paid out by the company in respect of depreciation charged to the statement of profit or loss and other comprehensive income.
- Cash flows relating to the purchase and sale of non-current assets are shown in the investing activities section.

- The dividends received deducted here will be added in the investing activities section.
- The operating activities section is calculated differently for the direct method – see page 175.

LAYOUT OF A STATEMENT OF CASH FLOWS

A statement of cash flows uses a common layout which can be amended to suit the particular needs of the company for which it is being prepared. The example layout shown on page 162 (with specimen figures included) is commonly used. It is suggested that you study a recent statement of cash flows for a large public limited company – the web directory at the beginning of this book lists some sources.

The diagram below shows the contents of a statement of cash flows using the indirect method. Note that the direct method is discussed on page 175 where we will see that it is only the operating activities section which is set out in a different way.

---

statement of cash flows (indirect method)

Operating activities
- Profit from operations (ie profit, before deduction of tax and interest)
- Depreciation charge for the year (see page 166 for treatment of a gain or a loss on sale of non-current assets)
- Less dividends received (shown in investing activities)
- Changes in inventories, trade and other receivables and payables
- Less interest paid
- Less taxes paid on income (eg corporation tax)

Investing activities
- Inflows: sale proceeds from property, plant and equipment, intangibles, and other non-current assets
- Outflows: purchase cost of property, plant and equipment, intangibles, and other non-current assets
- Interest received
- Dividends received

Financing activities
- Inflows: receipts from increase in share capital (note: no cash inflow from a bonus issue of shares – see page 69), raising/increase of loans
- Outflows: repayment of share capital/loans, and finance lease liabilities
- Dividends paid

STATEMENT OF CASH FLOWS: INDIRECT METHOD

ABC LIMITED
STATEMENT OF CASH FLOWS FOR THE YEAR ENDED 31 DECEMBER 20-6

	£	£
Net cash used in/from operating activities		78,000
Cash flows from investing activities		
Purchase of non-current assets	−125,000	
Proceeds from sale of non-current assets	15,000	
Interest received	10,000	
Dividends received	−	
Net cash used in/from investing activities		−100,000
Cash flows from financing activities		
Proceeds from issue of share capital	275,000	
Repayment of share capital	−	
Proceeds from long-term borrowings	−	
Repayment of long-term borrowings	−140,000	
Dividends paid (note: amount paid during year)	−22,000	
Net cash used in/from financing activities		113,000
Net increase/decrease in cash and cash equivalents		91,000
Cash and cash equivalents at beginning of year		105,000
Cash and cash equivalents at end of year		196,000

RECONCILIATION OF PROFIT FROM OPERATIONS TO NET CASH FROM OPERATING ACTIVITIES

	£
Profit from operations (note: before tax and interest)	75,000
Adjustments for:	
Depreciation for year	10,000
Decrease in inventories	2,000
Increase in trade and other receivables	−5,000
Increase in trade and other payables	7,000
Cash used in/from operations	89,000
Interest paid (note: amount paid during year)	−5,000
Income taxes paid (note: amount paid during year)	−6,000
Net cash used in/from operating activities	78,000

notes on the layout of a statement of cash flows

■ The separate amounts shown for each section can, if preferred, be detailed in a note to the statement of cash flows. The operating activities section is invariably set out in detail as a note below the statement of cash flows, with just the figure for net cash from operating activities (see example opposite) being shown on the statement – see grey line.

■ Money amounts shown in brackets (or a minus sign) indicate a deduction or, where the figure is a sub-total, a negative figure.

■ The changes in the main working capital items of inventories, trade and other receivables, and trade and other payables have an effect on cash balances. For example, a decrease in inventory increases cash, while an increase in trade receivables reduces cash.

■ IAS 7 allows some flexibility in the way in which companies present their statements of cash flows. In particular, the cash flows from interest and dividends received and paid can be classified as operating or investing or financing activities – in AAT Assessments interest received and dividends received are always treated as investing activities (note that for AAT, interest paid is shown as an operating activity, and dividends paid is shown as a financing activity).

■ Cash flows arising from taxes on income – eg corporation tax – are always classified as operating activities, unless they can be specifically identified with financing and investing activities.

■ The statement of cash flows concludes with a figure for the net increase or decrease in cash and cash equivalents for the year. This is calculated from the subtotals of each of the three sections of the statement. Added to this is the amount of cash and cash equivalents at the beginning of the year. Thus the final figure of the statement is that of cash and cash equivalents at the end of the year.

Case Study

STATEMENT OF CASH FLOWS

situation

The statements of financial position of Newtown Trading Company Limited for 20-5 and 20-6 are shown on the next page.

Prepare a statement of cash flows for the year ended 31 December 20-6 and comment on the main points highlighted by the statement. Note the following points:

• Extract from the statement of profit or loss and other comprehensive income for 20-6:

	£
Profit from operations	9,400
Interest paid	–400
Profit before tax	9,000
Tax	–1,500
Profit for the year	7,500

• Dividends of £1,500 were paid in 20-5, and £2,000 in 20-6.
• During 20-6 the property was revalued at £125,000.

Tutorial note:

When preparing a statement of cash flows from financial statements, take a moment or two to establish which is the earlier year and which is the later year. In this Case Study they are set out from left to right, ie 20-5 followed by 20-6. In some Assessments, the later year is shown first, ie 20-6 followed by 20-5.

NEWTOWN TRADING COMPANY LIMITED
STATEMENT OF FINANCIAL POSITION AS AT 31 DECEMBER

	20-5			20-6		
	£	£	£	£	£	£
ASSETS	Cost	Dep'n	Net	Cost or reval'n	Dep'n	Net
Non-current assets						
Property	75,000	–	75,000	125,000	–	125,000
Plant and equipment	22,200	6,200	16,000	39,000	8,900	30,100
	97,200	6,200	91,000	164,000	8,900	155,100
Current assets						
Inventories			7,000			11,000
Trade and other receivables			5,000			3,700
Cash and cash equivalents			1,000			500
			13,000			15,200
Total assets			104,000			170,300
EQUITY AND LIABILITIES						
Equity						
Share capital			80,000			90,000
Share premium			1,500			2,500
Revaluation reserve			–			50,000
Retained earnings			11,000			16,500
Total equity			92,500			159,000
Non-current liabilities						
Debentures			5,000			3,000
Current liabilities						
Trade and other payables			5,500			6,800
Tax liabilities			1,000			1,500
			6,500			8,300
Total liabilities			11,500			11,300
Total equity and liabilities			104,000			170,300

solution

NEWTOWN TRADING COMPANY LIMITED
STATEMENT OF CASH FLOWS FOR THE YEAR ENDED 31 DECEMBER 20-6

	£	£
Net cash used in/from operating activities (see below)		9,300
Cash flows from investing activities		
Purchase of non-current assets (plant and equipment)	−16,800	
Net cash used in/from investing activities		−16,800
Cash flows from financing activities		
Issue of ordinary shares at a premium		
ie £10,000 + £1,000 =	11,000	
Repayment of debentures	−2,000	
Dividends paid	−2,000	
Net cash used in/from financing activities		7,000
Net increase/decrease in cash and cash equivalents		−500
Cash and cash equivalents at beginning of year		1,000
Cash and cash equivalents at end of year		500

RECONCILIATION OF PROFIT FROM OPERATIONS TO NET CASH FROM OPERATING ACTIVITIES

	£
Profit from operations (before tax and interest)	9,400
Adjustments for:	
Depreciation for year*	2,700
Increase in inventories	−4,000
Decrease in trade and other receivables	1,300
Increase in trade and other payables	1,300
Cash used in/from operations	10,700
Interest paid	−400
Income taxes paid	−1,000
Net cash used in/from operating activities	9,300

*   Depreciation charged: £8,900 − £6,200 = £2,700

notes on the statement of cash flows

The liability for tax – which is a current liability at 31 December 20-5 – is paid in 20-6. Likewise, the current liability for tax at 31 December 20-6 will be paid in 20 7 (and will appear on that year's statement of cash flows).

The dividend is the amount **paid** during 20-6, ie £2,000.

The revaluation of the property (increase in the value of the non-current asset, and revaluation reserve recorded in the equity section) does not feature in the statement of cash flows because it is a non-cash transaction. Remember that the amount of the revaluation will also be shown as other comprehensive income in the statement of profit or loss and other comprehensive income.

how useful is the statement of cash flows?

The following points are highlighted by the statement on the previous page:

- cash generated from operations is £10,700 (this is before interest and tax is paid for the year)

- net cash from operating activities is £9,300

- a purchase of plant and equipment of £16,800 has been made, financed partly by operating activities, and partly by an issue of shares at a premium

- the bank balance during the year has fallen by £500, ie from £1,000 to £500

In conclusion, the picture shown by the statement of cash flows is that of a business which is generating cash from its operating activities and using the cash to build for the future.

GAIN OR LOSS ON DISPOSAL OF NON-CURRENT ASSETS

carrying amount and sale proceeds

When a company disposes of non-current assets it is most unlikely that the resultant sale proceeds will be equal to the carrying amount (cost/revaluation less accumulated depreciation) – there will be a gain or loss on disposal.

dealing with a gain or loss on disposal

The accounting solution is to transfer any small gain or loss on disposal – non-cash items – to the statement of profit or loss and other comprehensive income. However, such a gain or loss on disposal must be handled with care when preparing a statement of cash flows because, in such a statement we have to adjust for non-cash items when calculating the net cash from operating activities; at the same time we must separately identify the amount of the proceeds of sale of non-current assets in the investing activities section.

Case Study

GAIN OR LOSS ON DISPOSAL OF NON-CURRENT ASSETS

situation

H & J Wells Limited is an electrical contractor. For the year ended 30 June 20-6 its statement of profit or loss and other comprehensive income is as follows:

	£	£
Gross profit		37,500
Expenses:		
General expenses	−23,000	
Provision for depreciation: plant	−2,000	
equipment	−3,000	
		−28,000
Profit from operations		9,500

gain on disposal

During the course of the year the company has sold the following non-current asset; the effects of the disposal transaction have not yet been recorded in the statement of profit or loss and other comprehensive income:

		£
Plant:	cost price	1,000
	depreciation to date	−750
	carrying amount	250
	proceeds of sale	350

As the plant has been sold for £100 more than the carrying amount, this gain on disposal is shown in the statement of profit or loss and other comprehensive income, as follows:

	£	£
Gross profit		37,500
Gain on disposal of non-current assets		100
		37,600
Expenses:		
General expenses	−23,000	
Provision for depreciation: plant	−2,000	
equipment	−3,000	
		−28,000
Profit from operations		9,600

The statement of cash flows, based on the amended statement of profit or loss and other comprehensive income, will include the following figures:

**STATEMENT OF CASH FLOWS (EXTRACT) OF H & J WELLS LIMITED
FOR THE YEAR ENDED 30 JUNE 20-6**

	£	£
Cash flows from operating activities		
Profit from operations	9,600	
Adjustments for:		
Depreciation for year	5,000	
Gain on disposal of non-current assets	−100	
Increase/decrease in inventories	. . .	
Increase/decrease in trade and other receivables	. . .	
Increase/decrease in trade and other payables	. . .	
Net cash used in/from operating activities		14,500
Cash flows from investing activities		
Purchase of non-current assets	−. . .	
Proceeds from disposal of non-current assets	350	
Net cash used in/from investing activities		350

Note that the gain on disposal of non-current assets is deducted in the operating activities section because it is non-cash income. (Only the sections of the statement of cash flows affected by the disposal are shown above.)

loss on disposal

If the plant in the Case Study had been sold for £150, this would have given a loss on disposal of £100. This amount would be debited to the statement of profit or loss and other comprehensive income, to give an amended profit from operations of £9,400. The effect on the statement of cash flows would be twofold:

1   In the operating activities section, loss on disposal of non-current assets of £100 would be added; the net cash from operating activities remains at £14,500 (which proves that both gain and loss on disposal of non-current assets are items which do not affect cash)

2   In the investing activities section, proceeds from disposal of non-current assets would be £150

conclusion: disposal of non-current assets

The rule for dealing with a gain or a loss on disposal of non-current assets in a statement of cash flows is:

■   add the amount of the loss on disposal, or deduct the amount of the gain on disposal, to or from the profit from operations when calculating the net cash from operating activities

- show the total disposal proceeds, ie the amount of the payment received, as proceeds from sale of non-current assets in the investing activities section

The Case Study below incorporates calculations for a gain on disposal of non-current assets.

REVALUATION OF NON-CURRENT ASSETS

From time to time some non-current assets are revalued upwards and the amount of the revaluation is recorded as other comprehensive income and is taken to the statement of financial position. The most common asset to be treated in this way is property. The value of the non-current asset is increased and the amount of the revaluation is placed to a revaluation surplus in the equity section of the statement of financial position where it increases the total equity of the company. As a revaluation is purely a 'book' adjustment, ie no cash has changed hands, it does not feature in a statement of cash flows – see the Case Study of Newtown Trading Company Limited on pages 163 to 166.

PREPARING FOR ASSESSMENT

In AAT Assessments there are two tasks which require financial statements to be drafted. In Chapter 3 we have already seen (page 72) the two tasks for preparing statements of profit or loss, changes in equity, and financial position. The alternative two tasks in assessments focus on the statement of cash flows. Here you will be provided with a statement of profit or loss and other comprehensive income for a single year and statements of financial position for two years:

- in the first task you will be required to prepare a reconciliation of profit from operations to net cash from operating activities and a statement of cash flows
- in the second task you will be required to draft a statement of changes in equity (see page 174)

Both of these tasks use the same statements of profit or loss and other comprehensive income and financial position. Blank layouts are provided and, in the AAT Assessment, you select narrative items from pick lists and enter money amounts into gap fill boxes. Pro-formas for workings are also provided, as appropriate, in the assessment and partial marks can be obtained from these in the event of errors being made in the main layouts for the statements. Note that pro-formas for layouts and workings – in the format used in AAT Assessments – are provided in the Appendix of this book.

In the Case Study which follows we see how the aspects of the statement of cash flows and the statement of changes in equity are prepared from the statements of profit or loss and other comprehensive income and financial position – ie the two tasks for this type of AAT Assessment.

STATEMENT OF CASH FLOWS

situation

You have been asked to prepare the statement of cash flows and changes in equity for Doddington Ltd for the year ended 31 December 20X6.

The most recent statement of profit or loss and statement of financial position (with comparatives for the previous year) of Doddington Ltd are set out below.

Doddington Ltd **Statement of profit or loss for the year ended 31 December 20X6**	
Continuing operations	*£000*
Revenue	755
Cost of sales	–546
Gross profit	209
Dividends received	6
Gain on disposal of property, plant and equipment	10
Distribution costs	–115
Administrative expenses	–79
Profit from operations	31
Finance costs	–3
Profit before tax	28
Tax	–7
Profit for the period from continuing operations	21

Doddington Ltd		
Statement of financial position as at 31 December 20X6		
	20X6	**20X5**
	£000	*£000*
ASSETS		
Non-current assets		
Property, plant and equipment	275	200
Current assets		
Inventories	74	50
Trade receivables	120	80
Cash and cash equivalents	0	10
	194	140
Total assets	469	340
EQUITY AND LIABILITIES		
Equity		
Share capital	220	200
Share premium	10	0
Retained earnings	70	64
Total equity	300	264
Non-current liabilities		
Bank loans	60	0
	60	0
Current liabilities		
Trade payables	87	72
Tax liabilities	7	4
Bank overdraft	15	0
	109	76
Total liabilities	169	76
Total equity and liabilities	469	340

Further information:

- The total depreciation charge for the year was £36,000.
- Property, plant and equipment costing £40,000 with accumulated depreciation of £20,000 was sold in the year.
- All sales and purchases were on credit. Other expenses were paid for in cash.
- A dividend of £15,000 was paid during the year.

required

(a) Prepare a reconciliation of profit from operations to net cash from operating activities for Doddington Ltd for the year ended 31 December 20X6.

(b) Prepare the statement of cash flows for Doddington Ltd for the year ended 31 December 20X6.

(c) Draft the statement of changes in equity for Doddington Ltd for the year ended 31 December 20X6.

solution

(a)   Doddington Ltd

Reconciliation of profit from operations to net cash from operating activities	
	£000
Profit from operations	31
Adjustments for:	
Depreciation	36
Dividends received	−6
Gain on disposal of property, plant and equipment	−10
Adjustment in respect of inventories	−24
Adjustment in respect of trade receivables	−40
Adjustment in respect of trade payables	15
Cash generated by operations	2
Tax paid	−4
Interest paid	−3
Net cash from operating activities	−5

Tutorial note for AAT Assessments:

- 'profit from operations' is always the starting point for tasks which require the preparation of this reconciliation
- dividends received are always treated as investing activities – therefore they are deducted in the calculation of cash generated by operations

(b)   **Doddington Ltd**

Statement of cash flows for the year ended 31 December 20X6	
	£000
Net cash from operating activities	−5
Investing activities	
Dividends received	6
Proceeds on disposal of property, plant and equipment	30
Purchases of property, plant and equipment	−131
Net cash used in investing activities	−95
Financing activities	
Bank loans raised	60
Proceeds of share issue	30
Dividends paid	−15
Net cash from financing activities	75
Net increase/decrease in cash and cash equivalents	−25
Cash and cash equivalents at beginning of year	10
Cash and cash equivalents at end of year	−15

Workings

Proceeds on disposal of property, plant and equipment	*£000*
Carrying amount of property, plant and equipment sold	20
Gain on disposal	10
Proceeds =	30

Purchases of property, plant and equipment	*£000*
Property, plant and equipment at start of year	200
Depreciation charge	−36
Carrying amount of property, plant and equipment sold	−20
Property, plant and equipment at end of year	−275
Total property, plant and equipment additions =	−131

(c) **Doddington Ltd**

Statement of changes in equity for the year ended 31 December 20X6

	Share capital	Share premium	Retained earnings	Total equity
	£000	£000	£000	£000
Balance at 1 January 20X5	200	0	64	264
Changes in equity for 20X6				
Profit for the period			21	21
Dividends			−15	−15
Issue of share capital	20	10		30
Balance at 31 December 20X6	220	10	70	300

how useful is the statement of cash flows?

While the type of AAT Assessment task considered here will not ask you to comment on the statement of cash flows, aspects of cash flows can feature in tasks which require the interpretation of financial statements (see Chapter 7).

The following points are highlighted by the statement of cash flows of Doddington Ltd for the year ended 31 December 20X6:

- although there is a reasonable profit from operations of £31,000, the cash generated from operations is just £2,000 – insufficient to cover the tax and interest paid

- inventories, trade receivables and trade payables have increased – in particular trade receivables – so that a net £49,000 of cash has been used

- non-current assets of £131,000 have been purchased which have been almost financed by the £120,000 from the sale of non-current assets, the bank loan raised, and the proceeds of the share issue

- with a net decrease of £25,000 in cash and cash equivalents during the year, it might have been prudent to pay a smaller dividend

The company appears to be expanding, with increases in non-current assets, current assets and current liabilities. Despite the share issue and the loan raised, quite a lot of the expansion has been financed through the bank. It might have been better to have obtained more long-term finance rather than using a bank overdraft.

STATEMENT OF CASH FLOWS: THE DIRECT METHOD

So far in this chapter we have focussed on preparing the statement of cash flows using the **indirect method**. Thus the operating activities section starts with the profit from operations. As an alternative, IAS 7 allows the **direct method**. For the operating activities section this method, instead of starting with profit, shows cash flows as follows:

- cash received from the sale of goods
- cash paid to suppliers and employees
- interest paid
- tax paid

As an example of the direct method we will use the statement of cash flows of ABC Limited shown on page 162. The cash (used in)/from operations is calculated in the following way (with specimen figures included):

Cash flows from operating activities	£
Cash received from the sale of goods	759,000
Cash paid to suppliers and employees	–670,000
Cash used in/from operations	89,000
Interest paid	–5,000
Tax paid	–6,000
Net cash (used in)/from operating activities	78,000

Note that the figure of £89,000 for cash from operations and the £78,000 net cash from operating activities are the same as the indirect method on page 162. The statement of cash flows presented using the direct method is shown on the next page.

To summarise the direct method:

- only the operating activities section is set out differently from the indirect method
- cash receipts and cash payments are shown in the calculation of cash (used in)/from operations

Note that AAT's Assessment requires you to have knowledge of the examples of cash flows to be classified as operating activities when using the direct method.

STATEMENT OF CASH FLOWS: DIRECT METHOD

ABC LIMITED
STATEMENT OF CASH FLOWS FOR THE YEAR ENDED 31 DECEMBER 20-6

	£	£
Net cash used in/from operating activities		78,000
Cash flows from investing activities		
Purchase of non-current assets	−125,000	
Proceeds from sale of non-current assets	15,000	
Interest received	10,000	
Dividends received	−	
Net cash used in/from investing activities		−100,000
Cash flows from financing activities		
Proceeds from issue of share capital	275,000	
Repayment of share capital	−	
Proceeds from long-term borrowings	−	
Repayment of long-term borrowings	−140,000	
Dividends paid (note: amount paid during year)	−22,000	
Net cash used in/from financing activities		113,000
Net increase/decrease in cash and cash equivalents		91,000
Cash and cash equivalents at beginning of year		105,000
Cash and cash equivalents at end of year		196,000

Calculation of cash from operating activities	£
Cash flows from operating activities	
Cash received from the sale of goods	759,000
Cash paid to suppliers and employees	−670,000
Cash used in/from operations	89,000
Interest paid	−5,000
Tax paid	−6,000
Net cash used in/from operating activities	78,000

LINKS TO THE STATEMENT OF FINANCIAL POSITION

As the statement of cash flows is one of the main financial statements prepared at the end of an accounting period, it needs to be read in conjunction with the statement of financial position. In order to help the user of the statement of cash flows, IAS 7 requires that there should be explanatory notes on cash and cash equivalents.

cash and cash equivalents

Companies must disclose the components of cash and cash equivalents and reconcile the amounts shown in the statement of cash flows with the figures from the statement of financial position. Thus, for ABC Limited (see previous page) the reconciliation could be shown as follows, with specimen figures used:

Reconciliation of cash and cash equivalents

	31 December 20-5	31 December 20-6
	£	£
Cash	20,000	26,000
Overdraft	–45,000	–20,000
Short-term deposits	130,000	190,000
Cash and cash equivalents	105,000	196,000

INTERPRETING THE STATEMENT OF CASH FLOWS

The statement of cash flows is important because it identifies the sources of cash flowing into the company and shows how they have been used. To get an overall view of the company, we need to read the statement in conjunction with the other main financial statements – profit or loss and other comprehensive income and financial position – and also in the context of the previous year's statements.

The following points should be borne in mind:

■ Like the other financial statements, the statement of cash flows uses the money measurement concept. This means that only items which can be recorded in money terms can be included; also we must be aware of the effect of inflation if comparing one year with the next.

■ Look for positive cash flows from the operating activities section. In particular, look at the subtotal 'cash (used in)/from operations' – this shows the cash from revenue-producing activities before the payment of interest and tax.

■ Make a comparison between the amount of profit and the amount of cash generated from operations. Identify the reasons for major differences between these figures – look at the changes in inventories, trade and other receivables, and trade and other payables, and put them into context. For example, it would be a warning sign if there were large increases in these items in a company with falling profits, and such a trend would put a strain on the liquidity of the business. Also consider the company's policies on collecting trade receivables and potential for bad (irrecoverable) debts, payment to trade payables (is the company paying too quickly?) and control of inventories (are surpluses building up?).

■ Look at the figure for 'net cash (used in)/from operating activities', ie the cash from operations after interest and tax have been paid. If it is a positive figure, it shows that the company has been able to meet its interest and tax obligations to loan providers and the tax authorities.

■ The investing activities section of the statement shows the amount of investment made during the year (eg the purchase of non-current assets). In general there should be a link between the cost of the investment and an increase in loans and/or share capital – it isn't usual to finance non-current assets from short-term sources, such as a bank overdraft.

■ In the financing activities section of the statement, where there has been an increase in loans and/or share capital, look to see how the money has been used. Was it to buy non-current assets or other investments, or to finance inventory and trade receivables, or other purposes?

■ Look at the amount of dividends paid – this is an outflow of cash that will directly affect the change in the bank balance. As a quick test, the amount of net cash from operating activities should, in theory, be sufficient to cover dividends paid; if it doesn't, then it is likely that the level of dividends will have to be reduced in future years.

■ The statement of cash flows, as a whole, links profit with changes in cash. Both of these are important: without profits the company cannot generate cash (unless it sells non-current assets), and without cash it cannot pay bills as they fall due.

Chapter Summary

■ The objective of a statement of cash flows is to show an overall view of money flowing in and out of a company during an accounting period.

■ IAS 7 is the international financial reporting standard that sets out the requirements of statements of cash flows.

■ A statement of cash flows is divided into three sections:

1 operating activities – the main revenue-producing activities of the business, together with the payment of interest and tax

2 investing activities – the acquisition and disposal of non-current assets, and some other investments

3 financing activities – receipts from the issue of new shares, payments to cover the repayment of shares, changes in long-term borrowings

■ There are two methods of setting out the operating activities section: the direct method and the indirect method.

■ Limited companies are required to include a statement of cash flows as a part of their financial statements.

	statement of cash flows	shows an overall view of money flowing in and out of a company during an accounting period using either the direct method or the indirect method
	cash from operations	profit from operations (ie before deduction of tax and interest), add depreciation for the year, add loss (or deduct gain) on disposal of non-current assets, deduct investment income, together with changes in inventories, trade and other receivables, and trade and other payables
	net cash from operating activities	cash generated from operations (see above), deduct interest paid in period, deduct taxes paid on income in period
	investing activities	cost of purchase and/or proceeds of disposal of non-current assets; dividends received; interest received
	financing activities	issue or repayment of share capital and/or long-term borrowings; dividends paid
	cash	cash on hand and demand deposits
	cash equivalents	short-term, highly liquid investments that can easily be converted into cash

Activities

- A blank photocopiable pro-forma in the format used in AAT Assessments – of the statement of cash flows is included in the Appendix – it is advisable to enlarge it to full A4 size. Blank workings sheets are also included in the Appendix.
- Pro-formas and workings sheets are also available to download from www.osbornebooks.co.uk

6.1 An increase in inventories will have a negative impact on cash flow in the calculation of net cash flow from operating activities.

   True / False

6.2 A gain on disposal of property, plant and equipment will have a negative impact on cash flow in the calculation of net cash flow from operating activities.

   True / False

6.3 A decrease in trade payables will have a positive impact on cash flow in the calculation of net cash flow from operating activities.

   True / False

6.4 An increase in trade receivables will have a positive impact on cash flow in the calculation of net cash flow from operating activities.

   True / False

6.5 A loss on disposal of property, plant and equipment will have a positive impact on cash flow in the calculation of net cash flow from operating activities.

   True / False

6.6 A cash receipt from the sale of property, plant and equipment will be classified as an investing activity in the statement of cash flows.

   True / False

6.7 When preparing a statement of cash flows using the direct method, which of the following cash flows are used?

1. cash paid to suppliers and employees
2. cash received from the sale of goods
3. tax paid
4. interest paid

		✓
(a)	1 and 2	
(b)	1, 2 and 3	
(c)	3 and 4	
(d)	all of them	

6.8 The following information relates to a company for the year ended 30 June 20X1.

Profit from operations (after deducting depreciation of £5,000) is £12,400

	At 30.6.20X1	At 30.6.20X0
	£	£
Inventories	3,600	3,900
Trade receivables	4,800	4,200
Trade payables	4,100	3,700

What is the net cash generated from operating activities (prior to any tax and interest paid)?

		✓
(a)	£17,500	
(b)	£17,400	
(c)	£18,700	
(d)	£12,500	

6.9 Dewa Ltd has a profit from operations of £25,000 for 20X1. The company's statement of profit or loss and other comprehensive income and statement of financial position show the following:

	£
depreciation charge	8,000
decrease in inventories	3,000
increase in trade and other receivables	5,000
increase in trade and other payables	2,000

What is the cash from operations for 20X1?

		✓
(a)	£33,000 inflow	
(b)	£37,000 inflow	
(c)	£13,000 inflow	
(d)	£43,000 inflow	

6.10 Sumner Ltd has a loss from operations of £8,000 for 20X2. The company's statement of profit or loss and other comprehensive income and statement of financial position show the following:

	£
depreciation charge	7,500
increase in inventories	2,500
increase in trade and other receivables	1,500
decrease in trade and other payables	1,000

What is the cash from operations for 20X2?

		✓
(a)	£4,500 inflow	
(b)	£2,500 outflow	
(c)	£5,500 outflow	
(d)	£4,500 outflow	

6.11 Zhang Ltd has a profit from operations of £12,500 for 20X3. The company's statement of profit or loss and other comprehensive income and statement of financial position show the following:

	£
depreciation charge	8,500
gain on disposal of property, plant and equipment	3,500
decrease in inventories	2,500
increase in trade and other receivables	3,000
decrease in trade and other payables	2,000

What is the cash from operations for 20X3?

		✓
(a)	£26,000 inflow	
(b)	£15,000 inflow	
(c)	£16,000 inflow	
(d)	£32,000 inflow	

6.12 You have been asked to prepare the statement of cash flows for Minster Ltd for the year ended 31 March 20X1.

The most recent statement of profit or loss and statement of financial position (with comparatives for the previous year) of Minster Ltd are set out below.

Minster Ltd – Statement of profit or loss for the year ended 31 March 20X1

Continuing operations	£000
Revenue	2,749
Cost of sales	−1,312
Gross profit	1,437
Dividends received	25
Gain on disposal of property, plant and equipment	53
Distribution costs	−624
Administrative expenses	−347
Profit from operations	544
Finance costs	−54
Profit before tax	490
Tax	−115
Profit for the year from continuing operations	375

Minster Ltd – Statement of financial position as at 31 March 20X1

	20X1	20X0
	£000	£000
ASSETS		
Non-current assets		
Property, plant and equipment	3,640	2,490
Current assets		
Inventories	145	138
Trade receivables	185	196
Cash and cash equivalents	133	0
	463	334
Total assets	4,103	2,824
EQUITY AND LIABILITIES		
Equity		
Share capital	1,500	1,000
Share premium	750	500
Retained earnings	582	432
Total equity	2,832	1,932
Non-current liabilities		
Bank loans	1,000	600
	1,000	600
Current liabilities		
Trade payables	156	145
Tax liabilities	115	107
Bank overdraft	0	40
	271	292
Total liabilities	1,271	892
Total equity and liabilities	4,103	2,824

Further information:

- The total depreciation charge for the year was £365,000.
- Property, plant and equipment costing £260,000 with accumulated depreciation of £95,000 was sold in the year.
- All sales and purchases were on credit. Other expenses were paid for in cash.
- A dividend of £225,000 was paid during the year.

Required:

(a) Prepare a reconciliation of profit from operations to net cash from operating activities for Minster Ltd for the year ended 31 March 20X1.

(b) Prepare the statement of cash flows for Minster Ltd for the year ended 31 March 20X1.

6.13   You have been asked to prepare the statement of cash flows and changes in equity for Velani Ltd for the year ended 31 March 20X2.

The most recent statement of profit or loss and statement of financial position (with comparatives for the previous year) of Velani Ltd are set out below.

Velani Ltd – Statement of profit or loss for the year ended 31 March 20X2

Continuing operations	£000
Revenue	53,600
Cost of sales	−36,420
Gross profit	17,180
Dividends received	45
Loss on disposal of property, plant and equipment	−110
Distribution costs	−11,163
Administrative expenses	−4,032
Profit from operations	1,920
Finance costs	−109
Profit before tax	1,811
Tax	−347
Profit for the year from continuing operations	1,464

Velani Ltd – Statement of financial position as at 31 March 20X2

	20X2 £000	20X1 £000
ASSETS		
Non-current assets		
Property, plant and equipment	12,832	9,911
Current assets		
Inventories	5,057	5,168
Trade receivables	5,341	4,730
Cash and cash equivalents	0	1,360
	10,398	11,258
Total assets	23,230	21,169
EQUITY AND LIABILITIES		
Equity		
Share capital	8,000	6,000
Share premium	2,000	1,000
Retained earnings	6,052	5,183
Total equity	16,052	12,183
Non-current liabilities		
Bank loans	0	2,280
	0	2,280
Current liabilities		
Trade payables	6,721	6,410
Tax liabilities	347	296
Bank overdraft	110	0
	7,178	6,706
Total liabilities	7,178	8,986
Total equity and liabilities	23,230	21,169

Further information:
- The total depreciation charge for the year was £1,520,000.
- Property, plant and equipment costing £450,000 with accumulated depreciation of £210,000 was sold in the year.
- All sales and purchases were on credit. Other expenses were paid for in cash.
- A dividend of £595,000 was paid during the year.

Required:

(a)   Prepare a reconciliation of profit from operations to net cash from operating activities for Velani Ltd for the year ended 31 March 20X2.

(b)   Prepare the statement of cash flows for Velani Ltd for the year ended 31 March 20X2.

(c)   Draft the statement of changes in equity for Velani Ltd for the year ended 31 March 20X2.

7 Interpretation of financial statements

this chapter covers...

The statements of profit or loss and financial position of limited companies are often interpreted by means of accounting ratios in order to assess strengths and weaknesses. Comparisons can be made between:

■ *consecutive years for the same company*

■ *similar companies in the same industry*

■ *industry averages and the ratios for a particular company*

The financial statements of a business can be interpreted in the areas of profitability, liquidity, efficient use of resources and financial position.

In this chapter we examine:

■ *the importance of interpretation of financial statements*

■ *the main accounting ratios and performance indicators*

■ *a commentary on trends shown by the main accounting ratios*

■ *how to report on the financial situation of a company*

■ *limitations in the interpretation of financial statements*

> **Note:** *in AAT Assessments it is usual to calculate accounting ratios to the nearest one decimal place, eg 10.78 is shown as 10.8, and 10.23 is shown as 10.2.*

INTERESTED PARTIES

Interpretation of financial statements is not always made by an accountant; interested parties – as we have seen in Chapter 1 (page 7) – include:

- **managers** of the company, who need to make financial decisions affecting the future development of the company

- **banks**, who are being asked to lend money to finance the company

- **suppliers**, who wish to assess the likelihood of receiving payment

- **customers**, who wish to be assured of continuity of supplies in the future

- **shareholders**, who wish to be assured that their investment is sound

- prospective **investors**, who wish to compare relative strengths and weaknesses

- **employees** and **trade unions**, who wish to check on the financial prospects of the company

- **government** and **government agencies**, eg HM Revenue & Customs, who wish to check they are receiving the amount due to them

We saw in Chapter 1 how the *Conceptual Framework for Financial Reporting* requires that financial statements provide users with details of:

- financial position
- financial performance
- changes in financial position

From the financial statements the interested party will be able to calculate the main ratios, percentages and performance indicators. By doing this, the strengths and weaknesses of the company will be highlighted and appropriate conclusions can be drawn.

ACCOUNTING RATIOS AND THE ELEMENTS OF FINANCIAL STATEMENTS

The general term 'accounting ratios' is usually used to describe the calculations aspect of interpretation of financial statements. The term 'ratio' is, in fact, partly misleading because the performance indicators include percentages, time periods, as well as ratios in the strict sense of the word.

The main themes covered by the interpretation of financial statements are:

- **profitability** – the relationship between profit and revenue, assets, equity and capital employed

- **liquidity** – the stability of the company on a short-term basis

- **use of resources** – the effective and efficient use of assets and liabilities

- **financial position** – the way in which the company has been financed

In Chapter 1 we saw how the elements of financial statements are the building blocks from which financial statements are constructed. The elements are defined by the *Conceptual Framework for Financial Reporting* and comprise (see also page 10):

- assets

- liabilities

- equity

- income

- expenses

Accounting ratios make use of the elements in the interpretation of financial statements – the relationship between elements is what we are measuring, together with any changes from one year to the next, or between different companies in the same industry, or an industry average. The main themes of interpretation of financial statements use the elements as follows:

- **profitability** – measures the relationship between income and expenses; also the profits or losses measured against equity

- **liquidity** – focuses on the relationship between assets and liabilities

- **use of resources** – analyses how efficiently assets and liabilities have been used by the company

- **financial position** – compares the relationship between the equity and the non-current liabilities of the company

For example, one measure of the profitability of a company is to compare the profits or losses with the equity, as follows:

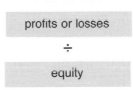

To illustrate this, the first two years' financial statements of a company show the relationship to be:

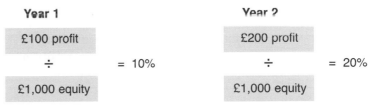

Thus it can be seen that an increase in the profit in year two has had an effect on the performance of the company because the relationship between profit and equity has changed from year 1.

MAKING USE OF ACCOUNTING RATIOS

It is important when examining a set of financial statements and calculating accounting ratios to relate them to reference points or standards. These points of reference might be to:

■ establish trends from past years, to provide a standard of comparison

■ benchmark against another similar company in the same industry

■ compare against industry averages

Above all, it is important to understand the relationships between ratios: one ratio may give an indication of the state of the company, but this needs to be supported by other ratios. Ratios can indicate symptoms, but the cause will then need to be investigated.

Another use of ratios is to estimate forward the likely profit or financial position of a company. For example, it might be assumed that the same gross profit percentage as last year will also apply next year; thus, given an estimated increase in revenue, it is a simple matter to estimate gross profit. In a similar way, by making use of ratios, operating profit (profit before finance costs and tax) and the statement of financial position can be forecast.

Whilst all of the ratios calculated in this chapter use figures from the statements of profit or loss and financial position, the statement of cash flows is important too. It assists in confirming the views shown by the accounting ratios and provides further evidence of the position.

Tutorial note:

ACCOUNTING RATIOS FOR PROFITABILITY

- Study the table and financial statements on the next two pages. They show the ways in which the profitability of a company is assessed.

- Then read the section entitled 'Profitability' which follows.

- Note that the accounting ratios from the financial statements of Wyvern Trading Company Limited are calculated and discussed in the Case Study on pages 208-213.

PROFITABILITY

One of the main objectives of a company is to make a profit. Profitability ratios examine the relationship between profit and revenue, assets, equity and capital employed. Before calculating the profitability ratios, it is important to read the statement of profit or loss in order to review the figures.

The key profitability ratios are illustrated on the next page. We will be calculating and discussing the accounting ratios from these figures in the Case Study on pages 208-213.

gross profit percentage

$$\frac{Gross\ profit}{Revenue} \times \frac{100}{1}$$

This expresses, as a percentage, the gross profit (revenue minus cost of sales) in relation to revenue. For example, a gross profit percentage of 20 per cent means that for every £100 of revenue, the gross profit is £20.

The gross profit percentage (or margin) should be similar from year-to-year for the same company. It will vary between companies in different areas of business, eg the gross profit percentage on jewellery is considerably higher than that on food. A significant change from one year to the next, particularly a fall in the percentage, requires investigation into the buying and selling prices.

Gross profit percentage, and also operating profit percentage (see below), need to be considered in context. For example, a supermarket may well have a lower gross profit percentage than a small corner shop but, because of the supermarket's much higher revenue, the amount of profit will be much higher. Whatever the type of business, gross profit – both as an amount and a percentage – needs to be sufficient to cover the overheads (expenses), and then to give an acceptable return on investment.

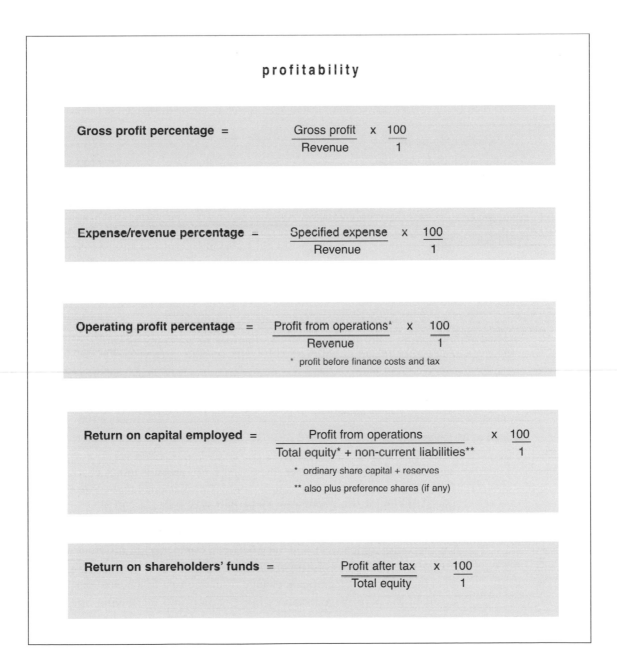

profitability

Gross profit percentage = $\dfrac{\text{Gross profit}}{\text{Revenue}} \times \dfrac{100}{1}$

Expense/revenue percentage – $\dfrac{\text{Specified expense}}{\text{Revenue}} \times \dfrac{100}{1}$

Operating profit percentage = $\dfrac{\text{Profit from operations}^{*}}{\text{Revenue}} \times \dfrac{100}{1}$

* profit before finance costs and tax

Return on capital employed = $\dfrac{\text{Profit from operations}}{\text{Total equity* + non-current liabilities**}} \times \dfrac{100}{1}$

* ordinary share capital + reserves

** also plus preference shares (if any)

Return on shareholders' funds = $\dfrac{\text{Profit after tax}}{\text{Total equity}} \times \dfrac{100}{1}$

Wyvern Trading Company Limited

STATEMENT OF PROFIT OR LOSS

for the year ended 31 December 20-1

	£000	£000
Continuing operations		
Revenue		1,430
Opening inventories	200	
Purchases	1,000	
	1,200	
Closing inventories	−240	
Cost of sales		−960
Gross profit		470
Distribution costs		−150
Administrative expenses		−140
Profit from operations		180
Finance costs		−10
Profit before tax		170
Tax		−50
Profit for the year from continuing operations		120

Statement of changes in equity (extract)

Retained earnings	
Balance at 1 January 20-1	180
Profit for the year	120
	300
Dividends paid	−100
Balance at 31 December 20-1	200

STATEMENT OF FINANCIAL POSITION (extract)

Capital employed (total equity + non-current liabilities)	1,550
Total equity (ordinary share capital + reserves)	1,450

Note: Items used in the ratios on the previous page are shown in bold type on a grey background

expense/revenue percentage

$$\frac{Specified\ expense}{Revenue} \quad x \quad \frac{100}{1}$$

A large expense or overhead item can be expressed as a percentage of revenue: for example, the relationship between advertising and revenue might be found to be 10 per cent in one year, but 20 per cent the next year. This could indicate that an increase in advertising had failed to produce a proportionate increase in revenue.

Note that each expense falls into one of three categories of cost:

1   fixed costs, or

2   variable costs, or

3   semi-variable costs

Fixed costs remain constant despite other changes. Variable costs alter with changed circumstances, such as increased output or revenue. Semi-variable costs combine both a fixed and a variable element, eg hire of a car at a basic (fixed) cost, with a (variable) cost per mile.

It is important to appreciate the nature of costs when interpreting accounts: for example, if revenue this year is twice last year's figure, not all expenses will have doubled.

operating profit percentage

$$\frac{Profit\ from\ operations^*}{Revenue} \quad x \quad \frac{100}{1}$$

profit before finance costs and tax

The operating profit percentage uses profit before finance costs and tax. Note that, in accounting terminology, profit from operations is often referred to as the 'net profit'.

As with gross profit percentage, the operating profit (net profit) percentage should be similar from year-to-year for the same company, and should also be comparable with other companies in the same line of business. Net profit percentage should, ideally, increase from year-to-year, which indicates that the overhead costs are being kept under control. Any significant fall should be investigated to see if it has been caused by:

■   a fall in gross profit percentage

■   and/or an increase in one particular expense, eg wages and salaries, advertising, etc

return on capital employed (ROCE)

Return on capital employed expresses the profit of a company in relation to the capital employed. The percentage return is best thought of in relation to other investments, eg a bank might offer a return of five per cent. A person setting up a company is investing a sum of money in that company, and the profit is the return that is achieved on that investment. However, it should be noted that the risks in running a company are considerably greater than depositing the money with a bank, and an additional return to allow for the extra risk is needed.

The calculation of return on capital employed for limited companies must take note of their different methods of financing. It is necessary to distinguish between the ordinary shareholders' investment (equity) and the capital employed by the company, which includes preference shares and non-current liabilities, such as debentures and long-term loans.

The calculation for capital employed is:

	Ordinary share capital
add	*Reserves (capital and revenue)*
equals	*Total equity*
add	*Preference share capital (if any)*
add	*Non-current liabilities*
equals	*Capital employed*

The reason for including preference shares and non-current liabilities (such as debentures/long-term loans) in the capital employed is that the company has the use of the money from these contributors for the foreseeable future, or certainly for a fixed time period.

The calculation of return on capital employed is:

$$\frac{\textit{Profit from operations}}{\textit{Total equity* + non-current liabilities**}} \quad x \quad \frac{\textit{100}}{\textit{1}}$$

*   *ordinary share capital + reserves*

** *plus preference shares (if any)*

Return on capital employed is also known as the **primary ratio** – see page 204.

return on shareholders' funds

$$\frac{Profit\ after\ tax}{Total\ equity} \times \frac{100}{1}$$

Return on shareholders' funds focuses on the return for the ordinary shareholders. It indicates the return the company is making on their funds, ie ordinary shares and reserves. The economic decision as to whether they remain as ordinary shareholders is primarily whether they could get a better return elsewhere.

Note that, when calculating return on equity, use the profit for the year, ie after tax, which is the amount of profit available to the ordinary shareholders.

Tutorial note:

ACCOUNTING RATIOS FOR LIQUIDITY, USE OF RESOURCES AND FINANCIAL POSITION

- Study the ratios table and financial statements below and on the next page. They show the ways in which the liquidity, use of resources, and financial position of a company are assessed.

- Then read the sections which follow.

- Note that the accounting ratios from the financial statements of Wyvern Trading Company Limited are calculated and discussed in the Case Study on pages 208-213.

---

liquidity

Current ratio =
(or working capital ratio)

$$\frac{Current\ assets}{Current\ liabilities} = x : 1$$

Acid test ratio –
(or quick ratio/liquid capital ratio)

$$\frac{Current\ assets - inventories}{Current\ liabilities} = x : 1$$

LIQUIDITY

Liquidity ratios measure the financial stability of a company, ie the ability of a company to pay its way on a short-term basis. Here we focus our attention on the current assets and current liabilities sections of the statement of financial position.

The key liquidity ratios are shown on page 201; these are linked to the statement of financial position of Wyvern Trading Company Limited. The ratios are calculated and discussed in the Case Study on pages 208-213.

working capital

Working capital = Current assets – Current liabilities

Working capital (often called *net current assets*) is needed by all companies in order to finance day-to-day trading activities. Sufficient working capital enables a company to hold adequate inventories, allow a measure of credit to its customers (trade receivables), and to pay its suppliers (trade payables) on the due date.

current ratio (or working capital ratio)

$$\text{Current ratio} \quad = \quad \frac{\text{Current assets}}{\text{Current liabilities}} \quad = \quad x : 1$$

Current ratio uses figures from the statement of financial position and measures the relationship between current assets and current liabilities. Although there is no ideal current ratio, an acceptable ratio is about 2:1, ie £2 of current assets to every £1 of current liabilities. However, a company in the retail trade may be able to work with a lower ratio, eg 1.5:1 or even less, because it deals mainly in cash and so does not have a large figure for receivables. A current ratio can be too high: if it is above 3:1 an investigation of the make-up of current assets and current liabilities is needed: eg the company may have too many inventories, too many trade receivables, or too much cash, or even too few trade payables.

acid test ratio (or quick ratio/liquid capital ratio)

$$\text{Acid test ratio} \quad = \quad \frac{\text{Current assets} \quad - \quad \text{inventories}}{\text{Current liabilities}} \quad = \quad x : 1$$

The acid test ratio is so called because, like the litmus test in chemistry, in accounting it gives a clear indication of the health of a company's finance. It uses the current assets and current liabilities from the statement of financial position, but inventories are omitted. This is because inventories are the least

Wyvern Trading Company Limited
STATEMENT OF FINANCIAL POSITION
as at 31 December 20-1

ASSETS	
Non-current assets	*£000*
Property, plant and equipment	1,280
Current assets	
Inventories	240
Trade receivables	150
Cash and cash equivalents	135
	525
Total assets	1,805
EQUITY AND LIABILITIES	
Equity	
Ordinary shares	1,250
Retained earnings	200
Total equity	1,450
Non-current liabilities	
10% Debentures	100
	100
Current liabilities	
Trade payables	205
Tax payable	50
	255
Total liabilities	355
Total equity and liabilities	1,805

STATEMENT OF PROFIT OR LOSS (extract)

Cost of sales	960
Revenue	1,430

Note: Items used in ratios are shown in bold type with a grey background.

liquid current asset: they have to be sold, turned into trade receivables, and then the cash has to be collected. Thus the acid test ratio provides a direct comparison between trade receivables/cash and short-term liabilities. The balance between liquid assets, that is trade receivables and cash, and current liabilities should, ideally, be about 1:1, ie £1 of liquid assets to each £1 of current liabilities. At this ratio a company is expected to be able to pay its current liabilities from its liquid assets; a figure below 1:1, eg 0.75:1, indicates that the company would have difficulty in meeting the demands of trade payables. However, as with the current ratio, some companies are able to operate with a lower acid test ratio than others.

USE OF RESOURCES

Use of resources measures how efficiently the management controls the current aspects of the company – principally inventories, trade receivables and trade payables. Like all accounting ratios, comparison needs to be made either with figures for the previous year, or with a similar company.

inventory holding period and inventory turnover

$$\text{Inventory holding period (days)} = \frac{\text{Inventories}}{\text{Cost of sales}} \quad x \quad 365 \text{ days}$$

Inventory holding period is the number of days' inventories held on average. This figure will depend on the type of goods sold by the company. For example, a market trader selling fresh flowers, who finishes each day when sold out, will have an inventory holding period of one day. By contrast, a jewellery shop – because it may hold large quantities of jewellery – will have a much longer inventory holding period, perhaps sixty or ninety days, or longer. Nevertheless, it is important for a company to keep its inventory holding period as short as possible, subject to being able to meet the needs of most of its customers. A company which is improving in efficiency will generally have a shorter inventory holding period comparing one year with the previous one, or with the inventory holding period of similar companies.

$$\text{Inventory turnover (times per year)} = \frac{\text{Cost of sales}}{\text{Inventories}} = x \text{ times}$$

Inventory turnover is the number of times a year that the inventory is turned over. An inventory turnover of, say, twelve times a year means that about thirty days' inventories are held.

Note that inventory holding period and turnover can only be calculated where a company buys and sells goods; it cannot be used for a company that provides a service.

use of resources

Inventory holding period (days) = $\dfrac{\text{Inventories}}{\text{Cost of sales}}$ x 365 days

Inventory turnover (times per year) = $\dfrac{\text{Cost of sales}}{\text{Inventories}}$ = x times

Trade receivables collection period (days) = $\dfrac{\text{Trade receivables}}{\text{Revenue}}$ x 365 days

Trade payables payment period (days) = $\dfrac{\text{Trade payables}}{\text{Cost of sales}}$ x 365 days

Working capital cycle (days) = Inventory days + Receivable days – Payable days

Asset turnover (non-current assets) ratio = $\dfrac{\text{Revenue}}{\text{Non-current assets}}$ = x times

Asset turnover (net assets) ratio = $\dfrac{\text{Revenue}}{\text{Total assets} - \text{current liabilities}}$ = x times

financial position

Interest cover = $\dfrac{\text{Profit from operations}}{\text{Finance costs}}$ = x times

Gearing = $\dfrac{\text{Non-current liabilities}}{\text{Total equity} + \text{non-current liabilities}}$ x $\dfrac{100}{1}$

trade receivables' collection period (days)

$$\frac{Trade\ receivables}{Revenue} \quad x \quad 365\ days$$

This calculation shows how many days, on average, trade receivables take to pay for goods sold to them by the company. The collection time can be compared with that for the previous year, or with that of a similar company. In the UK, most trade receivables should make payment within about 30 days; however, with international trade, it will take longer for the proceeds to be received. A comparison from year-to-year of the collection period is a measure of the company's efficiency at collecting the money that is due to it and we are looking for some reduction in trade receivables' days over time. Ideally trade receivables' days should be shorter than trade payables' days, thus indicating that money is being received from trade receivables before it is paid out to trade payables.

trade payables' payment period (days)

$$\frac{Trade\ payables}{Cost\ of\ sales} \quad x \quad 365\ days$$

This calculation is the opposite aspect to that of trade receivables: here we are measuring the speed it takes to make payment to trade payables. While trade payables can be a useful temporary source of finance, delaying payment too long may cause problems. This ratio is most appropriate for companies that buy and sell goods; it cannot be used for a company that provides a service; it is also difficult to interpret when a company buys in some goods and, at the same time, provides a service, eg an hotel. Generally, though, we would expect to see the trade payables' days period longer than the trade receivables' days, ie money is being received from trade receivables before it is paid out to trade payables. We would also be looking for a similar figure for trade payables' days from one year to the next: this would indicate a stable company.

working capital cycle

Working capital cycle = Inventory days + Receivable days – Payable days

This is a further use of the ratios covering the working capital items of inventory, trade receivables and trade payables. The working capital cycle measures the period of time between payment for goods received into inventory and the collection of cash from customers in respect of their sale. The shorter the time between the initial outlay and the ultimate collection of cash, the lower the amount of working capital needed by the business.

Comparison needs to be made – either with the working capital cycle for the previous year, or with a similar company. The working capital cycle will show either a better position, ie the time has been reduced, or a worse position, ie the time has been increased.

There are three ways in which a company can seek to reduce the working capital cycle:

■ reduce inventory (and lower the number of days that inventory is held)

■ speed up the rate of debt collection (and lower the number of receivable days)

■ slow down the rate of payment to suppliers (and increase the number of payable days)

However, it may not be possible to put these into practice as there could be unintended consequences – reducing inventory might mean that a poorer service is offered to customers, speeding up debt collection might mean that customers seek other suppliers who offer better terms, and slowing payment to suppliers might mean that they refuse to supply unless payment is made immediately.

asset turnover ratio: non-current assets, net assets

$$\frac{Revenue}{Non\text{-}current\ assets} = x\ times \qquad \frac{Revenue}{Total\ assets - current\ liabilities} = x\ times$$

These two ratios measure the efficiency of the use of assets – either non-current assets or net assets – in generating revenue. An increasing ratio from one year to the next indicates greater efficiency. A falling ratio may be caused either by a decrease in revenue, or an increase in assets – perhaps caused by the purchase or revaluation of non-current assets, or increased inventories, or increased trade receivables as a result of poor credit control.

Different types of businesses will have very different asset turnover ratios. For example a supermarket, with high revenue and relatively few assets, will have a very high figure; by contrast, an engineering company, with lower revenue and a substantial investment in non-current and current assets, will have a much lower figure.

FINANCIAL POSITION

Financial position measures the strength and long-term financing of the company. Two ratios are calculated – interest cover and gearing. Interest cover considers the ability of the company to meet (or cover) its finance costs from its profit from operations; gearing focuses on the balance in the long-term funding of the company between monies from loan providers and monies from equity shareholders.

Both ratios look at aspects of loan finance and it is important to remember that both interest and loan repayments must be made on time; if they are not the loan provider may well be able to seek payment by forcing the company to sell assets and, in the worst case, may well be able to force the company into liquidation.

interest cover

$$\frac{Profit\ from\ operations}{Finance\ costs} = x\ times$$

The interest cover ratio, linked closely to gearing, considers the safety margin (or cover) of profit over the finance costs of a company. For example, if the profit from operations was £10,000, and finance costs were £5,000, this would give interest cover of two times, which is a low figure. If the finance costs were £1,000, this would give interest cover of ten times which is a higher and much more acceptable figure. Thus, the conclusion to draw is that the higher the interest cover, the better (although there is an argument for having some debt).

gearing

$$\frac{Non\text{-}current\ liabilities}{Total\ equity + non\text{-}current\ liabilities} \quad x \quad \frac{100}{1}$$

Whilst the liquidity ratios seen earlier focus on whether the company can pay its way in the short-term, gearing is concerned with long-term financial stability. Here we measure how much of the company is financed by non-current liabilities (such as debentures and long-term loans) against the capital employed (total equity + non-current liabilities). The higher the gearing percentage, the less secure will be the financing of the company and, therefore, the future of the company. This is because debt is costly in terms of finance costs (particularly if interest rates are variable). It is difficult to set a standard for an acceptable gearing percentage: in general terms, most investors and lenders would not wish to see a gearing percentage of greater than 50%.

USE OF THE PRIMARY RATIO

Return on capital employed (see page 196) is perhaps the most effective ratio used in the interpretation of accounts. This is because it expresses profit in relation to the capital employed (total equity + non-current liabilities) and so is a direct measure of the efficiency of a company in using the capital available to it in order to generate profits.

Return on capital employed is often referred to as the primary ratio, since it can be broken down into the two secondary factors of:

■ operating profit percentage (see page 195)
■ asset turnover (net assets) (see page 203)

The relationship between the three can be expressed in the form of a 'pyramid of ratios' (where the ratio at the top of the pyramid is formed from and relates arithmetically to the other two ratios):

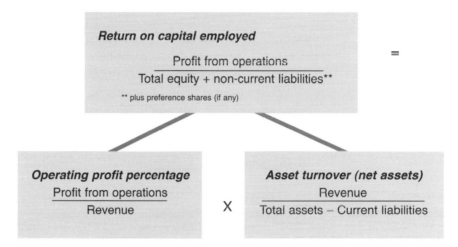

Note that the amounts for capital employed and net assets are the same – they are taken from different sides of the statements of financial position.

examples

■ **Company Aye** has revenue of £500,000, profit from operations of £50,000, and net assets/capital employed of £250,000. The pyramid of ratios is:

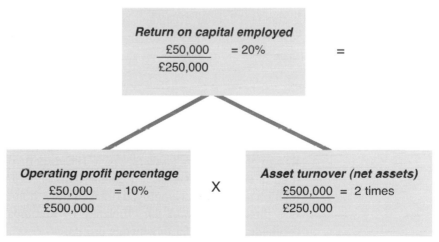

Thus it can be seen that, when the operating percentage is multiplied by the asset turnover (net assets), the answer is return on capital employed (the primary ratio):

10% x 2 times = 20% (primary ratio)

■ **Company Bee** has revenue of £1,000,000, profit from operations of £20,000, and net assets/capital employed of £100,000. The pyramid of ratios is:

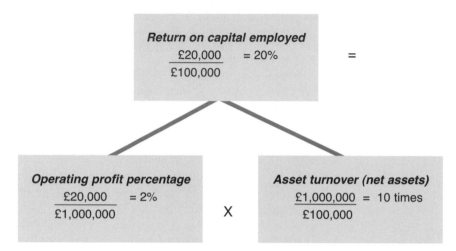

Here the primary ratio is made up of:

2% x 10 times = 20% (primary ratio)

By using the pyramid of ratios, we can get a better idea of how ratios relate one to another rather than considering them in isolation. Thus the primary ratio shows how the same return on capital employed can be achieved in different ways, depending on the type of business. It demonstrates the different ways of running a business – eg the supermarket (with low profit margins and high revenue) and the specialist shop (with higher profit margins, but lower revenue) – and how each achieves its return on capital employed.

INTERPRETATION OF FINANCIAL STATEMENTS

Interpretation of financial statements is much more than a mechanical process of calculating a number of ratios. It involves the analysis of the relationships between the elements within financial statements and the presentation of the information gathered in a meaningful way to interested parties.

It is important that a logical approach is adopted to the process of interpreting financial statements. The needs of the user – the person who has requested the information – must be the starting point. These needs are linked to the main themes of interpretation: profitability, liquidity, use of resources, and financial position. Users often include:

- potential investors – mainly concerned about the profitability of an investment in a company

- potential lenders – concerned with a borrower's liquidity, use of resources, and financial position

- potential buyers – investigating financial statements to assess a proposed supplier's profitability, liquidity, and financial position

The way in which the interpretation of financial statements is presented to the user must be appropriate to the needs of the user. Thus a letter is most appropriate for a potential investor, a report for a potential lender, and an email for a potential buyer (where both the buyer and the writer of the report work for the same company). Whichever form of presentation is used, take care over the layout and make sure that there are plenty of sub-sections to guide the user.

The form of the presentation to the user will usually include the following:

- calculation of ratios from financial statements

- an explanation of the meaning of each ratio (using language that can be understood by users with a non-financial background)

- comment on the financial position of the company as shown by the ratios (making comparisons against guideline standards where applicable – eg 2:1 for the current ratio – and against industry averages, when available); make use of the primary ratio (see pages 204-206), if appropriate

- a statement of how the financial position of the company has changed over the period covered by the financial statements – usually two years (looking for trends in the ratios and comment on what these mean and whether they show an improving or a worsening financial position; including comparisons against industry averages, when available)

- a conclusion which links back to the needs of the user (to invest in, or to lend to, the company, or to use as a supplier) and summarises against the themes of interpretation relevant to the user: profitability, liquidity, use of resources, and financial position

Two Case Studies which now follow put into practice an analytical approach to the interpretation of financial statements:

1 **Wyvern Trading Company Limited**

In the first we look at limited company financial statements from the point of view of a potential investor (for clarity, one year's statements are given although, in practice, more than one year would be used to establish a trend). The comments given indicate what should be looked for when analysing and interpreting a set of financial statements.

2 **Surgdressings Limited**

In the second we consider financial statements from the point of view of a potential buyer of products from the company. The interpretation seeks to assess the risk of switching to the supplier, and to make comparisons with industry average figures.

WYVERN TRADING COMPANY LIMITED: ACCOUNTING RATIOS

situation

The following are the financial statements of Wyvern Trading Company Limited. The business trades in office supplies and sells to the public through its three retail shops in the Wyvern area; it also delivers direct to businesses in the area from its modern warehouse on a local business park.

The financial statements and accounting ratios are to be considered from the viewpoint of a potential investor.

solution

We will now analyse the financial statements from the point of view of a potential investor. All figures shown are in £000s. The analysis starts on page 211 – note that the accounting ratios are calculated to the nearest one decimal place, in line with the practice of AAT Assessments.

Wyvern Trading Company Limited
STATEMENT OF PROFIT OR LOSS
for the year ended 31 December 20-1

	£000	£000
Continuing operations		
Revenue		1,430
Opening inventories	200	
Purchases	1,000	
	1,200	
Closing inventories	−240	
Cost of sales		−960
Gross profit		470
Distribution costs		−150
Administrative expenses		−140
Profit from operations		180
Finance costs		−10
Profit before tax		170
Tax		−50
Profit for the year from continuing operations		120

Statement of changes in equity (extract)

Retained earnings	
Balance at 1 January 20-1	180
Profit for the year	120
	300
Dividends paid	−100
Balance at 31 December 20-1	200

Wyvern Trading Company Limited
STATEMENT OF FINANCIAL POSITION as at 31 December 20-1

ASSETS

Non-current assets	*£000*
Property, plant and equipment	1,280
Current assets	
Inventories	240
Trade receivables	150
Cash and cash equivalents	135
	525
Total assets	1,805
EQUITY AND LIABILITIES	
Equity	
Ordinary shares	1,250
Retained earnings	200
Total equity	1,450
Non-current liabilities	
10% Debentures	100
	100
Current liabilities	
Trade payables	205
Tax payable	50
	255
Total liabilities	355
Total equity and liabilities	1,805

PROFITABILITY

Gross profit percentage

$$\frac{£470}{£1,430} \quad \times \quad \frac{100}{1} \qquad = \quad 32.9\%$$

Distribution costs to revenue

$$\frac{£150}{£1,430} \quad \times \quad \frac{100}{1} \qquad = \quad 10.5\%$$

Operating profit percentage

$$\frac{£180}{£1,430} \quad \times \quad \frac{100}{1} \qquad = \quad 12.6\%$$

Return on capital employed

$$\frac{£180}{£1,450 + £100} \quad \times \quad \frac{100}{1} \qquad = \quad 11.6\%$$

Return on shareholders' funds

$$\frac{£120}{£1,450} \quad \times \quad \frac{100}{1} \qquad = \quad 8.3\%$$

The gross and operating profit percentages seem to be acceptable figures for the type of business, although comparisons should be made with those of the previous accounting period. A company should always aim at least to hold its percentages and, ideally, to make a small improvement. A significant fall in the percentages may indicate a poor buying policy, poor pricing (perhaps caused by competition), and the causes should be investigated.

Distribution costs seem to be quite a high percentage of revenue. Comparisons need to be made with previous years to see if these are increasing or decreasing. It may be possible for increases in revenue not to have a significant effect on this cost.

Return on capital employed is satisfactory, but could be better. At 11.6% it is less than two percentage points above the ten per cent cost of the debentures (ignoring the tax advantages of issuing debentures). Return on shareholders' funds is 8.3%, but a potential shareholder needs to compare this with the returns available elsewhere.

LIQUIDITY

Current ratio

$$\frac{£525}{£255} \qquad = 2.1{:}1$$

Acid test ratio

$$\frac{(£525 - £240)}{£255} \qquad = 1.1{:}1$$

The current and acid test ratios are excellent: they are slightly higher than the expected 'norms' of 2:1 and 1:1 respectively (although many companies operate successfully with lower ratios); however, they are not too high which would be an indication of inefficient use of assets.

These two ratios indicate that the company is very solvent, with no short-term liquidity problems.

USE OF RESOURCES
Inventory holding period

$$\frac{£240 \times 365}{£960} = 91 \text{ days}$$

Trade receivables' collection period

$$\frac{£150 \times 365}{£1,430} = 38 \text{ days}$$

Trade payables' payment period

$$\frac{£205 \times 365}{£960} = 78 \text{ days}$$

Asset turnover (non-current assets)

$$\frac{£1,430}{£1,280} = 1.1:1$$

Asset turnover (net assets)

$$\frac{£1,430}{£1,550} = 0.9:1$$

This group of ratios shows the main weakness of the company: not enough business is passing through for the size of the company.

Inventory holding period is too long for an office supplies business: the inventories are turning over only every 91 days – surely it should be faster than this?

Trade receivables' collection period is acceptable on the face of it – 30 days would be better – but quite a volume of the revenue will be made through the retail outlets in cash. This amount should, if known, be deducted from the revenue before calculating the trade receivables' collection period: thus the collection period is, in reality, longer than that calculated.

Trade payables' payment period is very slow for this type of business – long delays could cause problems with suppliers in the future.

The asset turnover ratios say it all: this type of business should be able to obtain a much better figure:

• either, revenue needs to be increased using the same assets

• or, revenue needs to be maintained, but assets reduced

FINANCIAL POSITION

Interest cover

$$\frac{£180}{£10} \qquad = \quad 18 \text{ times}$$

Gearing

$$\frac{£100}{£1,450 + £100} \qquad \times \frac{100}{1} \qquad = \quad 6.5\%$$

The interest cover figure of 18 is very high and shows that the company has no problems in paying interest.

The gearing percentage is very low: anything up to 50% could be seen. A figure as low as 6.5% indicates that the company could borrow more money if it wished to finance, say, expansion plans (there are plenty of non-current assets for a lender – such as a bank – to take as security for a loan). At the present level of gearing there is a very low risk to potential investors.

CONCLUSION

This appears to be a profitable company, although there may be some scope for cutting down somewhat on the distribution costs (administrative expenses could be looked at too). The company offers a reasonable return on capital, although things could be improved.

The company is solvent and has good current and acid test ratios. Interest cover is high and gearing is very low – a good sign during times of variable interest rates.

The main area of weakness is in asset utilisation. It appears that the company could do much to reduce the days for inventory holding and the trade receivables' collection period; at the same time trade payables could be paid faster. Asset turnover is very low for this type of business and it does seem that there is much scope for expansion within the structure of the existing company. However, a potential investor will need to consider if the directors have the ability to focus on the weaknesses shown by the ratio analysis and to take steps to improve the company.

ASSESSING A SUPPLIER – SURGDRESSINGS LIMITED: ACCOUNTING RATIOS

situation

You work for the Wyvern Private Hospital plc. The company has been approached by a supplier of surgical dressings, Surgdressings Limited, which is offering its products at advantageous prices.

The Surgical Director of Wyvern Private Hospital is satisfied with the quality and suitability of the products offered and the Finance Director, your boss, has obtained the latest financial statements from the company which are set out on the next page.

You have been asked to prepare a report for the Finance Director recommending whether or not to use Surgdressings Limited as a supplier of surgical dressings to the Hospital. You are to use the information contained in the financial statements of Surgdressings Limited and the industry averages supplied. Included in your report should be:

* comments on the company's

  - profitability

  - liquidity

  - financial position

* consideration of how the company has changed over the two years

* comparison with the industry as a whole

The report should include calculation of the following ratios for the two years:

  - return on capital employed

  - operating profit percentage

  - acid test ratio

  - gearing

The relevant industry average ratios are as follows:

	20-5	20-4
Return on capital employed	11.3%	11.1%
Operating profit percentage	16.4%	16.2%
Acid test ratio	1.0:1	0.9:1
Gearing	31%	32%

SURGDRESSINGS LIMITED
Summary statement of profit or loss for the year ended 31 December

Continuing operations	20-5 £000	20-4 £000
Revenue	4,600	4,300
Cost of sales	−2,245	−2,135
Gross profit	2,355	2,165
Overheads	−1,582	−1,491
Profit for the year from continuing operations	773	674

Summary statement of financial position as at 31 December

ASSETS	20-5 £000	20-4 £000
Non-current assets	5,534	6,347
Current assets		
Inventories	566	544
Trade receivables	655	597
Cash and cash equivalents	228	104
	1,449	1,245
Total assets	6,983	7,592
EQUITY AND LIABILITIES		
Equity		
Share capital	2,300	2,000
Share premium	670	450
Retained earnings	1,375	1,140
Total equity	4,345	3,590
Non-current liabilities		
Long-term loan	1,824	3,210
	1,824	3,210
Current liabilities		
Trade payables	572	504
Tax payable	242	288
	814	792
Total liabilities	2,638	4,002
Total equity and liabilities	6,983	7,592

solution

REPORT

To: Finance Director, Wyvern Private Hospital plc

From: A Student

Date: today's date

Re: Analysis of Surgdressings Limited's financial statements 20-4/20-5

Introduction

The purpose of this report is to analyse the financial statements of Surgdressings Limited for 20-4 and 20-5 to determine whether the Hospital should use the company as a supplier of surgical dressings.

Calculation of ratios

The following ratios have been calculated:

	20-5		20-4	
	company	industry average	company	industry average
Return on capital employed	$\dfrac{773}{6,169}$ =12.5%	11.3%	$\dfrac{674}{6,800}$ = 9.9%	11.1%
Operating profit percentage	$\dfrac{773}{4,600}$ =16.8%	16.4%	$\dfrac{674}{4,300}$ = 15.7%	16.2%
Acid test ratio	$\dfrac{883}{814}$ = 1.1:1	1.0:1	$\dfrac{701}{792}$ = 0.9:1	0.9:1
Gearing	$\dfrac{1,824}{6,169^*}$ = 30%	31%	$\dfrac{3,210}{6,800^*}$ = 47%	32%

* total equity + non-current liabilities

Comment and analysis

- In terms of profitability, the company has improved from 20-4 to 20-5.
- Return on capital employed has increased from 9.9% to 12.5% – this means that the company is generating more profit in 20-5 from the available capital employed than it did in 20-4. The company has gone from being below the industry average in 20-4 to being better than the average in 20-5.
- Operating profit percentage has also improved, increasing from 15.7% in 20-4 to 16.8% in 20-5. This means that the company is generating more profit from revenue in 20-5 than it did in the previous year. In 20-4 the company was below the industry average but in 20-5 it is better than the average. As it is now performing better than the average, this suggests that it may continue to be successful in the future.

- The liquidity of the company has improved during the year.

- The acid test ratio has gone up from 0.9:1 to 1.1:1. This indicates that the liquid assets, ie receivables and cash, are greater than current liabilities in 20-5. The company has gone from being the same as the industry average in 20-4 to better than average in 20-5. Thus, in 20-5, Surgdressings Limited is more liquid than the average business in the industry.

- The financial position of the company has improved considerably during the year.

- In 20-4 gearing was high at 47%. In 20-5 the percentage of non-current liabilities to capital employed declined to 30%. A high gearing percentage is often seen as a risk to a company's long-term survival: in times of economic downturn, when profits fall, a high-geared company will have increasing difficulty in meeting the finance costs of debt – in extreme cases, a company could be forced into liquidation. In 20-4, the gearing percentage of Surgdressings Limited was much higher than the industry average, making it relatively more risky than the average of companies in the industry. The much improved percentage in 20-5 is now below the industry average, making it less risky than the average of other companies in the industry.

CONCLUSION

- Based solely on the information provided in the financial statements of Surgdressings Limited and the ratios calculated, it is recommended that the company is used by Wyvern Private Hospital as a supplier of surgical dressings.

- The company has increasing profitability, liquidity and financial position in 20-5 when compared with 20-4. It also compares favourably with other companies in the same industry and appears to present a lower risk than the average of the sector.

LIMITATIONS OF RATIO ANALYSIS

Although accounting ratios can usefully highlight strengths and weaknesses, they should always be considered as a part of the overall assessment of a company, rather than as a whole. We have already seen the need to place ratios in context and relate them to a reference point or standard. The limitations of ratio analysis should always be borne in mind.

retrospective nature of accounting ratios

Accounting ratios are usually retrospective, based on previous performance and conditions prevailing in the past. They may not necessarily be valid for making forward projections: for example, a large customer may become insolvent, so threatening the company with a bad (irrecoverable) debt, and also reducing revenue in the future.

differences in accounting policies

When the financial statements of a company are compared, either with previous years' figures, or with figures from a similar company, there is a danger that the comparative statements are not drawn up on the same basis as those currently being worked on. Different accounting policies, in respect of depreciation and inventory valuation for instance, may well result in distortion and invalid comparisons.

inflation

Inflation may prove a problem, as most financial statements are prepared on an historic cost basis, that is, assets and liabilities are recorded at their original cost. As a result, comparison of figures from one year to the next may be difficult. In countries where inflation is running at high levels any form of comparison becomes practically meaningless.

reliance on standards

We have already mentioned guideline standards for some accounting ratios, for instance 2:1 for the current ratio. There is a danger of relying too heavily on such suggested standards, and ignoring other factors in the statement of financial position. An example of this would be to criticise a company for having a low current ratio when the company sells the majority of its goods for cash and consequently has a very low trade receivables figure: this would in fact be the case with many well-known and successful retail companies.

other considerations

Economic: The general economic climate and the effect this may have on the nature of the business, eg in an economic downturn retailers are usually the first to suffer, whereas manufacturers feel the effects later.

State of the business: The chairman's report of the company should be read in conjunction with the financial statements (including the statement of cash flows) to ascertain an overall view of the state of the company. Of great importance are the products of the company and their stage in the product life cycle, eg is a car manufacturer relying on old models, or is there an up-to-date product range which appeals to buyers?

Comparing like with like: Before making comparisons between 'similar' companies, we need to ensure that we are comparing 'like with like'. Differences, such as the acquisition of assets – renting premises compared with ownership, leasing vehicles compared with ownership – will affect the profitability of the company and the structure of the statement of financial position; likewise, the long-term financing of a company – the balance between debt finance and equity finance – will also have an effect.

PREPARING FOR ASSESSMENT

In AAT Assessments the interpretation of financial statements using ratio analysis is assessed by means of two tasks.

In the first task, you will be provided with a statement of profit or loss (and possibly a statement of other comprehensive income) and a statement of financial position. You will be required to identify the formula for, and then calculate five ratios (note that all the ratios set out in this chapter are assessable). The formulas for the ratios are selected from pick lists and the calculated figures are entered into gap fill boxes.

In the second task, you will be presented with ratios, and sometimes additional information (eg an extract from the financial statements, including a statement of cash flows). You will be required to analyse and interpret these by reference to the ratios of a previous accounting period, a competitor or an industry average, and present the results to an identified party (eg potential investor, potential lender, potential buyer).

Chapter Summary	■ Accounting ratios are numerical values (percentages, time periods, ratios) extracted from the financial statements. They can be used to measure:
	– profitability
	– liquidity
	– use of resources
	– financial position

■ Accounting ratios are numerical values (percentages, time periods, ratios) extracted from the financial statements. They can be used to measure:
  - profitability
  - liquidity
  - use of resources
  - financial position

■ Comparisons need to be made with previous financial statements, or those of similar companies.

■ There are a number of limitations to be borne in mind when drawing conclusions from accounting ratios:
  - retrospective nature, based on past performance
  - differences in accounting policies
  - effects of inflation when comparing year-to-year
  - reliance on standards
  - economic and other factors

Key Terms

profitability   measures the relationship between profit and revenue, assets, equity and capital employed; ratios include:
  - gross profit percentage
  - expenses/revenue percentage
  - operating profit percentage
  - return on capital employed
  - return on shareholders' funds

liquidity   measures the financial stability of a company, ie the ability of a company to pay its way on a short-term basis; ratios include:
  - current ratio
  - acid test ratio

use of resources   measures how efficiently the management controls the current aspects of the company – principally inventories, trade receivables and trade payables; ratios include:
  - inventory turnover and holding period
  - trade receivables' collection period
  - trade payables' payment period
  - working capital cycle
  - asset turnover ratios

financial position   measures the strength and long-term financing of the company; ratios include:
  - interest cover
  - gearing

Activities

7.1   The following information is available:

	£
Sales revenue for the year	200,000
Purchases for the year	170,000
Opening inventories	40,000
Closing inventories	50,000

Gross profit percentage is:

		✓
(a)	10%	
(b)	15%	
(c)	20%	
(d)	25%	

7.2   Which **ONE** of the following would you not take into account when calculating the current ratio?

		✓
(a)	property, plant and equipment	
(b)	cash and cash equivalents	
(c)	trade receivables	
(d)	inventories	

7.3   Which **ONE** of the following would you not take into account when calculating the acid test (quick) ratio?

		✓
(a)	cash and cash equivalents	
(b)	trade receivables	
(c)	inventories	
(d)	trade payables	

7.4   The following information is available:

	£
Sales revenue for the year	450,000
Purchases for the year	250,000
Average inventories for the year	50,000

The inventory holding period is:

	✓
(a) 73 days	
(b) 41 days	
(c) 58 days	
(d) 88 days	

7.5   The calculation for interest cover is:

	✓
(a) non-current liabilities/finance costs	
(b) finance costs/non-current liabilities	
(c) profit from operations/finance costs	
(d) finance costs/profit from operations	

7.6   The following information is available:

	£
Non-current assets	350,000
Current assets	200,000
Non-current liabilities	100,000
Current liabilities	50,000
Total equity	400,000

Gearing percentage is:

	✓
(a) 20%	
(b) 37.5%	
(c) 27.3%	
(d) 50%	

7.7 The working capital cycle is:

		✓
(a)	inventory days + receivable days − payable days	
(b)	inventory days + payable days − receivable days	
(c)	payable days + receivable days − inventory days	
(d)	payable days + receivable days + inventory days	

Activities 7.8 to 7.13 relate to the statement of financial position of Perran Ltd:

	£000
Non-current assets	750
Current assets	
Inventories	75
Trade receivables	150
Cash and cash equivalents	25
	250
Total assets	1,000
Equity	
Share capital	300
Share premium	150
Retained earnings	200
Total equity	650
Non-current liabilities	
Bank loan	225
	225
Current liabilities	
Trade payables	75
Tax payable	50
	125
Total liabilities	350
Total equity and liabilities	1,000

7.8 Current ratio is:

		✓
(a)	1.4:1	
(b)	2.0:1	
(c)	0.25:1	
(d)	1.0:1	

7.9 Acid test (quick) ratio is:

		✓
(a)	1.4:1	
(b)	0.25:1	
(c)	2.0:1	
(d)	1.0:1	

7.10 The calculation for the gearing percentage is:

		✓
(a)	225/1,000 x 100	
(b)	225/475 x 100	
(c)	475/1,000 x 100	
(d)	225/875 x 100	

7.11 If sales revenue for the year is £3,000,000, the asset turnover (non-current assets) ratio is:

		✓
(a)	3.0:1	
(b)	0.33:1	
(c)	12.0:1	
(d)	4.0:1	

7.12 If sales revenue for the year is £3,000,000 (all sold on credit), the trade receivables' collection period is (rounded to the nearest day):

		✓
(a)	18 days	
(b)	9 days	
(c)	30 days	
(d)	91 days	

7.13   If cost of sales for the year is £2,250,000, the trade payables' collection period is (rounded to the nearest day):

✓

(a)	19 days	
(b)	24 days	
(c)	20 days	
(d)	12 days	

7.14   Botar Ltd has the following statement of profit or loss:

	£000
Continuing operations	
Revenue	350
Cost of sales	−160
Gross profit	190
Distribution costs	−65
Administrative expenses	−45
Profit from operations	80
Finance costs	−15
Profit before tax	65
Tax	−12
Profit for the year from continuing operations	53

Required:

(a)   State the formula that is used to calculate each of the following ratios:

   (1)   Gross profit percentage

   (2)   Administrative expenses/revenue percentage

   (3)   Operating profit percentage

   (4)   Interest cover

(b)   Calculate the above ratios (to the nearest one decimal place)

7.15   The following information is taken from the financial statements of Vanova Ltd:

	£000
Revenue	7,240
Profit from operations	1,390
Profit after tax	840
Non-current assets	3,250
Total assets	4,150
Total equity	3,580
Non-current liabilities	400
Current liabilities	170

Required:

(a)   State the formula that is used to calculate each of the following ratios:

(1)   Return on capital employed

(2)   Operating profit percentage

(3)   Return on shareholders' funds

(4)   Asset turnover (non-current assets)

(5)   Asset turnover (net assets)

(b)   Calculate the above ratios (to the nearest one decimal place)

7.16   The following information is taken from the statement of financial position of Swann Ltd:

	£000
Inventories	160
Trade receivables	125
Cash and cash equivalents	30
Trade payables	140
Non-current liabilities	200
Total equity	710
Further information:	
Revenue for year	1,540
Cost of sales for year	890

Required:

(a)   State the formula that is used to calculate each of the following ratios:

    (1)   Current ratio

    (2)   Acid test (quick) ratio

    (3)   Inventory turnover

    (4)   Inventory holding period

    (5)   Trade receivables collection period

    (6)   Trade payables payment period

    (7)   Gearing

    (8)   Working capital cycle

(b)   Calculate the above ratios (to the nearest one decimal place)

7.17   The Finance Director of Rudgard Limited is examining the company's business operations to ensure that they are making maximum use of their cash resources as profit margins are reducing and they are under pressure from the bank to reduce their overdraft.

She is particularly interested in Rudgard Ltd's performance in comparison with their competitors in the industry.

You have calculated the following ratios based on the company's latest financial statements and have also obtained each ratio's industry average for comparative purposes.

	Rudgard Limited	**Industry average**
Inventory turnover	4.5 times	5.4 times
Trade receivables collection period	44 days	39 days
Trade payables payment period	48 days	42 days
Asset turnover (net assets)	3.2 times	3.6 times

Required:

Prepare notes for the Financial Director of Rudgard Limited that include:

(a)   Comments on whether Rudgard Ltd has performed better or worse in respect of each of the calculated ratios, giving possible reasons, as compared to the industry averages.

(b)   Recommendations on how the company could improve their trade receivables collection period.

7.18 Nicola Lavendar, a shareholder in Gresham Plc, is debating whether to keep or sell her shares in the company. Her main concern is the level of return she is receiving from Gresham Plc, but she also wishes to ensure that her shareholding is safe.

She has asked you to analyse the company's most recent financial statements with a view to assisting her in her decision.

You have calculated the following three accounting ratios for Gresham Plc, for years 20X1 and 20X0, and an extract of the company's statement of cash flows for 20X1 is also provided below.

Accounting ratios

	20X1	20X0
Gearing	42%	34%
Asset turnover (non-current assets)	3.1 times	4.2 times
Interest cover	3.2 times	5.6 times

Gresham Plc – Statement of cash flows (extract) for year 20X1

	£000
Operating activities	40
Investing activities	(160)
Financing activities	100
Decrease in cash and cash equivalents	(20)

Required:

Prepare notes for Nicola that include:

(a) Comments on the relative performance of Gresham Plc in respect of the two years, giving possible reasons for any differences (the extract of the statement of cash flows may assist you in some aspects of this) based upon the ratios calculated.

(b) Advice to Nicola, with **ONE** principal reason only to support this, as to whether or not she should keep or sell her shares in the company.

7.19 Jake Matease plans to invest in Fauve Limited. This is a chain of retail outlets. He is going to meet the Managing Director of Fauve Limited to discuss the profitability of the company. To prepare for the meeting he has asked you to comment on the change in profitability and the return on capital of the company. He has given you the statements of profit or loss of Fauve Limited and the statements of financial position for the last two years. These are set out below:

Fauve Limited
Summary statement of profit or loss for the year ended 30 September

	20-1	20-0
	£000	£000
Continuing operations		
Revenue	4,315	2,973
Cost of sales	−1,510	−1,189
Gross profit	2,805	1,784
Distribution costs	−983	−780
Administrative expenses	−571	−380
Profit from operations	1,251	624
Finance costs	−45	−27
Profit before tax	1,206	597
Tax	−338	−167
Profit for the year from continuing operations	868	430

Note: A dividend of £300,000 was paid in 20-0, and of £340,000 in 20-1.

Fauve Limited
Summary statement of financial position as at 30 September

	20-1	20-0
	£000	£000
Non-current assets	6,663	4,761
Current assets	3,503	2,031
Total assets	10,166	6,792
Equity:		
ordinary shares of £1 each	4,000	1,703
retained earnings	3,930	3,402
Long-term loan	500	300
Current liabilities	1,736	1,387
Total equity and liabilities	10,166	6,792

Required:

Prepare a report for Jake Matease that includes the following:

(a) a calculation (to the nearest one decimal place) of the following ratios of Fauve Limited for each of the two years:
- return on capital employed
- operating profit percentage
- gross profit percentage
- asset turnover (net assets)

(b) an explanation of the meaning of each ratio and a comment on the performance of Fauve Limited as shown by each of the ratios

(c) a conclusion on how the overall performance has changed over the two years

7.20 The directors of Dowango Ltd have asked to have a meeting with you. They are intending to ask the bank for a further long-term loan to enable them to purchase a company which has retail outlets. The directors have identified two possible companies to take over and they intend to purchase the whole of the share capital of one of the two targeted companies.

The directors have obtained the latest financial statements of the two companies, in summary form and these are set out below:

Summary statements of profit or loss

	Company A	Company B
	£000	£000
Continuing operations		
Revenue	800	2,100
Cost of sales	−440	−1,050
Gross profit	360	1,050
Expenses	−160	−630
Profit for the year from continuing operations	200	420

Summary statements of financial position

	Company A	Company B
	£000	£000
Non-current assets	620	1,640
Current assets	520	2,240
Total assets	1,140	3,880
Equity	600	1,700
Long-term loan	400	1,100
Current liabilities	140	1,080
Total equity and liabilities	1,140	3,880

Required:

Advise the directors as to which of the two companies targeted for takeover is the more profitable and which one provides the higher return on capital. Your answer should include calculation of the following ratios (to the nearest one decimal place):

- return on capital employed
- operating profit percentage
- asset turnover (net assets)

You should also calculate and comment on at least **ONE** further ratio of your choice, for which you have sufficient information, which would be relevant to determining which of the companies is more profitable or provides the greater return on capital.

7.21 Rowan Healthcare plc is a private hospital group which has just lost its supplier of bandages. The company that has been supplying it for the last five years has gone into liquidation. The directors of Rowan Healthcare are concerned to select a new supplier which can be relied upon to supply the group with its needs for the foreseeable future. You have been asked by the finance director to analyse the financial statements of a potential supplier of bandages. You have obtained the latest financial statements of the company, in summary form, which are set out below.

Patch Limited
Summary statement of profit or loss for the year ended 30 September

	20-8	20-7
	£000	£000
Continuing operations		
Revenue	2,300	2,100
Cost of sales	−1,035	−945
Gross profit	1,265	1,155
Expenses	−713	−693
Profit for the year from continuing operations	552	462

Patch Limited
Summary statement of financial position as at 30 September

	20-8	20-7
	£000	£000
Non-current assets	4,764	5,418
Current assets		
Inventories	522	419
Trade receivables	406	356
Cash and cash equivalents	117	62
	1,045	837
Total assets	5,809	6,255
Share capital	1,100	1,000
Share premium	282	227
Retained earnings	2,298	2,073
Total equity	3,680	3,300
Long-term loan	1,654	2,490
Current liabilities		
Trade payables	305	254
Tax payable	170	211
	475	465
Total liabilities	2,129	2,955
Total equity and liabilities	5,809	6,255

You have also obtained the relevant industry average ratios which are as follows:

	20-8	20-7
Return on capital employed	9.6%	9.4%
Operating profit percentage	21.4%	21.3%
Acid test ratio	1.0:1	0.9:1
Gearing	33%	34%

Required:

Prepare a report for the finance director of Rowan Healthcare plc recommending whether or not to use Patch Ltd as a supplier of bandages. Use the information contained in the financial statements of Patch Ltd and the industry averages supplied.

Your answer should:
- comment on the company's profitability, liquidity and financial position;
- consider how the company has changed over the two years;
- include a comparison with the industry as a whole.

The report should include calculation (to the nearest one decimal place) of the following ratios for the two years:

(a)   Return on capital employed

(b)   Operating profit percentage

(c)   Acid test ratio

(d)   Gearing

8 Consolidated financial statements

this chapter covers...

This chapter examines the financial statements of groups of companies. These include a consolidated statement of profit or loss and a consolidated statement of financial position. Such consolidated financial statements show the position of the group as if it was a single economic entity. The chapter covers:

- *definitions of parent and subsidiary companies, and the group*

- *accounting for goodwill, post-acquisition profits, and non-controlling interests when using the acquisition method for preparing consolidated statements of financial position*

- *the use of fair values in consolidated accounts*

- *inter-company adjustments and profits*

- *consolidated statements of profit or loss*

Towards the end of the chapter we look at incorporating the results of associate companies – where fewer than half of the shares are owned – into the financial statements of the investor company.

THE ACCOUNTING SYSTEMS OF AN ORGANISATION

Throughout your earlier studies of accounting you will have been aware of how a business must adapt the accounting system to suit its particular needs. In the same way, a limited company's accounting systems are affected by a number of factors – these include the role of the company, its organisational structure, its administrative systems and procedures, and the nature of its business transactions. Provided that a company complies with the requirements of international financial reporting standards and the Companies Acts, it can arrange its accounting systems to suit its needs.

Up until now we have studied and prepared the financial statements of individual companies, eg Wyvern Trading Company Limited. Such financial statements are often referred to as **unitary** financial statements – because they relate to one company only. In this chapter we will study the financial statements of groups of companies – known as **consolidated** financial statements – where one company (the parent company) owns or controls one or more other companies (subsidiary companies).

Before commencing our studies of consolidated financial statements we will look at a Case Study which demonstrates two different ways of organising the accounting systems of large companies.

Case Study

CHOCOLAT LIMITED AND CHOC CABIN LIMITED: DIVISIONAL OR CONSOLIDATED?

situation

Both of these companies – Chocolat Limited and Choc Cabin Limited – manufacture high-quality chocolates and other confectionery which are sold through their own retail chains – shops on high streets and in shopping centres, and franchises located within department stores. Both companies also sell wholesale to major store chains, where the chocolates are boxed and branded under the name of the retailer.

The two companies are direct competitors, chasing the same market – their shops are to be found close to one another on many a high street or shopping centre. Despite their similarities, however, the way in which they organise their accounting systems is very different.

solution

Chocolat Limited – divisional accounting

This company uses a divisional approach to its accounting system, with a separate division for each of its main activities – manufacture, retail, and own-brand wholesale – illustrated as follows:

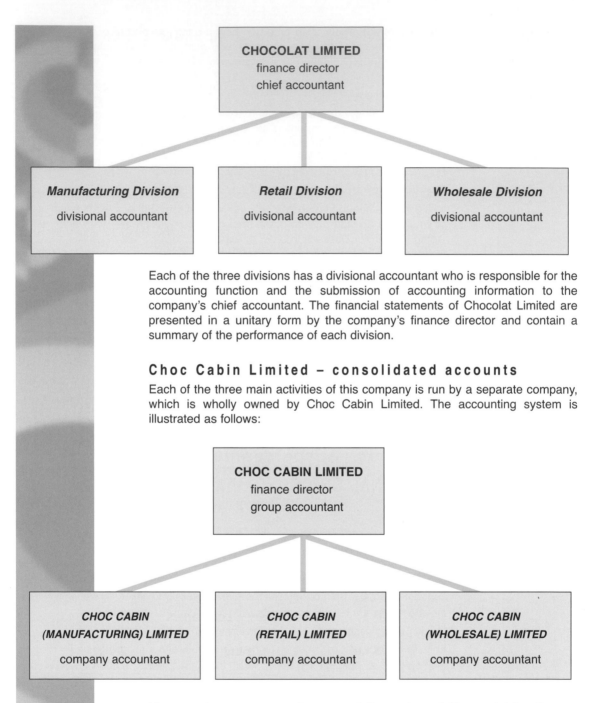

Each of the three divisions has a divisional accountant who is responsible for the accounting function and the submission of accounting information to the company's chief accountant. The financial statements of Chocolat Limited are presented in a unitary form by the company's finance director and contain a summary of the performance of each division.

Choc Cabin Limited – consolidated accounts

Each of the three main activities of this company is run by a separate company, which is wholly owned by Choc Cabin Limited. The accounting system is illustrated as follows:

Here, each company running one of the main activities maintains its own accounting system and is required to produce its own financial statements in accordance with the Companies Acts and international financial reporting standards – each has a company accountant to enable it to do so. As each company is wholly owned, it is a subsidiary company of Choc Cabin Limited, the parent company. In these circumstances, consolidated – or group – financial statements are produced in order to show a complete picture of the group. The parent company's group accountant will prepare the consolidated financial statements for presentation by the company's finance director.

conclusion

This Case Study shows two different accounting systems – unitary financial statements with the reporting of divisional performance, and consolidated financial statements with subsidiary companies.

As an organisation grows, it must adapt its accounting systems to suit its needs – no one system is correct in all circumstances.

The divisional method often suits a company that grows organically where new divisions are set up to meet the requirements of the business, eg "we will set up a wholesale division". By contrast, subsidiary companies are often acquired as going concern businesses in order to expand rapidly, eg "we need to expand, let us buy an existing wholesale business".

While subsidiary companies often have more autonomy than divisions, the preparation of consolidated financial statements is more complex – as we will see in this chapter – than that of unitary companies.

INTRODUCTION TO CONSOLIDATED FINANCIAL STATEMENTS

In recent years many companies have been taken over by other companies to form groups. Each company within a group maintains its separate legal entity, and so a group of companies may take the following form:

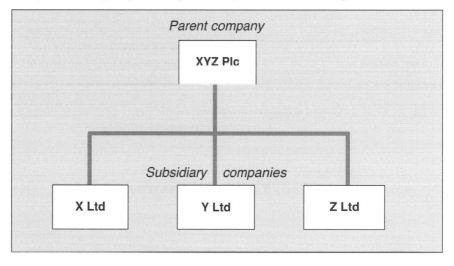

Two international financial reporting standards give guidance as to the accounting treatment for consolidated financial statements:

■ IFRS 3, *Business Combinations*

■ IFRS 10, *Consolidated Financial Statements*

IFRS 3 defines a business combination as 'a transaction or other event in which an acquirer obtains control of one or more businesses'. An acquirer is defined as 'the entity that obtains control of the acquiree'. An acquiree is defined as 'the business or businesses that the acquirer obtains control of in a business combination'. The acquisition date is the date on which the acquirer obtains control of the acquiree.

Control is defined by IFRS 10 as 'when it (the investor) is exposed, or has rights, to variable returns from its involvement with the investee and has the ability to affect those returns through its power over the investee'. Control is assumed to exist when the investor has power to direct the relevant activities of the investee, ie the activities of the investee that significantly affect the investee's returns.

Power to direct the relevant activities of the investee include:

■ rights in the form of voting rights of an investee (eg a majority – above 50 per cent – of the voting rights – although there may be circumstances where such ownership does not give power).

■ rights to appoint, reassign or remove members of an investee's key management personnel who have the ability to direct the relevant activities.

■ rights to appoint or remove another entity that directs the relevant activities.

■ rights to direct the investee to enter into, or veto any changes to, transactions for the benefit of the investor.

■ other rights (eg decision-making rights specified in a management contract) that give the ability to direct the relevant activities.

Although there are a variety of ways in which a business combination can be structured, we shall be studying the parent-subsidiary relationship in which the acquirer is the parent and the acquiree is the subsidiary. The key features of IFRS 3 are set out in the diagram opposite (the terms and techniques will be described in more detail later on).

PARENT AND SUBSIDIARY COMPANIES DEFINED

A group exists where one entity (the parent) controls, either directly or indirectly, another entity (the subsidiary). IFRS 10 gives the following definitions:

■ parent – an entity that controls one or more entities

■ subsidiary – an entity that is controlled by another entity

■ group – a parent and its subsidiaries

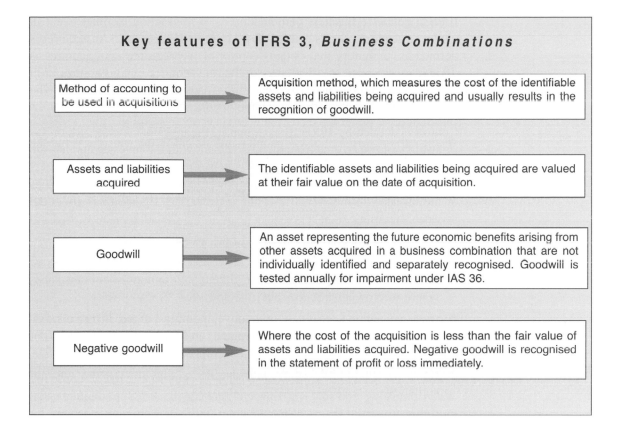

Key features of IFRS 3, *Business Combinations*

| Method of accounting to be used in acquisitions | → | Acquisition method, which measures the cost of the identifiable assets and liabilities being acquired and usually results in the recognition of goodwill. |

| Assets and liabilities acquired | → | The identifiable assets and liabilities being acquired are valued at their fair value on the date of acquisition. |

| Goodwill | → | An asset representing the future economic benefits arising from other assets acquired in a business combination that are not individually identified and separately recognised. Goodwill is tested annually for impairment under IAS 36. |

| Negative goodwill | → | Where the cost of the acquisition is less than the fair value of assets and liabilities acquired. Negative goodwill is recognised in the statement of profit or loss immediately. |

IFRS 10 requires that consolidated financial statements are to be prepared for a group. Such financial statements include a consolidated statement of profit or loss and a consolidated statement of financial position – these are designed to show the position of the group as if it was a single economic entity. (Note that there are some circumstances under which a parent need not present consolidated financial statements – eg if it is, itself, a subsidiary of a parent that produces consolidated financial statements.)

When a parent company does not own 100 per cent of the shares of a subsidiary company, then there will be some shares owned by outsiders, who are termed the non-controlling interest. For example, Adel Limited owns 75 per cent of the shares of Sade Limited – this creates a parent-subsidiary relationship, even though 25 per cent of Sade's shares are owned by outsiders, the **non-controlling interest**. IFRS 10 defines non-controlling interest as the 'equity in a subsidiary not attributable, directly or indirectly, to a parent'. On a consolidated statement of financial position, IFRS 10 requires the value of the non-controlling interest to be shown within equity, but separately from the equity of the owners of the parent (see page 246).

CONSOLIDATION PROCEDURES

To prepare consolidated financial statements, items from both the parent and the subsidiary's financial statements are combined by adding together assets, liabilities, income and expenses. The following steps are taken to present the information of the group as that of a single economic entity:

- the carrying amount of the parent's investment in the subsidiary and the parent's portion of equity in the subsidiary are eliminated or cancelled out against each other – this usually results in the recognition of goodwill

- non-controlling interest in the profit or loss of the subsidiary is identified

- non-controlling interest in the net assets of the subsidiary is identified and shown separately from the parent shareholders' equity; there are two elements of non-controlling interest:
  - the value at the date of acquisition
  - the share of changes in equity since the date of acquisition

As well as dealing with the above, any intragroup balances, transactions, income and expenses need to be eliminated in full. Such transactions take place between the parent and subsidiary companies, eg one company sells goods to another, both within the same group.

When preparing consolidated financial statements, IFRS 10 requires that uniform accounting policies should be used by the group.

We shall now study the three major calculations used in the preparation of a consolidated statement of financial position, each having a different relevant date:

1. goodwill – as at the date of acquisition of the subsidiary

2. post-acquisition profits – since the date of acquisition of the shares in the subsidiary

3. non-controlling interest – the stake of the other shareholders in the subsidiary at the date of the consolidated statement of financial position

In the Case Studies which follow, we look at the preparation of consolidated statements of financial position – starting with simple groups, and then incorporating calculations for goodwill, post-acquisition profits and non-controlling interest. Included in the Case Studies are tutorial notes which explain the calculations.

Case Study

SIMPLE GROUPS OF COMPANIES

situation

The summary statements of financial position of Pam Limited, a parent company, and Sam Limited, the subsidiary of Pam, are shown below as at 31 December 20-2. Sam Limited was acquired by Pam Limited as a subsidiary company on 31 December 20-2.

	Pam Ltd	Sam Ltd
	£000	£000
Investment in Sam:		
20,000 £1 ordinary shares at cost	40	–
Other assets	40	40
	80	40
Share capital (£1 ordinary shares)	60	20
Retained earnings	20	20
	80	40

solution

The first thing to look at is the percentage of shares owned in the subsidiary by the parent company. Here Pam Limited owns all 20,000 shares of Sam Limited, so the subsidiary is 100 per cent owned. Note that the shares have been bought at the financial year end, ie the date of the consolidated statement of financial position.

The method of preparing the consolidated statement of financial position of Pam Limited and its subsidiary Sam Limited is as follows:

1   the £40,000 cost of the investment in Sam (shown on Pam's statement of financial position) cancels out directly against the share capital (£20,000) and retained earnings (£20,000) of Sam and is not shown on the consolidated statement of financial position

2   add together the other assets of the two companies

3   show only the share capital and retained earnings of the parent company

The consolidated statement of financial position is shown in the far right column:

	Pam Ltd	Sam Ltd	Consolidated
	£000	£000	£000
Investment in Sam:			
20,000 £1 ordinary shares at cost	40	–	
Other assets	40	40	80
	80	40	80
Share capital (£1 ordinary shares)	60	20	60
Retained earnings	20	20	20
	80	40	80

Tutorial note:
The reason for cancelling out the amount of the investment against the share capital and retained earnings of the subsidiary is because the amounts record a transaction that has taken place within the group. It does not need reporting because the statement of financial position shows the group as if it was a single economic entity.

GOODWILL – POSITIVE AND NEGATIVE

situation

The summary statements of financial position of Peeble Limited, a parent company, and Singh Limited and Salvo Limited, its two subsidiaries, as at 31 December 20-3 appear below. The investments in Singh Limited and Salvo Limited were bought on 31 December 20-3.

	Peeble Ltd £000	Singh Ltd £000	Salvo Ltd £000
Non-current assets	30	25	20
Investment in Singh:			
20,000 £1 ordinary shares at cost	50		
Investment in Salvo:			
24,000 £1 ordinary shares at cost	25		
Current assets	30	25	20
	135	50	40
Share capital (£1 ordinary shares)	70	20	24
Retained earnings	45	20	6
	115	40	30
Current liabilities	20	10	10
	135	50	40

solution

Peeble Limited owns all the shares of Singh Limited and Salvo Limited – the subsidiaries are 100 per cent owned. The acquisitions have been bought at the financial year-end – the date of the consolidated statement of financial position.

As the cost price of the investment in the subsidiaries does not cancel out directly against the share capital and reserves, the difference represents goodwill:

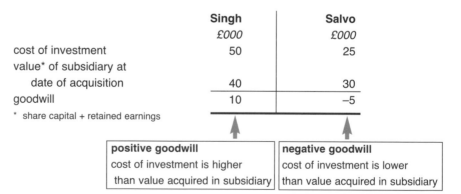

	Singh £000	Salvo £000
cost of investment	50	25
value* of subsidiary at date of acquisition	40	30
goodwill	10	–5

* share capital + retained earnings

positive goodwill	negative goodwill
cost of investment is higher than value acquired in subsidiary	cost of investment is lower than value acquired in subsidiary

The consolidated statement of financial position of Peeble Limited and its subsidiaries can now be prepared following the principles outlined in the previous Case Study. Positive goodwill is shown on the assets side of the consolidated statement of financial position, with negative goodwill added to the statement of profit or loss, thus increasing the figure for retained earnings. (Note, however, that IFRS 3 does say that, where negative goodwill is indicated, the first step should be to check the values used to ensure that they are correct in arriving at negative goodwill.)

PEEBLE LIMITED AND ITS SUBSIDIARIES
Consolidated statement of financial position as at 31 December 20-3

	£000
Goodwill	10
Other non-current assets 30 + 25 + 20	75
Current assets 30 + 25 + 20	75
	160
Share capital	70
Retained earnings 45 + 5 (negative goodwill)	50
Total equity	120
Current liabilities 20 + 10 + 10	40
	160

Tutorial note:
In future years, positive goodwill must be subject to an impairment test at least annually – see IAS 36, *Impairment of Assets* (pages 110-114).

Case Study

PRE-ACQUISITION AND POST-ACQUISITION PROFITS

situation

The summarised statements of financial position of Peat Limited, a parent company, and Stone Limited, its subsidiary, as at 31 December 20-4 appear as follows:

	Peat Ltd	Stone Ltd
	£000	£000
Non-current assets	80	25
Investment in Stone:		
20,000 £1 ordinary shares at cost	35	
Current assets	25	10
	140	35
Share capital (£1 ordinary shares)	100	20
Retained earnings	30	7
	130	27
Current liabilities	10	8
	140	35

Stone Limited was bought by Peat Ltd on 31 December 20-3, when Stone's retained earnings were £5,000 (note that Stone has earned £2,000 since the date of acquisition).

Ten per cent of the goodwill is to be written off as an impairment loss.

Tutorial note:

The retained earnings of the subsidiary at the date of acquisition are those that have been earned pre-acquisition: they are included in the goodwill calculation.

The retained earnings of the subsidiary after acquisition – post-acquisition profits – are earned while it is part of the group and are, therefore, part of the consolidated retained earnings shown on the consolidated statement of financial position. Such consolidated retained earnings are available for distribution as dividends to shareholders – provided that there is sufficient cash in the bank to pay the dividends.

solution

1 Peat Limited owns all the shares of Stone Limited, ie the subsidiary is 100% owned.

2 The calculation of goodwill in Stone is as follows:

	£000
cost of investment	35
value of subsidiary at date of acquisition 20 + 5	*25
positive goodwill	10

* £20,000 of share capital, plus £5,000 of retained earnings at date of acquisition
(ie pre-acquisition profits)

3 As ten per cent of the goodwill is to be written off as an impairment loss, £1,000 will be written off to the statement of profit or loss in 20-4, leaving £9,000 of goodwill to be shown in the statement of financial position.

4 The post-acquisition retained earnings of Stone for the consolidated statement of financial position are:

	£000
retained earnings at date of consolidated statement of financial position	7
retained earnings at date of acquisition of Stone	5
post-acquisition retained earnings	2

PEAT LIMITED AND ITS SUBSIDIARY
Consolidated statement of financial position as at 31 December 20-4

	£000
Goodwill 10 – 1	9
Other non-current assets 80 + 25	105
Current assets 25 + 10	35
	149
Share capital	100
Retained earnings 30 + 2 – 1*	31
Total equity	131
Current liabilities 10 + 8	18
	149

* goodwill written off to the statement of profit or loss

NON-CONTROLLING INTEREST

Tutorial note:

As noted earlier (page 239), non-controlling interest occurs where the parent company does not own all the shares in the subsidiary company, eg a subsidiary is 75 per cent owned by a parent company; the 25 per cent of shares not owned by the parent is the non-controlling interest.

The amount shown for non-controlling interest on the consolidated statement of financial position usually reflects the value of the subsidiary held by the non-controlling shareholders, and is shown on the equity side (share capital and retained earnings), and identified separately.

situation

The summarised statements of financial position of Pine Limited, a parent company, and Spruce Limited, its subsidiary, as at 31 December 20-5 are shown below.

The investment in Spruce was bought on 31 December 20-4, when Spruce's retained profit was £8,000.

Twenty per cent of the goodwill is to be written off as an impairment loss.

	Pine Ltd	Spruce Ltd
	£000	£000
Non-current assets	80	25
Investment in Spruce:		
15,000 £1 ordinary shares at cost	26	
Current assets	25	12
	131	37
Share capital (£1 ordinary shares)	100	20
Retained earnings	21	12
	121	32
Current liabilities	10	5
	131	37

solution

1. Pine Limited owns 75 per cent of the shares of Spruce Limited, ie 15,000 shares out of 20,000 shares. Thus the non-controlling interest is 25 per cent of Spruce.

2. The calculation of goodwill in Spruce is as follows:

	£000
cost of investment	26
value of subsidiary at date of acquisition	
20 + 8 = 28 x 75% owned =	21
positive goodwill	5

Note that, for the goodwill calculation, the value of the subsidiary at date of acquisition is reduced to the percentage of shares owned, here 75 per cent.

3   As twenty per cent of the goodwill is to be written off as an impairment loss, £1,000 will be written off to the statement of profit or loss in 20-5, leaving £4,000 of goodwill to be shown on the statement of financial position.

4   The post-acquisition profits of Spruce for the consolidated statement of financial position are:

	£000
retained earnings at date of consolidated statement of financial position	12
retained earnings at date of acquisition of Spruce	8
post-acquisition retained earnings	4
75% owned	3

Note that, for the calculation of post-acquisition retained earnings, the amount is reduced to the percentage of shares owned, here 75 per cent.

5   The non-controlling interest in Spruce is:

	£000
value at date of consolidated statement of financial position	32
25% non-controlling interest	8

Note that, for the calculation of the non-controlling interest, the amount is reduced to the percentage of shares owned, here 25 per cent, ie the non-controlling interest is valued at its proportionate share of net assets.

PINE LIMITED AND ITS SUBSIDIARY
Consolidated statement of financial position as at 31 December 20-5

	£000
Goodwill 5 – 1	4
Other non-current assets 80 + 25	105
Current assets 25 + 12	37
	146
Share capital	100
Retained earnings 21 + 3 – 1*	23
	123
Non-controlling interest	8
Total equity	131
Current liabilities 10 + 5	15
	146

* goodwill written off to the statement of profit or loss

Tutorial note:

When there is a non-controlling interest, note that we do not reduce the value of the subsidiary's assets and liabilities in the consolidated statement of financial position to allow for non-controlling shareholders – what we are saying is that the parent company has *control* over the subsidiary's assets and liabilities.

The amount shown for the non-controlling interest on the consolidated statement of financial position is the value of the subsidiary held *at the date of the consolidated statement of financial position.*

Non-controlling interest is identified separately on the equity side (share capital and retained earnings) of the consolidated statement of financial position in order to show the overall view of the group.

FAIR VALUES IN CONSOLIDATED FINANCIAL STATEMENTS

When a parent company acquires a majority holding of shares in a subsidiary company, it acquires both control of the subsidiary and also control of the subsidiary's assets and liabilities. IFRS 3 requires that the cost of the business acquired is to be measured at the fair values of all the identifiable* assets and liabilities that existed at the date of acquisition.

identifiable = either separable from the entity (eg capable of being sold) or arising from contractual or other legal rights

Fair value is 'the price that would be received to sell an asset or paid to transfer a liability in an orderly transaction between market participants at the measurement date' (IFRS 3, *Business Combinations*). For example, the fair value of land and buildings would be the market value, for plant and equipment it would also be the market value, for raw materials it would be the current replacement cost.

Fair value has an effect on the calculations for goodwill, non-controlling interest (where applicable), and sometimes on post-acquisition profits:

- goodwill, which is the cost of the investment in the subsidiary, less the fair value of the subsidiary's identifiable assets and liabilities

- non-controlling interest, which is the proportion of the subsidiary, based on the fair value of the subsidiary's identifiable assets and liabilities

- post-acquisition profits, which will be affected where the use of fair value for non-current assets leads to a different depreciation charge from that based on historic costs

The procedure for dealing with fair values is to restate the subsidiary's statement of financial position using fair values. Increases in the valuation of assets are credited to revaluation reserve; decreases are debited to revaluation reserve. Any changes to the value of liabilities are also passed through revaluation reserve. Note that, to be dealt with in this way, the fair value of identifiable assets and liabilities must be capable of being measured reliably.

The Case Study which follows shows how fair values affect the calculations for the consolidated statement of financial position.

Case Study

FAIR VALUES IN CONSOLIDATED FINANCIAL STATEMENTS

situation

On 31 December 20-6, Pipe Limited bought 75 per cent of the share capital of Soil Limited at a cost of £37,000. At that date the two companies' statements of financial position were as follows:

	Pipe Ltd	Soil Ltd
	£000	£000
Non-current assets	60	18
Investment in Soil:		
9,000 £1 ordinary shares at cost	37	
Current assets	20	16
	117	34
Share capital (£1 ordinary shares)	80	12
Retained earnings	24	16
	104	28
Current liabilities	13	6
	117	34

At the date of acquisition

- the fair value of Soil's non-current assets was £30,000

- the fair value of Soil's current assets was £12,000

The non-controlling interest is to be valued at its proportionate share of net assets.

solution

1   We must incorporate the fair values into Soil's statement of financial position as follows:

	£000	£000
Non-current assets (increase in value)		
debit non-current assets account	12	
credit revaluation reserve		12
Current assets (reduction in value)		
debit revaluation reserve	4	
credit current assets		4

2   Thus Soil's statement of financial position is:

	before	adjustment	after
	£000	£000	£000
Non-current assets	18	+ 12	30
Current assets	16	− 4	12
	34	+ 8	42
Share capital	12	−	12
Revaluation reserve	−	+ 12 ⎫	8
		− 4 ⎭	
Retained earnings	16	−	16
	28	+ 8	36
Current liabilities	6	−	6
	34	+ 8	42

3 Goodwill is:

	£000
cost of investment	37
value of subsidiary at date of acquisition	
fair value of 36 (see above) x 75% owned	27
positive goodwill	10

4 Non-controlling interest is:

	£000
value at date of consolidated statement of financial position	36
25% non-controlling interest	9

5 There will be no post-acquisition profits at 31 December 20-6, as this is the date at which the investment in the subsidiary is being made.

PIPE LIMITED AND ITS SUBSIDIARY
Consolidated statement of financial position as at 31 December 20-6

	£000
Goodwill	10
Other non-current assets 60 + 30 (at fair value)	90
Current assets 20 + 12 (at fair value)	32
	132
Share capital	80
Retained earnings	24
	104
Non-controlling interest	9
Total equity	113
Current liabilities 13 + 6	19
	132

Tutorial note:

Goodwill will be tested for impairment at least annually.

There may be an adjustment each year to post-acquisition profits if the use of fair values leads to an additional depreciation charge.

INTER-COMPANY ADJUSTMENTS

We have already seen the need to cancel out the inter-company balances of investment in the subsidiary company (shown in the parent company's statement of financial position) against the share capital and reserves (shown in the subsidiary company's statement of financial position). Other inter-company amounts also have to be cancelled out or adjusted against each other when preparing consolidated statements of financial position.

receivables, payables and loans

Where there are receivables, payables and loans between companies that are part of the same group, they cancel out against each other and do not show on the consolidated statement of financial position.

Example 1

Beech Limited has sold goods to Cedar Limited for £5,000. Both Beech and Cedar are subsidiaries of Ash Limited. At the date of the consolidated statement of financial position Cedar has not yet paid Beech for the goods, so:

- Beech has an asset of receivables, including the £5,000 due from Cedar
- Cedar has a liability of payables, including the £5,000 due to Beech

For the consolidated statement of financial position of Ash Limited and its subsidiaries, the inter-company balance of receivables and payables will not be shown because it is between group companies.

Example 2

Ash Limited has made a loan to Beech Limited of £10,000. The loan shows:

- as an asset on Ash's statement of financial position
- as a liability on Beech's statement of financial position

For the consolidated statement of financial position, the loan will not be shown because it is an inter-company balance within the group.

inter-company profits

Inter-company profits occur when one group company sells goods to another company within the group. If the goods have then been sold to buyers outside the group, then no adjustment to the consolidated statement of financial position is necessary as the profit has been realised. However, when some or all of the goods remain in the inventory of a group company at the date of the consolidated statement of financial position, then an adjustment for unrealised inter-company profits must be made.

For example, Able Limited and Baker Limited are parent company and subsidiary company respectively. Able sells goods which cost it £1,000 to Baker for £1,500. A consolidated statement of financial position is prepared before Baker sells any of the goods. The £500 profit made by Able is included in its statement of profit or loss, whilst the value of the inventory held by Baker includes Able's profit. For the consolidated statement of financial position:

- the statement of profit or loss of Able is reduced by £500
- the inventory of Baker is reduced by £500

This accounting adjustment ensures that the inventory of the group is stated in the consolidated statement of financial position at cost to the group (or net realisable value, if lower) and that no unrealised profit is shown in the group financial statements. Note that, if some of the goods had been sold by Baker, then only the profit on the proportion remaining in the group would be adjusted.

When a partly-owned subsidiary has sold goods to another group company and there are unrealised inter-company profits at the date of the consolidated statement of financial position, non-controlling interest needs to be adjusted for its share of the unrealised profits. This is illustrated in the Case Study which follows.

Case Study

INTER-COMPANY ADJUSTMENTS

situation

The summary statements of financial position of Pearl Limited, a parent company, and Sea Limited, its subsidiary, as at 31 December 20-7 are shown below.

The investment in Sea Limited was bought on 31 December 20-6, when Sea's retained earnings were £10,000. At that date there were no material differences between the book value and fair value of any of the assets of Sea.

In 20-7 Pearl writes off ten per cent of the goodwill on the acquisition of Sea as an impairment loss.

In November 20-7, Sea sold goods costing £5,000 to Pearl at a price of £7,000. At 31 December 20-7 half of those goods were unsold by Pearl.

	Pearl Ltd £000	Sea Ltd £000
Investment in Sea:		
12,000 £1 ordinary shares at cost	28	
Loan to Sea	10	
Current assets	62	61
	100	61
Share capital (£1 ordinary shares)	60	20
Retained earnings	20	16
	80	36
Current liabilities	20	15
Loan from Pearl		10
	100	61

solution

1 Pearl Limited owns 60 per cent of the shares in Sea Limited, ie 12,000 shares out of 20,000 shares.

2 The calculation of goodwill is as follows:

	£000
cost of investment	28
value of subsidiary at date of acquisition	
20 + 10 = 30 x 60% owned =	18
positive goodwill	10

As ten per cent of the goodwill is to be written off as an impairment loss, £1,000 will be written off to the statement of comprehensive income in 20-7, leaving £9,000 of goodwill to be shown in the statement of financial position.

3 **Inter-company adjustments:**

Loan

The £10,000 loan from Pearl to Sea cancels out for the consolidated statement of financial position, ie the asset of Pearl cancels out against the liability of Sea.

Inter-company profits:

Of the £2,000 profit made when Sea sold goods to Pearl at the date of the consolidated statement of financial position, £1,000 is unrealised (because the goods remain in Pearl's inventory). For the consolidated statement of financial position:

- the statement of profit or loss of Sea is reduced by £1,000
- the inventory of Pearl is reduced by £1,000

Tutorial note:

It is always advisable to make the inter-company adjustments before calculating post-acquisition profits and non-controlling interest. By doing this, non-controlling shareholders (if any) will be charged or credited with their share of adjustments which affect the subsidiary company.

---

4 The post-acquisition profits of Sea are:

	£000
retained earnings at date of consolidated statement of financial position:	
16 − 1 unrealised profit	15
retained earnings at date of acquisition	10
post-acquisition profits	5
60% owned	3

5 The non-controlling interest in Sea is valued at its proportionate share of net assets:

	£000
value at date of consolidated statement of financial position:	
36 − 1 unrealised profit	35
40% non-controlling interest	14

PEARL LIMITED AND ITS SUBSIDIARY
Consolidated statement of financial position as at 31 December 20-7

	£000
Goodwill 10 – 1 (impairment loss)	9
Current assets 62 – 1 (inventory) + 61	122
	131
Share capital	60
Retained earnings 20 – 1 (impairment loss) + 3	22
	82
Non-controlling interest	14
Total equity	96
Current liabilities 20 + 15	35
	131

PREPARING FOR ASSESSMENT

A logical approach towards preparing consolidated statements of financial position provides a good framework for AAT's Assessment. This approach is set out below in five steps which – for steps three, four and five – make use of the workings tables provided in the Assessment. You are welcome to photocopy these pages to help with your first few consolidated statements of financial position. (Note that blank workings tables can be downloaded from www.osbornebooks.co.uk)

Step 1: Establish the group structure

Identify the structure of the group – it will help to complete the following table:

Structure of the group	
Name of parent company	
Name of subsidiary company	
Percentage control of the parent	
Date of acquisition	
Date of consolidated Statement of Financial Position	

Step 2: Calculate the net assets of the subsidiary

The net assets of the subsidiary should be calculated both at the **date of acquisition** and at the **date of the consolidated statement of financial position**. The calculation is set out in the following table:

Net assets of subsidiary	Date of acquisition £000	Date of consolidated SFP £000
Share capital		
Share premium		
Revaluation reserve*		
Retained earnings		
Net assets of subsidiary =		

* Be prepared to incorporate a further revaluation if an activity/assessment tells you that the fair value of any of the subsidiary's assets is higher than the carrying amount – the difference is usually credited to revaluation reserve.

Step 3: Calculate the goodwill on consolidation

Goodwill is calculated as a proportion of the net assets of the subsidiary **at the date of acquisition**. Note that activities and assessment tasks will state if there is to be any impairment of goodwill. The calculation is set out in the following table:

Goodwill	£000
Price paid	
Share capital – attributable to parent	–
Share premium – attributable to parent	–
Revaluation reserve – attributable to parent	–
Retained earnings – attributable to parent	–
Impairment	–
Goodwill =	

Notes:

- Price paid is usually identifiable from the non-current assets section of the parent's statement of financial position – look for 'Investment in (name of subsidiary)'.

- The amounts attributable to the parent are taken from step 2:

  date of acquisition column x percentage control of the parent

  Note that these amounts are deducted from price paid to give an intermediate figure for goodwill prior to impairment, if any (there may not be a spare line for this intermediate calculation in the table provided in AAT Assessments).

- Impairment, if any, will be stated in activities and assessments either as a percentage (eg 25%) or as a time period (eg over four years = 25% per year).

Step 4: Calculate the non-controlling interest

The non-controlling interest (NCI) is calculated as a proportion (the percentage not held by the parent) of the net assets of the subsidiary **at the**

date of the consolidated statement of financial position. The calculation is set out in the following table:

Non-controlling interest (NCI)	£000
Share capital – attributable to NCI	
Share premium – attributable to NCI	
Revaluation reserve – attributable to NCI	
Retained earnings – attributable to NCI	
Non-controlling interest =	

Note that amounts attributable to the non-controlling interest are taken from step 2:

date of consolidated SFP column x NCI's percentage held

Step 5: Group retained earnings

Group retained earnings comprises 100% of the parent's retained earnings, plus/minus the increase/decrease in the subsidiary's retained earnings **since the date of acquisition** and multiplied by the parent's percentage control. The proportion attributable to the parent is calculated by comparing the two money columns for retained earnings from step 2; the difference is multiplied by the percentage control of the parent, from step 1.

Retained earnings is set out in the following table:

Retained earnings	£000
Parent (100%)	
Subsidiary – attributable to parent	
Impairment	–
Retained earnings =	

Note that impairment, if any, is deducted in the group retained earnings calculation; any amount for impairment shown in step 3 is transferred into this box.

summary

These five steps provide a logical approach to the main calculations used in consolidated statements of financial position. It only remains to record the figures in the statement of financial position layout given in the assessment and then to add together other assets and liabilities of the parent and subsidiary, ie non-current assets (excluding the investment in the subsidiary), inventories, trade receivables, trade payables and loans. In some consolidated SFPs there may be an added requirement to cancel out loans and sales made between group companies – the treatment of these inter-company transactions is explained on pages 249-253.

<table>
<tr><td>**Case Study**</td><td colspan="2"># THE CONSOLIDATED STATEMENT OF FINANCIAL POSITION</td></tr>
</table>

Tutorial note:

This Case Study demonstrates how the calculations for goodwill, post-acquisition profits and non-controlling interest and retained earnings can be presented in the workings format used in AAT Assessments. A pro-forma layout for the consolidated statement of financial position is given in the Appendix.

situation

Ace plc has one subsidiary undertaking, Bec Limited, which it acquired on 1 April 20-8. The statements of financial position of the two companies as at 31 March 20-9 are set out below.

Statements of financial position as at 31 March 20-9		
ASSETS	**Ace plc**	**Bec Ltd**
Non-current assets	*£000*	*£000*
Property, plant and equipment	45,210	27,480
Investment in Bec Limited	23,000	–
	68,210	27,480
Current assets		
Inventories	21,450	4,222
Trade and other receivables	9,874	6,486
Cash and cash equivalents	1,458	127
	32,782	10,835
Total assets	100,992	38,315
EQUITY AND LIABILITIES		
Equity		
Share capital	38,000	12,000
Share premium	11,000	6,000
Retained earnings	22,526	11,740
Total equity	71,526	29,740
Non-current liabilities		
Long-term loans	14,000	4,000
Current liabilities		
Trade and other payables	11,234	4,445
Tax payable	4,232	130
	15,466	4,575
Total liabilities	29,466	8,575
Total equity and liabilities	100,992	38,315

Further information:

• The share capital of Bec Limited consists of ordinary shares of £1 each. Ownership of these shares carries voting rights in Bec Limited. There have been no changes to the balances of share capital and share premium during the year. No dividends were paid or proposed by Bec Limited during the year.

- Ace plc acquired 7,200,000 shares in Bec Limited on 1 April 20-8.
- On 1 April 20-8 the balance of retained earnings of Bec Limited was £9,640,000.
- The fair value of the non-current assets of Bec Limited at 1 April 20-8 was £29,800,000. The carrying amount of the non-current assets at 1 April 20-8 was £25,800,000. The revaluation has not been recorded in the books of Bec Limited (ignore any effect on the depreciation for the year).
- Included in trade and other receivables for Ace plc and in trade and other payables for Bec Limited is an inter-company transaction for £3,000,000 that took place in early March 20-9.
- The directors of Ace plc have concluded that goodwill has been impaired by 25% during the year.
- Ace plc has decided non-controlling interest will be valued at its proportionate share of net assets.

Draft the consolidated statement of financial position of Ace plc and its subsidiary undertaking as at 31 March 20-9.

solution

Step 1: Establish the group structure

Identify the structure of the group – it will help to complete the following table:

Structure of the group	
Name of parent company	Ace plc
Name of subsidiary company	Bec Limited
Percentage control of the parent	*60%
Date of acquisition	1 April 20-8
Date of consolidated Statement of Financial Position	31 March 20-9

* 7,200,000 shares/12,000,000 shares

Step 2: Calculate the net assets of the subsidiary

Net assets of subsidiary	Date of acquisition	Date of consolidated SFP
	£000	£000
Share capital	12,000	12,000
Share premium	6,000	6,000
Revaluation reserve	*4,000	4,000
Retained earnings	9,640	11,740
Net assets of subsidiary =	31,640	33,740

* At date of acquisition, the non-current assets of Bec Limited had the following values:

	£000
Fair value	29,800
Carrying amount	25,800
Difference	4,000

As fair value is higher than carrying amount, this increase must be recorded in Bec Limited's accounts

	£000	£000
debit non-current assets	4,000	
credit revaluation reserve		4,000

Step 3: Calculate the goodwill on consolidation

Goodwill	£000
Price paid	23,000
Share capital – attributable to parent	–7,200
Share premium – attributable to parent	–3,600
Revaluation reserve – attributable to parent	–2,400
Retained earnings – attributable to parent	–5,784
	4,016
Impairment	*–1,004
Goodwill =	3,012

* 25% of £4,016 written off as an impairment loss

Step 4: Calculate the non-controlling interest

Non-controlling interest (NCI)	£000
Share capital – attributable to NCI	4,800
Share premium – attributable to NCI	2,400
Revaluation reserve – attributable to NCI	1,600
Retained earnings – attributable to NCI	4,696
Non-controlling interest =	13,496

Step 5: Group retained earnings

Retained earnings	£000
Parent (100%)	22,526
Subsidiary – attributable to parent	*1,260
Impairment	–1,004
Retained earnings =	22,782

* 60% x (£11,740 - £9,640)

Inter-company transaction

The inter-company transaction is deducted from both trade and other receivables and trade and other payables to give:

• trade and other receivables £9,874 + £6,486 - £3,000 = £13,360

• trade and other payables £11,234 + £4,445 - £3,000 = £12,679

The consolidated statement of financial position can now be prepared as shown on the next page (note: asset and liability calculations are shown for your reference).

ACE PLC AND ITS SUBSIDIARY
Consolidated statement of financial position as at 31 March 20-9

ASSETS	£000
Non-current assets	
Goodwill	3,012
Property, plant and equipment 45,210 + 27,480 + 4,000 increase to fair value	76,690
	79,702
Current assets	
Inventories 21,450 + 4,222	25,672
Trade and other receivables 9,874 + 6,486 – 3,000	13,360
Cash and cash equivalents 1,458 + 127	1,585
	40,617
Total assets	120,319
EQUITY AND LIABILITIES	
Equity	
Share capital	38,000
Share premium	11,000
Retained earnings	22,782
	71,782
Non-controlling interest	13,496
Total equity	85,278
Non-current liabilities	
Long-term loans 14,000 + 4,000	18,000
	18,000
Current liabilities	
Trade and other payables 11,234 + 4,445 – 3,000	12,679
Tax payable 4,232 + 130	4,362
	17,041
Total liabilities	35,041
Total equity and liabilities	120,319

CONSOLIDATED STATEMENTS OF PROFIT OR LOSS

The consolidated statement of profit or loss, like the consolidated statement of financial position, is intended to show the position of the group as if it was a single economic entity. The consolidated statement of profit or loss shows the shareholders of the parent company how much profit has been earned by the parent company and the subsidiaries, with a deduction for the proportion of profit due to non-controlling interests. The diagram below shows the format of a consolidated statement of profit or loss; as the diagram demonstrates, the figures are merged from the statements of profit or loss of the parent company and the subsidiaries.

Format of consolidated statement of profit or loss

Continuing operations

Revenue	parent + subsidiaries – inter-company sales
Cost of sales*	see below
Gross profit	parent + subsidiaries – inter-company unrealised profit
Distribution costs	parent + subsidiaries
Administrative expenses	parent + subsidiaries
Profit/(loss) from operations	parent + subsidiaries
Finance costs	parent + subsidiaries
Profit/(loss) before tax	parent + subsidiaries
Tax	parent + subsidiaries

Profit/(loss) for the year
from continuing operations   parent + subsidiaries

Attributable to:

Equity holders of the parent	parent + profit of wholly-owned subsidiaries + parent's share of profit of partly-owned subsidiaries
Non-controlling interest	non-controlling interest's share of subsidiaries' profit

* Cost of sales:	
opening inventories	parent + subsidiaries
+ purchases	parent + subsidiaries – inter-company purchases
– closing inventories	parent + subsidiaries – inter-company unrealised profit

---

notes on the statement of profit or loss

- the full profit of subsidiaries is shown, with a separate note of the proportion of the profit due to the non-controlling interest

- inter-company transactions are deducted for
    - inter-company sales
    - inter-company purchases
    - inter-company unrealised profit

Two Case Studies follow which demonstrate the preparation of consolidated statements of profit or loss – firstly for a simple group, secondly incorporating inter-company transactions. The layout follows that shown in the diagram. Note that workings tables – in the format used in AAT Assessments – are shown as part of the solutions.

Case Study

STATEMENT OF PROFIT OR LOSS FOR SIMPLE GROUPS

situation

The summary statements of profit or loss of Pack Limited, a parent company, and Sack Limited, its subsidiary, for the year-ended 31 December 20-8 are shown below.

Pack Limited bought 80 per cent of the ordinary shares of Sack Limited on 1 January 20-6.

	Pack Ltd	Sack Ltd
Continuing operations	£000	£000
Revenue	115	60
Cost of sales	−65	−28
Gross profit	50	32
Distribution costs	−5	−8
Administrative expenses	−15	−12
Profit before tax	30	12
Tax	−8	−2
Profit for the year from continuing operations	22	10

Notes: There were no impairment losses on goodwill during the year.

solution

1 The figures from the statements of profit or loss are merged.

2 The after-tax profit for the year of Sack is £10,000; of this 20 per cent, ie £2,000 is due to the non-controlling interest.

PACK LIMITED AND ITS SUBSIDIARY

Consolidated statement of profit or loss for the year ended 31 December 20-8

Continuing operations		£000
Revenue	see workings below	175
Cost of sales	see workings below	−93
Gross profit	50 + 32	82
Distribution costs	5 + 8	−13
Administrative expenses	15 + 12	−27
Profit from operations	30 + 12	42
Finance costs		−
Profit before tax		42
Tax	8 + 2	−10
Profit for the year from continuing operations		32

Attributable to:		
Equity holders of the parent	22 + (80% x 10*)	30
Non-controlling interest	20% x 10*	2
		32

* Sack's after-tax profit for the year

Revenue	£000
Pack Ltd	115
Sack Ltd	60
Revenue =	175

Cost of sales	£000
Pack Ltd	65
Sack Ltd	28
Cost of sales =	93

Case Study

GROUP STATEMENT OF PROFIT OR LOSS WITH ADJUSTMENTS

situation

The summary statements of profit or loss of Perch Limited, a parent company, and Skate Limited, its subsidiary for the year ended 31 December 20-9 are shown on the next page.

Perch Limited bought 75 per cent of the shares of Skate Limited on 1 January 20-9.

During the year to 31 December 20-9, Perch sold goods costing £20,000 to Skate at a price of £40,000; at the year end half of these goods were unsold by Skate.

Notes:

- Dividends paid during the year were:

    Perch Limited, £50,000

    Skate Limited, £12,000

- There were no impairment losses on goodwill during the year.

	Perch Ltd	Skate Ltd
Continuing operations	*£000*	*£000*
Revenue	400	150
Opening inventories	100	50
+ Purchases	300	100
− Closing inventories	150	40
Cost of sales	−250	−110
Gross profit	150	40
Distribution costs	−40	−10
Administrative expenses	−50	−10
Dividend from subsidiary	9	
Profit before tax	69	20
Tax	−20	−4
Profit for the year from continuing operations	49	16

solution

Tutorial note:

Inter-company revenue, purchases and unrealised profit are deducted from revenue, purchases and closing inventories respectively before the figures are shown in the consolidated statement of profit or loss.

The dividend of the subsidiary company has been correctly recorded by Perch to show the proportion paid to the parent company – this will not be shown on the consolidated statement of profit or loss because it is an inter-company transaction.

The after-tax profit of Skate is £16,000; of this 25 per cent, ie £4,000, is due to the non-controlling interest with the rest, ie £12,000, due to the parent.

PERCH LIMITED AND ITS SUBSIDIARY

Consolidated statement of profit or loss for the year ended 31 December 20-9

Continuing operations		£000
Revenue	see workings below	510
Cost of sales	see workings below	−330
Gross profit		180
Distribution costs	40 + 10	−50
Administrative expenses	50 + 10	−60
Profit from operations		70
Finance costs		−
Profit before tax		70
Tax	20 + 4	−24
Profit for the year from continuing operations		46

Attributable to	£000
Equity holders of the parent	42
Non-controlling interest (25% x £16)	4
Profit for the period from continuing operations =	46

Workings

Revenue	£000
Perch Ltd	400
Skate Ltd	150
Total inter-company adjustment	−40
Revenue =	510

Cost of sales	£000
Perch Ltd	250
Skate Ltd	110
Total inter-company adjustment	*−30
Cost of sales =	330

* purchases −40, unrealised profit 10 = cost of sales −30

ASSOCIATE COMPANIES

participating interest and significant influence

An associate is defined by IAS 28, *Investments in Associates and Joint Ventures*, as 'an entity over which the investor has significant influence'. The relationship is that of investor and investee (the associate company).

The exercise of **significant influence** is where the investor has the power to participate in the financial and operating policy decisions – such as the expansion or contraction of the business, changes in products, markets, activities – of the investee but is not in control of those policies.

As a general guideline, an associate company is where an investor owns between 20 per cent and 50 per cent of the ordinary shares of another company. However, ownership of shares by itself is not enough to establish an associate company relationship: ownership must be accompanied by the exercise of significant influence.

IAS 28 suggests that the existence of significant influence by an investor is usually evidenced by one or more of the following:

■ representation on the board of directors of the investee (the associate company)
■ participation in policy-making processes
■ material transactions between the investor and the investee
■ interchange of managerial personnel
■ provision of essential technical information

As we have seen earlier in this chapter, an ordinary share ownership above 50 per cent usually indicates a subsidiary company relationship. Thus an investment in an associate company is a substantial investment but which is not as significant as a subsidiary company.

equity method of accounting

The equity method is the usual way of accounting for the results of associate companies:

■ initially the investment in the associate company is recognised at cost
■ the investor's share of subsequent profits or losses of the investee is added to, or deducted from, the carrying amount of the investment
■ the investor's share of the investee's profit or loss is recognised in the investor's statement of profit or loss
■ distributions received from the investee reduce the carrying amount of the investment
■ the investor's share of other comprehensive income of the investee (eg

revaluation of property) is recognised in the investor's other comprehensive income and adjusted to the carrying amount of the investment

In the investor's financial statements, the key features of the equity method are:

■ in the **statement of profit or loss** (see diagram below) show the investor's share of the associated company's profit after tax

■ in the **statement of financial position**

    – the investment in the associate company is to be included and separately disclosed as a non-current asset

    – any goodwill arising on the investor's acquisition of its associate is included in the carrying amount of the associate (note that, as goodwill of associate companies is not shown separately in the investor's statement of financial position, the entire carrying amount is tested for impairment – see IAS 36, *Impairment of Assets*, pages 110-114)

    – distributions received from the investee reduce the carrying amount of the investment

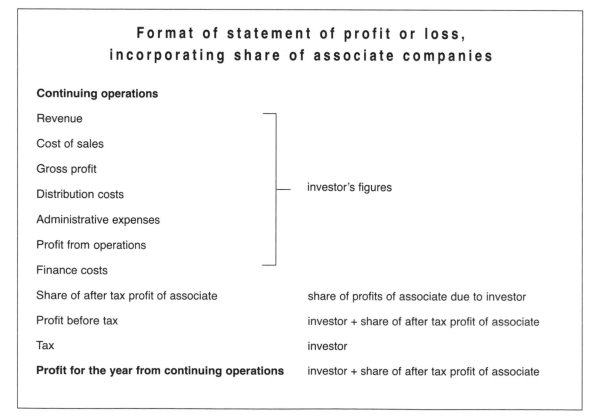

Format of statement of profit or loss, incorporating share of associate companies

Continuing operations

Revenue

Cost of sales

Gross profit

Distribution costs   investor's figures

Administrative expenses

Profit from operations

Finance costs

Share of after tax profit of associate	share of profits of associate due to investor
Profit before tax	investor + share of after tax profit of associate
Tax	investor
Profit for the year from continuing operations	investor + share of after tax profit of associate

The accounting policies of the investor are to be applied consistently and, if there are differences between those of investor and investee, adjustments are to be made when the associate's financial statements are used by the investor. (Note that the accounting treatment of investments in joint ventures is not assessed by AAT.)

ASSOCIATE COMPANIES

This Case Study shows the effect of transactions on the financial statements of the investor – using the equity method of accounting. Note that for AAT Assessments you will not be required to draft financial statements, but you must have an understanding of the key features of an investor/associate relationship.

situation

(a) On 31 December 20X1, Icod Ltd bought 25 per cent of the share capital of Arona Ltd, its associated company, at a cost of £300,000.

Explain how this transaction will be recorded in the financial statements of Icod Ltd, using the equity method of accounting.

(b) In the year ended 31 December 20X2 the following events occurred for Arona Ltd:
- a profit of £100,000 (after tax) was made for the year
- a dividend of £60,000 was paid
- property was revalued from £500,000 to £620,000

Explain how each of these events will be recorded in the financial statements of Icod Ltd, using the equity method of accounting. Show the resultant carrying amount of the investment in the associate after each has taken place in the order shown above.

solution

(a) In Icod Ltd's statement of financial position the investment in Arona Ltd is recognised initially at cost (as a non-current asset):

Investment in associate	£300,000

Icod Ltd's bank balance will be reduced as a result of paying for the investment.

(b) *A profit of £100,000 (after tax) was made for the year by the associate*

Icod Ltd's 25 per cent share of the profit of its associate is £25,000. As this profit was earned by the associate after the date of acquisition, the amount is recognised in the investor's statement of profit or loss on the line above profit before tax:

Share of after tax profit of associate	£25,000

At the same time, in Icod Ltd's statement of financial position, the carrying amount of the investment is increased to recognise the investor's share of the profit of the associate:

Investment in associate	£325,000

A dividend of £60,000 was paid by the associate

Icod Ltd's 25 per cent share of the dividend paid by its associate is £15,000.

This distribution received from the investee reduces the carrying amount of the investment:

Investment in associate	£310,000

(Icod Ltd's bank balance will be increased as a result of receiving the dividend payment.)

Property of the associate was revalued from £500,000 to £620,000

Icod Ltd's 25 per cent share of the increase of £120,000 is £30,000.

This amount is recognised in the investor's statement of profit or loss and other comprehensive income as other comprehensive income:

Other comprehensive income for the year	
Gain on revaluation of property of associate	£30,000

At the same time, in Icod Ltd's statement of financial position, the carrying amount of the investment is increased to recognise the investor's share of the other comprehensive income of the investee:

Investment in associate	£340,000

summary

Under the equity method of accounting:

- the investment in an associate is initially recognised at cost
- as the investee makes profits or losses after the date of acquisition:
  - the investor's share is recognised in the investor's statement of profit or loss
  - the carrying amount of the investment is increased or decreased to recognise the investor's share of the profit or loss

- distributions (eg dividends) received from an investee reduce the carrying amount of the investment
- if the investee has other comprehensive income (eg revaluation of property):

    the investor's share is recognised in the investor's statement of profit or loss and other comprehensive income

    – the carrying amount of the investment is increased to recognise the investor's share

DISCLOSURE IN CONSOLIDATED FINANCIAL STATEMENTS

The international financial reporting standards IFRS 3, *Business Combinations*, and IFRS 10, *Consolidated Financial Statements*, cover the techniques of consolidated accounting for parent and subsidiary companies and set out the detailed disclosures required in group accounts. IAS 28, *Investments in Associates and Joint Ventures*, deals with accounting for associate companies.

The published financial statements of limited companies – which are readily available to shareholders and interested parties – include, where appropriate, group financial statements (including statements of profit or loss, financial position, and cash flows) which disclose the consolidated financial performance and financial position of the parent company and its subsidiary companies; the financial statements also incorporate the results of associate companies. Thus the user is assured that the financial statements have been prepared in accordance with international financial reporting standards.

Chapter Summary

- Companies adapt their accounting systems to suit the needs of the organisation.

- Consolidated financial statements are designed to show the position of a group – parent company and subsidiary companies – as if it was a single economic entity.

- There are three major calculations in the preparation of a consolidated statement of financial position:
    - goodwill, calculated as at the date of acquisition of the subsidiary
    - post-acquisition profits, calculated since the date of acquisition of the shares in the subsidiary
    - non-controlling interest, calculated at the date of the consolidated statement of financial position

- The use of fair values affects:
    - goodwill, which is calculated as the cost of the investment in the subsidiary, less the fair value of the subsidiary's identifiable assets and liabilities
    - non-controlling interest, which is the proportion of the subsidiary, based on the fair value of the subsidiary's identifiable assets and liabilities
    - post-acquisition profits, which will be affected where the use of fair value for non-current assets leads to a different depreciation charge from that based on historic costs

- Inter-company adjustments may have to be made when preparing consolidated statements of financial position for:
    - receivables, payables and loans, which cancel out between companies within the group
    - inter-company profits, eg on sale of goods, which are unrealised at the date of the consolidated statement of financial position

- When preparing a consolidated statement of profit or loss:
    - the full profit of subsidiaries is shown, with a separate deduction for the proportion of the profit due to the non-controlling interest
    - inter-company transactions are deducted for inter-company sales, inter-company purchases, and inter-company unrealised profit

- An associate company is where an investor owns generally between 20 per cent and 50 per cent of the ordinary shares of another company and exercises significant influence over its financial and operating policies.

■ The equity method is the usual way of accounting for the results of associate companies:

– initially the investment in the associate company is recognised at cost on the investor's statement of financial position

– the investor's share of subsequent profits or losses are added to, or deducted from, the carrying amount of the investment

– the investor's share of the investee's profit or loss is recognised in the investor's statement of profit or loss

– distributions received from the investee reduce the carrying amount of the investment

– the investor's share of other comprehensive income of the investee (eg revaluation of property) is recognised in the investor's other comprehensive income and adjusted to the carrying amount of the investment

Key Terms

parent	an entity that controls one or more entities
subsidiary	an entity that is controlled by another entity
group	a parent and its subsidiaries
parent company/ subsidiary company	a parent company has a subsidiary where any of the following apply: – has a majority of the voting rights – has the right to appoint, reassign or remove members of an investee's key management personnel – has the right to appoint or remove another entity that directs the relevant activities of the investee – has the right to direct the investee to enter into, or veto any changes to, transactions for the benefit of the investor – has other rights that give the ability to direct the relevant activities of the investee
acquisition method	method of accounting used in acquisitions which measures the cost of assets and liabilities being acquired and usually results in the recognition of goodwill

goodwill	the excess of the cost of the acquisition over the fair value of the identifiable assets and liabilities acquired
fair value	'the price that would be received to sell an asset or paid to transfer a liability in an orderly transaction between market participants at the measurement date' (IFRS 3, *Business Combinations*)
post-acquisition profits	profits earned by a subsidiary since the date of acquisition
non-controlling interest	'equity in a subsidiary not attributable, directly or indirectly, to a parent' (IFRS 10, *Consolidated Financial Statements*)
associate company	'an entity over which the investor has significant influence and that is neither a subsidiary nor an interest in a joint venture' (IAS 28, *Investments in Associates*)
significant influence	where the investor takes part in the financial and operating policy decisions but is not in control of those policies
equity method	method of accounting for associate companies by which the investor values its investment so as to reflect its interest in the investee

Activities

- Blank photocopiable pro-formas in the format used in AAT Assessments – of the consolidated statement of profit or loss, and the consolidated statement of financial position are included in the Appendix – it is advisable to enlarge them to full A4 size. Blank workings sheets are also included in the Appendix.

- Pro-formas and workings sheets are also available to download from www.osbornebooks.co.uk

8.1 Carline plc invested £420,000 in 240,000 ordinary shares of £1 each in Foss Limited. At the date of acquisition the equity of Foss Limited comprised £300,000 in share capital and £160,000 in retained earnings.

What is the value of goodwill at the date of acquisition?

		✓
(a)	£220,000	
(b)	£368,000	
(c)	£60,000	
(d)	£52,000	

8.2 At 31 March 20X1 the equity of Richmond Limited comprises £160,000 in share capital and £96,000 in retained earnings. The parent company, Hampton plc, currently owns 120,000 of £1 ordinary shares in Richmond Limited.

What is the value of the non-controlling interest at 31 March 20X1?

		✓
(a)	£64,000	
(b)	£192,000	
(c)	£24,000	
(d)	£40,000	

8.3 Tennyson plc owns 60% of the ordinary shares on Donne Limited. Revenue for the year ended 31 March 20X1 is: Tennyson £550,000, Donne £355,000. The revenue of Tennyson plc includes goods sold to Donne Limited for £35,000. All of these goods still remain in the inventory of Donne Limited at the end of the year.

What is the value for revenue that will be shown in the consolidated statement of profit or loss for Tennyson plc and its subsidiary undertaking for the year ended 31 March 20X1?

		✓
(a)	£870,000	
(b)	£940,000	
(c)	£905,000	
(d)	£515,000	

8.4   At 31 December 20X4 the statement of financial position of a parent company shows inventories of £40,000. At the same date its sole subsidiary company shows inventories of £25,000. In November 20X4 the subsidiary company had sold goods costing £8,000 to the parent company at a price of £11,000. At 31 December 20X4 two-thirds of these goods were unsold by the parent company.

What is the valuation to be shown for inventories on the consolidated statement of financial position at 31 December 20X4?

		✓
(a)	£67,000	
(b)	£65,000	
(c)	£64,000	
(d)	£63,000	

8.5   At 31 December 20X2 the statement of financial position of a parent company shows non-current liabilities of £65,000. At the same date its sole subsidiary company shows non-current liabilities of £85,000. In November 20X2 the parent company made a long-term loan to the subsidiary of £50,000. No loan repayments have been made, or are due in the year to 31 December 20X3.

What is the amount to be shown for non-current liabilities on the consolidated statement of financial position at 31 December 20X2?

		✓
(a)	£150,000	
(b)	£100,000	
(c)	£200,000	
(d)	£65,000	

8.6   How does IFRS 3, *Business Combinations*, define the following?

(a)   an acquiree

(b)   an acquirer

(c)   a business combination

(d)   goodwill

8.7   **(a)**   How does IFRS 3, *Business Combinations*, define fair value?

(b)   Explain the effect of fair values on:

(1)   goodwill

(2)   post-acquisition profits

(3)   non-controlling interest

8.8 IFRS 10, *Consolidated Financial Statements*, sets out the key aspects to be applied in the preparation and presentation of consolidated financial statements for a group of entities under the control of a parent.

(a) What is meant by:

(1) a parent?

(2) a group?

(b) How is a subsidiary defined?

(c) How is non-controlling interest defined?

8.9 IFRS 10, *Consolidated Financial Statements*, defines control as 'when an investor is exposed, or has rights, to variable returns from its involvement with the investee and has the ability to affect those returns through its power over the investee'.

Explain the circumstances under which control is assumed to exist.

8.10 Exe Plc acquired 75% of the issued share capital and voting rights of Lyn Ltd on 1 April 20X0 for £1,400,000. At that date Lyn Ltd had issued share capital of £1,000,000 and retained earnings of £560,000.

Extracts from the statements of financial position for the two companies one year later at 31 March 20X1 are as follows:

	Exe Plc £000	Lyn Ltd £000
ASSETS		
Non-current assets		
Investment In Lyn Ltd	1,400	
Property, plant and equipment	2,640	1,327
	4,040	1,327
Current assets	1,725	855
Total assets	5,765	2,182
EQUITY AND LIABILITIES		
Equity		
Share capital	2,000	1,000
Share premium	0	0
Retained earnings	890	592
Total equity	2,890	1,592
Non-current liabilities	830	320
Current liabilities	2,045	270
Total liabilities	2,875	590
Total equity and liabilities	5,765	2,182

Further information:

- Included within the current assets of Exe Plc and in the current liabilities of Lyn Ltd is an inter-company transaction for £50,000 that took place in early March 20X1.

- Exe Plc has decided that non-controlling interest will be valued at their proportionate share of net assets.

Required:

Draft the consolidated statement of financial position for Exe Plc and its subsidiary undertaking as at 31 March 20X1.

8.11 Carr Plc acquired 80% of the issued share capital and voting rights of Foss Ltd on 1 January 20X0 for £2,600,000. At that date Foss Ltd had issued share capital of £1,500,000, share premium of £400,000 and retained earnings of £680,000.

Extracts from the statements of financial position for the two companies one year later at 31 December 20X0 are as follows:

	Carr Plc	Foss Ltd
	£000	£000
ASSETS		
Non-current assets		
Investment in Foss Ltd	2,680	
Property, plant and equipment	4,120	2,260
	6,800	2,260
Current assets	2,395	1,695
Total assets	9,195	3,955
EQUITY AND LIABILITIES		
Equity		
Share capital	4,500	1,500
Share premium	500	400
Retained earnings	1,070	740
Total equity	6,070	2,640
Non-current liabilities	1,050	270
Current liabilities	2,075	1,045
Total liabilities	3,125	1,315
Total equity and liabilities	9,195	3,955

Further information:

- Carr Plc has decided that non-controlling interest will be valued at their proportionate share of net assets.

- At 1 January 20X0 the fair value of the non-current assets of Foss Ltd was £150,000 more than the book value. This revaluation has not been recorded in the books of Foss Ltd (ignore any effect on the depreciation for the year).

- On 1 October 20X0, Carr Plc made an interest-free long-term loan of £80,000 to Foss Ltd, and classified it as part of its investment in Foss Ltd. Foss Ltd has classified the loan as a non-current liability in its financial statements. No loan repayments have yet been made.

- The directors of Carr Plc have calculated that goodwill has been impaired by £70,000 during the year.

Required:

Draft the consolidated statement of financial position for Carr Plc and its subsidiary undertaking as at 31 December 20X0.

8.12 Alasmith plc has one subsidiary undertaking, Jones Limited, which it acquired on 1 October 20-3. The statements of financial position of Alasmith plc and Jones Limited as at 30 September 20-4 are set out below.

Statements of financial position as at 30 September 20-4

	Alasmith plc	Jones Ltd
	£000	£000
Tangible non-current assets	56,320	39,320
Investment in Jones Limited	26,680	–
	83,000	39,320
Current assets		
Inventories	13,638	5,470
Trade and other receivables	7,839	3,218
Cash and cash equivalents	1,013	1,184
	22,490	9,872
Total assets	105,490	49,192
Equity		
Called up share capital	25,000	6,000
Share premium	10,000	4,000
Retained earnings	40,248	25,200
	75,248	35,200
Long-term loan	20,000	8,850
Current liabilities		
Trade and other payables	8,733	4,288
Accruals	450	543
Tax payable	1,059	311
	10,242	5,142
Total equity and liabilities	105,490	49,192

Further information:

- The share capital of Jones Limited consists of ordinary shares of £1 each. There have been no changes to the balances of share capital and share premium during the year. No dividends were paid by Jones Limited during the year.
- Alasmith plc acquired 3,600,000 shares with voting rights in Jones Limited on 1 October 20-3.
- At 1 October 20-3 the balance of retained earnings of Jones Limited was £19,800,000.
- The fair value of the non-current assets of Jones Limited at 1 October 20-3 was £43,470,000. The carrying amount of the non-current assets at 1 October 20-3 was £35,470,000. The revaluation has not been recorded in the books of Jones Limited (ignore any effect on the depreciation for the year).
- For the year to 30 September 20-4, Alasmith plc has written off ten per cent of the goodwill on the acquisition of Jones Limited as an impairment loss.
- Alasmith plc has decided non-controlling interest will be valued at its proportionate share of net assets.

Required:

Draft the consolidated statement of financial position of Alasmith plc and its subsidiary undertaking as at 30 September 20-4.

8.13   The summary statements of profit or loss of Tom Limited, a parent company, and Ben Limited, its subsidiary, for the year ended 31 December 20X2 are as follows:

	Tom Ltd	Ben Ltd
Continuing operations	*£000*	*£000*
Revenue	800	400
Opening inventories	200	150
Purchases	600	300
Closing inventories	−300	−200
Cost of sales	−500	−250
Gross profit	300	150
Distribution costs	−80	−40
Administrative expenses	−100	−40
Dividends from Ben Limited	30	–
Profit from operations	150	70
Finance costs	−20	−10
Profit before tax	130	60
Tax	−40	−20
Profit for the year from continuing operations	90	40

Further information:

- Tom Limited bought 75 per cent of the shares of Ben Limited on 1 January 20X2.

- During the year to 31 December 20X2 Tom sold goods costing £12,000 to Ben at a price of £20,000; Ben had sold all of these goods by the year end for £24,000.

- Dividends paid during the year were:

    Tom Limited, £100,000

    Ben Limited, £40,000

- There were no impairment losses on goodwill during the year.

Required:

Prepare the consolidated statement of profit or loss of Tom Limited and its subsidiary for the year ended 31 December 20X2.

8.14 The managing director of Perran plc has asked you to prepare the consolidated statement of profit or loss for the group. The company has one subsidiary undertaking, Porth Limited. The statements of profit or loss for the two companies for the year ended 31 March 20X6 are as follows:

Statements of profit or loss for the year ended 31 March 20X6

	Perran plc	Porth Limited
Continuing operations	*£000*	*£000*
Revenue	36,450	10,200
Cost of sales	−18,210	−5,630
Gross profit	18,240	4,570
Distribution costs	−5,735	−1,210
Administrative expenses	−4,295	−450
Dividends received from Porth Limited	750	−
Profit from operations	8,960	2,910
Finance costs	−1,720	−300
Profit before tax	7,240	2,610
Tax	−1,950	−530
Profit for the year from continuing operations	5,290	2,080

Further information:

- Perran plc acquired 75% of the ordinary share capital of Porth Ltd on 1 April 20X5.

- During the year Porth Limited sold goods which had cost £500,000 to Perran plc for £750,000. All of the goods had been sold by Perran plc by the end of the year.

- Dividends paid during the year were:

    Perran plc, £2,500,000

    Porth Limited, £1,000,000

- There were no impairment losses on goodwill during the year.

Required:

Draft the consolidated statement of profit or loss for Perran plc and its subsidiary undertaking for the year ended 31 March 20X6.

8.15   Fleet Plc acquired 75% of the issued share capital and voting rights of Drake Ltd on 1 April 20X0.

Extracts from each company's statement of profit or loss for the year ended 31 March 20X1 are shown below:

	Fleet Plc	Drake Ltd
	£000	*£000*
Continuing operations		
Revenue	33,200	12,400
Cost of sales	−19,400	−8,200
Gross profit	13,800	4,200
Other income	600	0
Distribution costs and administrative expenses	−11,100	−2,600
Profit before tax	3,300	1,600

Further information:

- During the year, Fleet Plc sold goods which had cost £280,000 to Drake Ltd for £440,000. Half of these goods still remain in inventories at the end of the year.

- Other income of Fleet Plc consists of a dividend of £300,000 received from Drake Ltd and rental income received from another company.

Required:

Draft the consolidated statement of profit or loss for Fleet Plc and its subsidiary undertaking up to and including the profit before tax line for the year ended 31 March 20X1.

8.16 Avon Plc acquired 60% of the issued share capital and voting rights of Severn Ltd on 1 April 20X0.

Extracts of each company's statement of profit or loss for the year ended 31 March 20X1 are shown below:

	Avon Plc	Severn Ltd
	£000	£000
Continuing operations		
Revenue	60,240	30,180
Cost of sales	−35,790	−24,630
Gross profit	24,450	5,550
Other income	650	0
Distribution costs and administrative expenses	−15,330	−3,190
Profit before tax	9,770	2,360
Tax	−1,840	−330
Profit for the period from continuing operations	7,930	2,030

Further information:

- During the year, Severn Ltd sold goods which had cost £120,000 to Avon Plc for £180,000. One-third of these goods still remain in inventories at the end of the year.

- Other income of Avon Plc consists of a dividend of £450,000 received from Severn Ltd and rental income received from another company.

Required:

Draft the consolidated statement of profit or loss for Avon Plc and its subsidiary undertaking for the year ended 31 March 20X1.

8.17 IAS 28, *Investments in Associates and Joint Ventures*, sets out the key features of an investor/investee relationship.

(a) How is an associate defined?

(b) What is meant by significant influence?

(c) Explain the equity method of accounting.

8.18   Under IAS 28, *Investments in Associates and Joint Ventures*, which of the following are evidence of significant influence by an investor?

1.   holding 19 per cent of the voting power of the investee

2.   representation on the board of directors of the investee

3.   interchange of management personnel

4.   material transactions between the investor and the investee

		✓
(a)	1 and 2	
(b)	2 and 3	
(c)	2, 3 and 4	
(d)	all of them	

8.19   Under IAS 28, *Investments in Associates and Joint Ventures*, which of the following are features of the equity method of accounting?

1.   The investment in an associate is initially recognised at cost.

2.   After acquisition, the carrying amount of the investment is increased to recognise the investor's share of the profit of the investee.

3.   Distributions received from an investee increase the carrying amount of the investment.

4.   The revaluation of property, plant and equipment by the investee does not alter the carrying amount of the investment for the investor.

		✓
(a)	1 and 2	
(b)	2 and 3	
(c)	3 and 4	
(d)	all of them	

Answers to activities

CHAPTER 1: PURPOSE OF FINANCIAL STATEMENTS

1.1   (c)   equity = assets – liabilities

1.2   (b)   profits or losses = income – expenses

1.3   (c)   68,350   26,800   41,550

1.4

	Income	Expenses	Profit/(Loss)
	£	£	£
(a)	76,400	73,900	2,500

1.5   Business A   Liabilities £31,600

Business B   Assets £92,000

Business C   Equity £58,500

Business D   Liabilities £48,600

1.6   Business M   Profit £16,600

Business N   Expenses £85,700

Business O   Income £64,400

Business P   Expenses £99,000

1.7   **(a)**   An **asset** is a resource controlled by the entity as a result of past events and from which future economic benefits are expected to flow to the entity.

A **liability** is a present obligation of the entity arising from past events, the settlement of which is expected to result in an outflow from the entity of resources embodying economic benefits.

Equity is the residual interest in the assets of the entity after deducting all its liabilities.

(b)   (1)   This transaction will increase the assets of the business by £2,500 (inventories) and will increase the liabilities by £2,500 (trade payables).

(2)   This transaction will decrease the assets by £2,500 (inventories) but also increase the assets by £3,500 (cash), giving a net increase of assets of £1,000 and increase the equity of £1,000 (profit).

(c)   The accounting equation after the two transactions will be:

Assets £13,500 – Liabilities £7,000 = Equity £6,500

(d)   A simple statement of profit or loss will be

	£
Revenue	3,500
Cost of sales	−2,500
Profit	1,000

1.8   **statement of profit or loss and other comprehensive income**

Measures the financial performance of the company for a particular time period (the accounting period).

statement of financial position

Lists the assets, liabilities and equity of the company at the end of the accounting period.

statement of cash flows

Links the profit of the company with changes in assets and liabilities, and the effect on the cash of the company.

1.9   **(a)**   The objective of general purpose financial reporting is to provide financial information about the reporting entity that is useful to existing and potential investors, lenders and other creditors in making decisions about providing resources to the entity.

   (b)   1.   Existing and potential investors

   2.   Lenders

   3.   Other creditors

1.10   **(a)**   **asset**

An asset is a resource controlled by the entity as a result of past events and from which future economic benefits are expected to flow to the entity.

liability

A liability is a present obligation of the entity arising from past events, the settlement of which is expected to result in an outflow from the entity of resources embodying economic benefits.

   (b)   **inventories**

   •   the entity controls the inventories which can either be sold to customers or can be used in the manufacture of products

   •   the inventories were bought in the past

   •   cash will be received when either the inventories or the manufactured products are sold, whether as a cash sale, or later for a credit sale

trade payables

- the entity has a present obligation to pay the trade payables in respect of current debts

- the debts were incurred from past transactions for goods or services

- cash will be paid to the trade payables within agreed timescales

1.11 income

Income is an increase in economic benefits during the accounting period in the form of inflows or enhancements of assets or decreases of liabilities that result in increases in equity, other than those relating to contributions from equity participants.

expenses

Expenses are decreases in economic benefits during the accounting period in the form of outflows or depletions of assets or incurrence of liabilities that result in decreases in equity, other than those relating to distributions to equity participants.

1.12 (a)

1. Relevance

2. Faithful representation

(b) Relevance

For information to be relevant it must:

- be capable of making a difference in the decisions made by users

- have predictive value, which helps users to predict future outcomes

- have confirmatory value, which helps users to confirm previous evaluations

Faithful representation

For the faithful representation of information it must:

- correspond to the effect of transactions or events

- as far as possible be complete (to include all information necessary for a user), neutral (without bias), and free from error (no errors in the description or process)

1.13 verifiability, timeliness, understandability, comparability

1.14 (a) Materiality

(b) Business entity

(c) Accruals

(d) Going concern

1.15 NOTES FOR THE DIRECTORS

(a) The elements in a statement of financial position and the balances in Machier Limited which fall under those elements are as follows:

Elements	Balances
Assets	Non-current assets, current assets
Liabilities	Current liabilities, non-current loan
Equity	Share capital, share premium, retained earnings

(b) The accounting equation is as follows:
(figures in £000)

Assets	−	Liabilities	= Equity
(£4,282 + £975)	−	(£749 + £2,800)	= £1,708
£5,257	−	£3,549	= £1,708

1.16 (a)
- **Financial position** is reported through a statement of financial position

- **Financial performance** is reported through a statement of profit or loss and other comprehensive income

- **Changes in financial position** are reported through a statement of cash flows

(b) An entity is an organisation such as a limited company, whose activities and resources are kept separate from those of the owner(s).

(c)

Examples of users	Economic decisions
• existing and potential investors	• when to buy, hold or sell shares in the company
• lenders	• to assess the security available for loans made to the company
• other creditors	• to assess the ability of the company to pay its suppliers and employees

Other decisions made by users include:

• to assess the stewardship of the management of the company

• to determine the distributable profits and dividends of the company

• to obtain figures for use in national statistics

• to assess the amount of tax payable on the profits of the company

• to regulate the activities of the company

CHAPTER 2: INTRODUCTION TO LIMITED COMPANY FINANCIAL STATEMENTS

2.1   (a) and (c) are FALSE; the remaining statements are TRUE.

2.2   **(a)**   •   Ordinary shares are the most commonly issued class of share. They take a share of the profits which remain after all other expenses of the business. The main risk of ordinary shares is that part or all of the value of the shares will be lost if the company loses money or becomes insolvent.

            •   Preference shares usually carry a fixed rate of dividend which is paid in preference to that of ordinary shareholders. In the event of the company ceasing to trade, the preference shareholders will also receive repayment of capital before the ordinary shareholders.

        (b)   •   Nominal value is the face value of a share which is entered in the accounts, eg 5p, 10p, 25p, 50p or £1.

            •   Market value is the price at which issued shares are traded, ie bought and sold.

        (c)   •   Capital reserves are created as a result of a non-trading profit; examples include revaluation reserve, share premium account.

            •   Revenue reserves are retained profits from the statement of profit or loss and other comprehensive income; examples include retained earnings, general reserve.

2.3   **(a)**   debenture interest is shown as an expense – under finance costs – in the statement of profit or loss and other comprehensive income

        (b)   directors' remuneration is shown as an expense – under administrative expenses – in the statement of profit or loss and other comprehensive income

        (c)   corporation tax is shown in the statement of profit or loss and other comprehensive income, and any amount not yet paid is shown as a current liability on the statement of financial position

        (d)   dividends paid are shown in the statement of changes in equity

        (e)   revaluation reserve is shown as a capital reserve as a part of the equity section of the statement of financial position

        (f)   goodwill is shown as an intangible asset in the non-current assets section of the statement of financial position; it is amortised in the same way as tangible non-current assets are depreciated

2.4   (b)   dividends paid

2.5   (c)   opening inventories

2.6   (b)   retained earnings

2.7   (d)   share premium

2.8   **(a)**   **Non-current liabilities** are those where repayment is more than twelve months from the date of the statement of financial position.

Examples include: bank loans, debentures – both where the repayment date is more than twelve months from the date of the statement of financial position.

(b)   **Current liabilities** are those where repayment is due within twelve months of the date of the statement of financial position.

Examples include: trade and other payables, bank overdraft (which is repayable on demand), and tax payable within the next twelve months.

2.9   (c)   non-current assets, plus current assets

2.10   (d)   issued share capital, plus capital and revenue reserves, plus non-current liabilities, plus current liabilities

2.11   (d)   £187,500*

* 300,000 shares of 50p each = £150,000 + (£150,000 x 25%)

2.12   Nelson Ltd – Statement of profit or loss for the year ending 31 March 20-2

	£000
Revenue	1,935
Cost of sales	−920
Gross profit	1,015
Administrative expenses	−361
Distribution costs	−534
Profit before tax	120
Tax	−15
Profit for the year from continuing operations	105

Workings

Cost of sales	£000
Opening inventories	140
Purchases	960
Closing inventories	−180
Cost of sales =	920

Administrative expenses	£000
Administrative expenses	285
Depreciation	*76
Administrative expenses =	361

* depreciation: plant and equipment £950 x 20% = £190 x 40% = £76

Distribution costs	£000
Distribution costs	420
Depreciation	*114
Distribution costs =	534

* depreciation as per administrative expenses, but at 60%

Nelson Ltd – Statement of financial position as at 31 March 20-2

ASSETS	£000
Non-current assets	
Property, plant and equipment	440
Current assets	
Inventories	180
Trade and other receivables	570
Cash and cash equivalents	35
	785
Total assets	1,225
EQUITY AND LIABILITIES	
Equity	
Share capital	500
Share premium	140
Retained earnings	310
Total equity	950
Current liabilities	
Trade and other payables	260
Tax liability	15
Total liabilities	275
Total equity and liabilities	1,225

Workings

Plant and equipment	£000
Plant and equipment – cost	950
Accumulated depreciation	*–510
Plant and equipment =	440

* £320 + £190

Retained earnings	£000
Retained earnings at 1 April 20-1	245
Profit for the year	105
Dividends paid	–40
Retained earnings =	310

2.13 Wentworth Ltd – Statement of profit or loss for the year ending 31 March 20-5

	£000
Revenue	2,125
Cost of sales	−1,330
Gross profit	795
Administrative expenses	−385
Distribution costs	−200
Profit from operations	210
Finance costs	−25
Profit before tax	185
Tax	−15
Profit for the year from continuing operations	170

Workings

Cost of sales	£000
Opening inventories	210
Purchases	1,220
Depreciation: plant and equipment	*90
Closing inventories	−190
Cost of sales =	1,330

* depreciation: plant and equipment £1,200 x 15% = £180 x 50% = £90

Administrative expenses	£000
Administrative expenses	340
Depreciation: plant and equipment	*45
Administrative expenses =	385

* depreciation as per cost of sales, but at 25%

Distribution costs	£000
Distribution costs	175
Depreciation: plant and equipment	*45
Prepayment	−20
Distribution costs =	200

* depreciation as per cost of sales, but at 25%

Wentworth Ltd – Statement of financial position as at 31 March 20-5

ASSETS	£000
Non-current assets	
Property, plant and equipment	660
Current assets	
Inventories	190
Trade and other receivables	250
Cash and cash equivalents	95
	535
Total assets	1,195
EQUITY AND LIABILITIES	
Equity	
Share capital	600
Share premium	80
Retained earnings	390
Total equity	1,070
Current liabilities	
Trade and other payables	110
Tax liability	15
Total liabilities	125
Total equity and liabilities	1,195

Workings

Plant and equipment	£000
Plant and equipment – cost	1,200
Accumulated depreciation	*-540
Plant and equipment =	660

* £360 + £180

Trade and other receivables	£000
Trade and other receivables	230
Prepayment	20
Trade and other receivables =	250

Retained earnings	£000
Retained earnings at 1 April 20-4	330
Profit for the year	170
Dividends paid	−110
Retained earnings =	390

2.14   Blenheim Ltd – Statement of profit or loss for the year ending 31 March 20-4

	£000
Revenue	3,650
Cost of sales	−2,080
Gross profit	1,570
Administrative expenses	−503
Distribution costs	−710
Profit from operations	357
Finance costs	−90
Profit before tax	267
Tax	−35
Profit for the year from continuing operations	232

Workings

Cost of sales	£000
Opening inventories	230
Purchases	2,100
Closing inventories	−250
Cost of sales =	2,080

Administrative expenses	£000
Administrative expenses	420
Bad (irrecoverable) debt	8
Depreciation: buildings	*25
Depreciation: plant and equipment	**50
Administrative expenses =	503

*   depreciation: buildings £500 x 5% = £25

**   depreciation: plant and equipment (£800 − £300) x 20% = £100 x 50% = £50

Distribution costs	£000
Distribution costs	650
Depreciation: plant and equipment	*50
Accrual	10
Distribution costs =	710

* depreciation as per administrative expenses

Blenheim Ltd – Statement of financial position as at 31 March 20-4

ASSETS	£000
Non-current assets	
Property, plant and equipment	3,750
Current assets	
Inventories	250
Trade and other receivables	182
Cash and cash equivalents	670
	1,102
Total assets	4,852
EQUITY AND LIABILITIES	
Equity	
Share capital	2,500
Retained earnings	587
Total equity	3,087
Non-current liabilities	
Bank loan	1,500
	1,500
Current liabilities	
Trade and other payables	230
Tax liability	35
	265
Total liabilities	1,765
Total equity and liabilities	4,852

Workings

Property, plant and equipment	£000
Land and buildings – value	3,500
Accumulated depreciation – land and buildings	*–150
Plant and equipment – cost	800
Accumulated depreciation – plant and equipment	**–400
Property, plant and equipment =	3,750

* £125 + £25

** £300 + £100

Trade and other receivables	£000
Trade and other receivables	190
Bad (irrecoverable) debt	–8
Trade and other receivables =	182

Trade and other payables	£000
Trade and other payables	170
Accruals – Trial balance	50
Additional distribution costs accrued	10
Trade and other payables =	230

Retained earnings	£000
Retained earnings at 1 April 20-3	495
Profit for the year	232
Dividends paid	–140
Retained earnings =	587

CHAPTER 3: PUBLISHED FINANCIAL STATEMENTS OF LIMITED COMPANIES

3.1 (a) 1 and 2

3.2 (b) 3 and 4

3.3 (d) all of them

3.4 (d) all of them

3.5 (a) all of them

3.6 (b) separate disclosure of the nature and amount

3.7 (a) **Chapelporth Ltd – Statement of profit or loss and other comprehensive income for the year ended 30 June 20-8**

	£
Profit from operations	135,000
Finance costs	–12,500
Profit before tax	122,500
Tax	–48,000
Profit for the year from continuing operations	74,500
Other comprehensive income for the year	0
Total comprehensive income for the year	74,500

(b) **Chapelporth Ltd – Statement of changes in equity for the year ended 30 June 20-8**

	Share capital	Other reserves	Retained earnings	Total equity
	£	£	£	£
Balance at 1 July 20-7	500,000	0	185,000	685,000
Changes in equity for 20-8				
Total comprehensive income			74,500	74,500
Dividends			–48,500	–48,500
Balance at 30 June 20-8	500,000	0	211,000	711,000

3.8 (a) **Mason Motors Ltd – Statement of profit or loss and other comprehensive income for the year ended 31 December 20-1**

	£
Profit from operations	75,000
Finance costs	−5,500
Profit before tax	69,500
Tax	−20,500
Profit for the year from continuing operations	49,000
Other comprehensive income for the year	0
Total comprehensive income for the year	49,000

(b) **Mason Motors Ltd – Statement of changes in equity for the year ended 31 December 20-1**

	Share capital £	Other reserves £	Retained earnings £	Total equity £
Balance at 1 January 20-1	300,000	0	100,000	400,000
Changes in equity for 20-1				
Total comprehensive income			49,000	49,000
Dividends			−30,000	−30,000
Transfer to general reserve		20,000	−20,000	0
Balance at 31 December 20-1	300,000	20,000	99,000	419,000

3.9 (b) £168,000

3.10 (a) (1) £250,000 (2) £75,000

3.11   Doddington Ltd – Statement of changes in equity for the year ended 31 December 20X2

	Share capital £	Other reserves £	Retained earnings £	Total equity £
Balance at 1 January 20X2	220,000	0	118,000	338,000
Changes in equity for 20X2				
Profit for the year			79,000	79,000
Dividends			−45,000	−45,000
Issue of share capital	110,000	66,000		176,000
Balance at 31 December 20X2	330,000	66,000	152,000	548,000

3.12   Martin Ltd – Statement of changes in equity for the year ended 30 June 20X5

	Share capital £	Other reserves £	Retained earnings £	Total equity £
Balance at 1 July 20X4	600,000	90,000	330,000	1,020,000
Changes in equity for 20X5				
Profit for the year			365,000	365,000
Dividends			−220,000	−220,000
Issue of share capital	150,000	90,000		240,000
Balance at 30 June 20X5	750,000	180,000	475,000	1,405,000

3.13   Bourne Ltd – Statement of changes in equity for the year ended 31 December 20-6

	Share capital £	Other reserves £	Retained earnings £	Total equity £
Balance at 1 January 20-6	75,000	0	19,400	94,400
Changes in equity for 20-6				
Total comprehensive income			68,200	68,200
Dividends			−10,000	−10,000
Balance at 31 December 20-6	75,000	0	77,600	152,600

Bourne Ltd – Statement of financial position as at 31 December 20-6

	£000
Assets	
Non-current assets	
Property, plant and equipment	184,500
Current assets	
Inventories	10,750
Trade and other receivables	42,500
Cash and cash equivalents	1,950
	55,200
Total assets	239,700
EQUITY AND LIABILITIES	
Equity	
Share capital	75,000
Retained earnings	77,600
Total equity	152,600
Non-current liabilities	
Bank loan	55,000
	55,000
Current liabilities	
Trade and other payables	17,250
Tax liability	14,850
	32,100
Total liabilities	87,100
Total equity and liabilities	239,700

Workings

Property, plant and equipment	£000
Land and buildings – value	175,000
Accumulated depreciation – land and buildings	–10,500
Plant and equipment – cost	25,000
Accumulated depreciation – plant and equipment	–5,000
Property, plant and equipment =	184,500

3.14 (a) Dudley Ltd – Statement of profit or loss and other comprehensive income for the year ended 31 March 20X1

	£000
Revenue	75,216
Cost of sales	−48,688
Gross profit	26,528
Distribution costs	−11,932
Administrative expenses	−9,194
Profit from operations	5,402
Finance costs	−300
Profit before tax	5,102
Tax	−1,100
Profit for the year from continuing operations	4,002
Other comprehensive income for the year	5,000
Total comprehensive income for the year	9,002

Workings

Cost of sales	£000
Opening inventories	4,683
Purchases	45,834
Closing inventories	−5,129
Depreciation	*3,300
Cost of sales =	48,688

* depreciation: buildings £50,000 x 2% x 60% = £600; plant and equipment (£32,000 − £14,000) x 25% x 60% = £2,700; total £3,300

Distribution costs	£000
Distribution costs	10,272
Accrual	10
Depreciation	*1,650
Distribution costs =	11,932

* depreciation as per cost of sales, but at 30%

Administrative expenses	£000
Administrative expenses	8,636
Bad (irrecoverable) debt	8
Depreciation	*550
Administrative expenses =	9,194

* depreciation as per cost of sales, but at 10%

(b)   Dudley Ltd – Statement of changes in equity for the year ended 31 March 20X1

	Share capital	Other reserves	Retained earnings	Total equity
	£000	£000	£000	£000
Balance at 1 April 20X0	60,000	10,000	33,021	103,021
Changes in equity for 20X1				
Total comprehensive income		5,000	4,002	9,002
Dividends			−1,500	−1,500
Issue of share capital				
Balance at 31 March 20X1	60,000	15,000	35,523	110,523

(c)   Dudley Ltd – Statement of financial position as at 31 March 20X1

	£000
Assets	
Non-current assets	
Property, plant and equipment	108,500
Current assets	
Inventories	5,129
Trade and other receivables	3,512
Cash and cash equivalents	1,742
	10,383
Total assets	118,883
EQUITY AND LIABILITIES	
Equity	
Share capital	60,000
Retained earnings	35,523
Revaluation reserve	15,000
Total equity	110,523
Non-current liabilities	
Bank loan	5,000
	5,000
Current liabilities	
Trade and other payables	2,260
Tax liability	1,100
	3,360
Total liabilities	8,360
Total equity and liabilities	118,883

Workings

Property, plant and equipment	£000
Land and buildings – value	100,000
Accumulated depreciation – land and buildings	*–5,000
Plant and equipment – cost	32,000
Accumulated depreciation – plant and equipment	**–18,500
Property, plant and equipment =	108,500

* £4,000 + £1,000

** £14,000 + £4,500

Trade and other receivables	£000
Trade and other receivables	3,520
Bad (irrecoverable) debt	–8
Trade and other receivables =	3,512

Trade and other payables	£000
Trade and other payables	2,140
Accruals – trial balance	110
Additional distribution costs accrued	10
Trade and other payables =	2,260

3.15 **(a)** **Avanzi Ltd – Statement of profit or loss and other comprehensive income for the year ended 31 March 20X1**

	£000
Revenue	22,400
Cost of sales	−11,935
Gross profit	10,465
Distribution costs	−3,350
Administrative expenses	−2,780
Profit from operations	4,335
Finance costs	−40
Profit before tax	4,295
Tax	−830
Profit for the year from continuing operations	3,465
Other comprehensive income for the year	0
Total comprehensive income for the year	3,465

Workings

Cost of sales	£000
Opening inventories	1,200
Purchases	11,500
Closing inventories	−1,315
Depreciation	*550
Cost of sales =	11,935

* depreciation: buildings £5,000 x 2% x 50% = £50; plant and equipment (£9,000 − £4,000) x 20% x 50% = £500; total £550

Distribution costs	£000
Distribution costs	3,000
Accrual	20
Depreciation	*330
Distribution costs =	3,350

* depreciation as per cost of sales, but at 30%

Administrative expenses	£000
Administrative expenses	2,550
Bad (irrecoverable) debt	10
Depreciation	*220
Administrative expenses =	2,780

* depreciation as per cost of sales, but at 20%

(b)   Avanzi Ltd – Statement of changes in equity for the year ended 31 March 20X1

	Share capital	Other reserves	Retained earnings	Total equity
	£000	*£000*	*£000*	*£000*
Balance at 1 April 20X0	4,000	1,000	2,050	7,050
Changes in equity for 20X1				
Total comprehensive income			3,465	3,465
Dividends			−1,050	−1,050
Issue of share capital	1,000	500		1,500
Balance at 31 March 20X1	5,000	1,500	4,465	10,965

(c)   Avanzi Ltd – Statement of financial position as at 31 March 20X1

	£000
Assets	
Non-current assets	
Property, plant and equipment	9,900
Current assets	
Inventories	1,315
Trade and other receivables	3,390
Cash and cash equivalents	600
	5,305
Total assets	15,205
EQUITY AND LIABILITIES	
Equity	
Share capital	5,000
Retained earnings	4,465
Share premium	1,500
Total equity	10,965
Non-current liabilities	
Bank loan	800
	800
Current liabilities	
Trade and other payables	2,610
Tax liability	830
	3,440
Total liabilities	4,240
Total equity and liabilities	15,205

Workings

Property, plant and equipment	£000
Land and buildings – value	7,000
Accumulated depreciation – land and buildings	*–1,100
Plant and equipment – cost	9,000
Accumulated depreciation – plant and equipment	**–5,000
Property, plant and equipment =	9,900

* £1,000 + £100

** £4,000 + £1,000

Trade and other receivables	£000
Trade and other receivables	3,400
Bad (irrecoverable) debt	–10
Trade and other receivables =	3,390

Trade and other payables	£000
Trade and other payables	2,400
Accruals – trial balance	190
Additional distribution costs accrued	20
Trade and other payables =	2,610

3.16   (a)   **Sutar Ltd – Statement of profit or loss and other comprehensive income for the year ended 31 March 20X3**

	£000
Revenue	31,710
Cost of sales	−14,997
Gross profit	16,713
Distribution costs	−7,094
Administrative expenses	−3,520
Profit from operations	6,099
Finance costs	−480
Profit before tax	5,619
Tax	−975
Profit for the year from continuing operations	4,644
Other comprehensive income for the year	500
Total comprehensive income for the year	5,144

Workings

Cost of sales	£000
Opening inventories	6,531
Purchases	15,525
Closing inventories	−7,878
Depreciation	*819
Cost of sales =	14,997

* depreciation: buildings £4,500 x 2% x 70% = £63; plant and equipment (£7,800 − £2,400) x 20% x 70% = £756; total £819

Distribution costs	£000
Distribution costs	6,842
Accrual	18
Depreciation	*234
Distribution costs =	7,094

* depreciation as per cost of sales, but at 20%

Administrative expenses	£000
Administrative expenses	3,378
Bad (irrecoverable) debt	25
Depreciation	*117
Administrative expenses =	3,520

* depreciation as per cost of sales, but at 10%

(b)   Sutar Ltd – Statement of changes in equity for the year ended 31 March 20X3

	Share capital	Other reserves	Retained earnings	Total equity
	£000	£000	£000	£000
Balance at 1 April 20X2	5,000	1,000	6,178	12,178
Changes in equity for 20X3				
Total comprehensive income		500	4,644	5,144
Dividends			−400	−400
Issue of share capital				
Balance at 31 March 20X3	5,000	1,500	10,422	16,922

(c)   **Sutar Ltd – Statement of financial position as at 31 March 20X3**

	£000
Assets	
Non-current assets	
Property, plant and equipment	12,666
Current assets	
Inventories	7,878
Trade and other receivables	5,430
Cash and cash equivalents	304
	13,612
Total assets	26,278
EQUITY AND LIABILITIES	
Equity	
Share capital	5,000
Retained earnings	10,422
Revaluation reserve	1,500
Total equity	16,922
Non-current liabilities	
Bank loan	6,000
	6,000
Current liabilities	
Trade and other payables	2,381
Tax liability	975
	3,356
Total liabilities	9,356
Total equity and liabilities	26,278

Workings

Property, plant and equipment	£000
Land and buildings – value	*9,000
Accumulated depreciation – land and buildings	**–654
Plant and equipment – cost	7,800
Accumulated depreciation – plant and equipment	***–3,480
Property, plant and equipment =	12,666

* £8,500 + £500

** £564 + £90

*** £2,400 + £1,080

Trade and other receivables	£000
Trade and other receivables	5,455
Bad (irrecoverable) debt	–25
Trade and other receivables =	5,430

Trade and other payables	£000
Trade and other payables	2,350
Accruals – trial balance	13
Additional distribution costs accrued	18
Trade and other payables =	2,381

CHAPTER 4: ACCOUNTING FOR ASSETS

4.1   (d)   £34,900

4.2   (d)   £18,000

4.3   (a)   An identifiable non-monetary asset without physical substance.

(b)   1.   Computer software

2.   Patents

Note: other examples include copyrights, customer lists, licences and marketing rights

(c)   1.   **Identifiability** – the asset is either separable from the entity and is capable of being sold or transferred, or it arises from contractual or other legal rights.

2.   **Control** – the entity has the power to obtain future economic benefits from the asset.

3.   **Future economic benefits** – includes revenue from the sale of products or services, cost savings, or other benefits.

4.4   (b)   trademarks

4.5   (a)   research expenditure

4.6   (a)   IAS 38, *Intangible Assets*, states that development can only be recognised on the statement of financial position when the entity can demonstrate all of the following:

•   the technical feasibility of completing the intangible asset so that it will be available for use or sale

•   its intention to complete the intangible asset and to use or sell it

•   its ability to use or sell the intangible asset

•   the way in which the intangible asset will generate probable future economic benefits

•   the availability of resources to complete the development and to use or sell the intangible asset

•   its ability to measure the development expenditure reliably

(b)   Included: direct costs (eg materials, labour, fees to register legal rights)

Excluded: general overheads (eg administrative expenses)

4.7   (c)   expenditure of £20,000, subject to satisfying certain criteria, may be recognised as an intangible asset.

4.8 **(a)** An impairment review is carried out in three steps:

STEP 1   The asset's carrying amount is ascertained.

STEP 2   The asset's recoverable amount is ascertained, being the higher of:

- fair value, less costs of disposal, and

- value in use, including cash from its ultimate disposal

STEP 3   If recoverable amount is greater than carrying value, there is no impairment. If carrying value is greater than recoverable amount, then the asset is impaired and should be written down to its recoverable amount.

Terms used:

Carrying amount is the amount at which an asset is recognised after deducting any accumulated depreciation/amortisation and accumulated impairment losses.

Recoverable amount is the higher of the asset's fair value, less costs of disposal, and its value in use.

Fair value is the price that would be received to sell an asset in an orderly transaction between market participants at the measurement date.

Value in use is the present value of the future cash flows expected to be derived from an asset.

(b) When an asset is impaired it should be written down to its recoverable amount on the statement of financial position. The amount of the impairment loss is recognised as an expense in the statement of profit or loss and other comprehensive income, unless it relates to a previously revalued asset, when it is debited to the revaluation reserve within equity (to the extent of the revaluation surplus for that particular asset).

4.9 **External sources of impairment**

- a significant fall in the asset's value

- adverse effects on the entity caused by technology, markets, the economy, laws

- increases in interest rates

- the market value of the entity is less than the carrying amount of net assets

Internal sources of impairment

- obsolescence or physical damage to the asset

- adverse effects on the asset of a significant reorganisation within the entity

- the economic performance of the asset is worse than expected

4.10 (d)   3 and 4

4.11 **Finance lease**

A lease is classified as a finance lease when substantially all the risks and rewards of ownership are transferred to the lessee.

Operating lease

A lease is classified as an operating lease when there is no substantial transfer of the risks and rewards of ownership to the lessee.

Alternatively: an operating lease is a lease other than a finance lease.

4.12 (a) A finance lease is initially recognised on the statement of financial position as an asset, together with a corresponding liability to the lessor.

The amount shown is the lower of:

- the fair value of the asset, and
- the present value of the minimum lease payments

(b) Under an operating lease, lease payments are recognised as an expense in the statement of profit or loss and other comprehensive income on a straight-line basis over the lease term (unless another basis is more representative of the time pattern of the user's benefit).

4.13 (a) **Sum-of-the-digits**

The interest is apportioned to the statement of profit or loss and other comprehensive income by reference to the sum of the number of years. This 'sum-of-the-digits' is calculated, for example, over three years as $1 + 2 + 3 = 6$. The digits then count down over the number of years: year one 3/6, year two 2/6, year three 1/6. In this way a larger amount of interest is charged in the early years, which then reduces over time.

Actuarial method

The actuarial method apportions the finance charges over the period of the lease so as to give a constant rate of interest on the capital amount of the lease. The rate of interest to be used is found either by using actuarial tables or by trial and error. It is a more accurate method of apportioning interest than the sum-of-the-digits method.

(b)

Year	Leasing payments due at start of year	Leasing payments during year	Finance charge
	£	£	£
20-1	20,000	5,000	2,400
20-2	15,000	5,000	1,800
20-3	10,000	5,000	1,200
20-4	5,000	5,000	600

4.14 (d) at the lower of cost and net realisable value

4.15 (d) £95,200

CHAPTER 5: ACCOUNTING FOR LIABILITIES AND THE STATEMENT OF PROFIT OR LOSS

5.1   **(a)**   A present obligation of the entity arising from past events, the settlement of which is expected to result in an outflow from the entity of resources embodying economic benefits.

   (b)   •   Goods or services bought on credit in the past

   •   Resulting in a present obligation of the entity

   •   Settlement of the obligation will result in an outflow of resources from the entity, ie payment will be made

5.2   (a)   is TRUE; (b) is FALSE

5.3   (a)   in the statement of profit or loss and other comprehensive income and as a current liability in the statement of financial position

5.4

Corporation tax charge	Corporation tax liability	
£	£	
25,000	30,000	✔

5.5

RATHOD LTD Statement of profit or loss (extract) for the year ended 31 March 20X4	
	£
Profit before tax	40,700
Tax	–9,500
Profit for the year	31,200

Rathod Ltd – Statement of financial position as at 31 March 20X4

ASSETS	£
Non-current assets	
Property, plant and equipment	125,000
Current assets	
Inventories	15,500
Trade receivables	22,400
Cash and cash equivalents	4,000
	41,900
Total assets	166,900
EQUITY AND LIABILITIES	
Equity	
Share capital	100,000
Retained earnings	*37,900
Total equity	137,900
Non-current liabilities	0
	0
Current liabilities	
Trade payables	19,500
Tax payable	9,500
	29,000
Total liabilities	29,000
Total equity and liabilities	166,900

* £ 29,200 at start + £31,200 profit for year – £22,500 dividends paid

5.6   (c)   at the lower of the fair value of the asset being leased and the present value of the minimum lease payments

5.7   **(a)**   A **provision** is a liability of uncertain timing and amount.

A provision differs from a liability such as trade payables because, with provisions, there is uncertainty as to the timing or amount of the future expenditure required to settle. This contrasts with trade payables where the goods or services have been received or supplied and the amount due has either been invoiced or agreed with the supplier.

(b)   A **contingent liability** is

- either a possible obligation arising from past events whose existence will be confirmed only by the occurrence or non-occurrence of one or more uncertain future events not wholly within the entity's control

- or a present obligation that arises from past events but is not recognised because:

    (1)   either it is not probable that an outflow of economic benefits will be required to settle the obligation

    (2)   or the obligation cannot be measured with sufficient reliability

The difference between a provision and a contingent liability is that a provision is probable (with more than a 50% likelihood of occurrence) whereas a contingent liability is either possible or remote (with less than a 50% likelihood of occurrence).

(c)   A **provision** is to be recognised as a liability in the financial statements when:

- an entity has a present obligation as a result of a past event

- it is probable that an outflow of economic benefits will be required to settle the obligation

- a reliable estimate can be made of the amount of the obligation

A provision should also be disclosed as a note to the financial statements, giving:

- details of changes in the amount of provisions between the beginning and end of the year

- a description of the provision(s) and expected timings of any resulting transfers

A **contingent liability** is not recognised in the financial statements; however, it should be disclosed as a note to the financial statements which includes:

- a brief description of the nature of the contingent liability

- an indication of the uncertainties relating to the amount or timing of any outflow

- the possibility of any reimbursement

Where a contingent liability is considered to be remote, then no disclosure is required in the notes to the financial statements.

5.8   (d)   recognised in the financial statements as a provision

5.9   True

5.10   **(a)**   Adjusting events provide evidence of conditions that existed at the end of the reporting period.

(b)   Non-adjusting events are indicative of conditions that arose after the end of the reporting period.

(c)   •   IAS 10 recognises that there may be events which occur, or information that becomes available, after the end of the financial year that need to be reflected in the financial statements

•   Any such changes can only be made in the period

-   after the end of the financial year

-   before the financial statements are authorised for issue

•   For adjusting events, if material, adjustments should be made to the amounts shown in the financial statements

•   For non-adjusting events no adjustment is made to the financial statements; instead, if material, they are disclosed by way of notes which explain the nature of the event and, where possible, give an estimate of its financial effect

5.11   (c)   1 and 2

5.12   False

5.13   **(a)**   Revenue is the gross inflow of economic benefits during the period arising in the course of the ordinary activities of an entity when those inflows result in increases in equity, other than increases relating to contributions from equity participants.

(b)   Fair value is the price that would be received to sell an asset or paid to transfer a liability in an orderly transaction between market participants at the measurement date.

(c)   •   sale of goods

•   rendering of services

•   interest, royalties and dividends

5.14   (a)   at the fair value of the consideration received or receivable

5.15   (d)   all of them

5.16   (a)   all of them

5.17 **(a)** Although the selling of the inventory is an event which happened after the year end, under IAS 10, *Events after the Reporting Period*, this is an example of an adjusting event. Such events provide evidence of conditions that existed at the end of the reporting period; if material, changes should be made to the amounts shown in the financial statements. The sale of inventory provides evidence as to the net realisable value of the inventory reported in the financial statements for the year under review. Under IAS 2, *Inventories*, inventories are to be valued at the lower of cost and net realisable value.

(b) A dividend declared or proposed on ordinary shares after the reporting period is, under IAS 10, an example of a non-adjusting event. Such events are indicative of conditions that arose after the reporting period; no adjustment is made to the financial statements – if material, they are disclosed by way of notes which explain the nature of the event and, where possible, give an estimate of its financial effect. The proposed ordinary dividend cannot be recorded as a liability at 30 September 20-6 as it was not a present obligation of the company at the financial year end. The details of the proposed dividend will be given in the notes to the financial statements, including the amount of £75,000.

(c) Under IAS 10, this is an example of a non-adjusting event after the reporting period. Although the employee was working for Gernroder Limited at the financial year end, the legal proceedings do not relate to conditions that existed at the year end. Instead, the legal proceedings are indicative of conditions that arose after the end of the reporting period and no adjustment is to be made to the financial statements. The amount of £20,000, if material, is to be disclosed by way of a note which explains the nature of the event and the financial effect.

CHAPTER 6: STATEMENT OF CASH FLOWS

6.1 True

6.2 True

6.3 False

6.4 False

6.5 True

6.6 True

6.7 (d) all of them

6.8 (a) £17,500*

* £12,400 + £5,000 + £300 − £600 + £400

6.9   (a)   £33,000* inflow

* £25,000 + £8,000 + £3,000 − £5,000 + £2,000

6.10   (c)   £5,500* outflow

* −£8,000 + £7,500 − £2,500 − £1,500 − £1,000

6.11   (b)   £15,000* inflow

* £12,500 + £8,500 − £3,500 + £2,500 − £3,000 − £2,000

6.12   (a)   **Minster Ltd**

Reconciliation of profit from operations to net cash from operating activities

	£000
Profit from operations	544
Adjustments for:	
Depreciation	365
Dividends received	−25
Gain on disposal of property, plant and equipment	−53
Adjustment in respect of inventories	−7
Adjustment in respect of trade receivables	11
Adjustment in respect of trade payables	11
Cash generated by operations	846
Tax paid	−107
Interest paid	−54
Net cash from operating activities	685

(b)   Minster Ltd

Statement of cash flows for the year ended 31 March 20X1

	£000
Net cash from operating activities	685
Investing activities	
Dividends received	25
Proceeds on disposal of property, plant and equipment	218
Purchases of property, plant and equipment	−1,680
Net cash used in investing activities	−1,437
Financing activities	
Bank loans raised	400
Proceeds of share issue	750
Dividends paid	−225
Net cash from financing activities	925
Net increase/decrease in cash and cash equivalents	173
Cash and cash equivalents at beginning of year	−40
Cash and cash equivalents at end of year	133

Workings

Proceeds on disposal of property, plant and equipment	*£000*
Carrying amount of property, plant and equipment sold	165
Gain on disposal	53
Proceeds =	218

Purchases of property, plant and equipment	*£000*
Property, plant and equipment at start of year	2,490
Depreciation charge	−365
Carrying amount of property, plant and equipment sold	−165
Property, plant and equipment at end of year	−3,640
Total property, plant and equipment additions =	−1,680

6.13 (a)

Velani Ltd

Reconciliation of profit from operations to net cash from operating activities

	£000
Profit from operations	1,920
Adjustments for:	
Depreciation	1,520
Dividends received	−45
Loss on disposal of property, plant and equipment	110
Adjustment in respect of inventories	111
Adjustment in respect of trade receivables	−611
Adjustment in respect of trade payables	311
Cash generated by operations	3,316
Tax paid	−296
Interest paid	−109
Net cash from operating activities	2,911

(b)

Velani Ltd

Statement of cash flows for the year ended 31 March 20X2

	£000
Net cash from operating activities	2,911
Investing activities	
Dividends received	45
Proceeds on disposal of property, plant and equipment	130
Purchases of property, plant and equipment	−4,681
Net cash used in investing activities	−4,506
Financing activities	
Bank loans repaid	−2,280
Proceeds of share issue	3,000
Dividends paid	−595
Net cash from financing activities	125
Net increase/decrease in cash and cash equivalents	−1,470
Cash and cash equivalents at beginning of year	1,360
Cash and cash equivalents at end of year	−110

Workings

Proceeds on disposal of property, plant and equipment	£000
Carrying amount of property, plant and equipment sold	240
Loss on disposal	−110
Proceeds =	130

Purchases of property, plant and equipment	£000
Property, plant and equipment at start of year	9,911
Depreciation charge	−1,520
Carrying amount of property, plant and equipment sold	−240
Property, plant and equipment at end of year	−12,832
Total property, plant and equipment additions =	−4,681

(c)

Velani Ltd

Statement of changes in equity for the year ended 31 March 20X2

	Share capital	Share premium	Retained earnings	Total equity
	£000	£000	£000	£000
Balance at 1 April 20X1	6,000	1,000	5,183	12,183
Changes in equity for 20X2				
Profit for the period			1,464	1,464
Dividends			−595	−595
Issue of share capital	2,000	1,000		3,000
Balance at 31 March 20X2	8,000	2,000	6,052	16,052

CHAPTER 7: INTERPRETATION OF FINANCIAL STATEMENTS

7.1   (c)   20%

7.2   (a)   property, plant and equipment

7.3   (c)   inventories

7.4   (a)   73 days

7.5   (c)   profit from operations/finance costs

7.6   (a)   20%

7.7   (a)   inventory days + receivable days – payable days

7.8   (b)   2.0:1

7.9   (a)   1.4:1

7.10   (d)   225/875 x 100

7.11   (d)   4.0:1

7.12   (a)   18 days

7.13   (d)   12 days

7.14

Ratio	(a) Formula	(b) Calculation of ratio for Botar Ltd (amounts in £000)
(1) Gross profit percentage	$\dfrac{\text{Gross profit}}{\text{Revenue}} \times 100$	$\dfrac{190}{350} \times 100 = 54.3\%$
(2) Admin expenses/ revenue percentage	$\dfrac{\text{Administrative expenses}}{\text{Revenue}} \times 100$	$\dfrac{45}{350} \times 100 = 12.9\%$
(3) Operating profit percentage	$\dfrac{\text{Profit from operations}}{\text{Revenue}} \times 100$	$\dfrac{80}{350} \times 100 = 22.9\%$
(4) Interest cover	$\dfrac{\text{Profit from operations}}{\text{Finance costs}}$	$\dfrac{80}{15} = 5.3 \text{ times}$

7.15

Ratio	(a) Formula	(b) Calculation of ratio for Vanova Ltd (amounts in £000)
(1) Return on capital employed	$\dfrac{\text{Profit from operations}}{\left(\begin{array}{c}\text{Total equity +}\\ \text{non-current liabilities}\end{array}\right)} \times 100$	$\dfrac{1,390}{3,580 + 400} \times 100 = 34.9\%$
(2) Operating profit percentage	$\dfrac{\text{Profit from operations}}{\text{Revenue}} \times 100$	$\dfrac{1,390}{7,240} \times 100 = 19.2\%$
(3) Return on shareholders' funds	$\dfrac{\text{Profit after tax}}{\text{Total equity}} \times 100$	$\dfrac{840}{3,580} \times 100 = 23.5\%$
(4) Asset turnover (non-current assets)	$\dfrac{\text{Revenue}}{\text{Non-current assets}}$	$\dfrac{7,240}{3,250} = 2.2 \text{ times}$
(5) Asset turnover (net assets)	$\dfrac{\text{Revenue}}{\text{Total assets} - \text{current liabilities}}$	$\dfrac{7,240}{4,150 - 170} = 1.8 \text{ times}$

7.16

Ratio	(a) Formula	(b) Calculation of ratio for Swann Ltd (amounts In £000)
(1) Current ratio	$\dfrac{\text{Current assets}}{\text{Current liabilities}}$	$\dfrac{315}{140} = 2.3{:}1$
(2) Acid test (quick) ratio	$\dfrac{\text{(Current assets} - \text{inventories)}}{\text{Current liabilities}}$	$\dfrac{315 - 160}{140} = 1.1{:}1$
(3) Inventory turnover	$\dfrac{\text{Cost of sales}}{\text{Inventory}}$	$\dfrac{890}{160} = 5.6 \text{ times}$
(4) Inventory holding period	$\dfrac{\text{Inventories}}{\text{Cost of sales}} \times 365 \text{ days}$	$\dfrac{160}{890} \times 365 = 65.6 \text{ days}$
(5) Trade receivables collection period	$\dfrac{\text{Trade receivables}}{\text{Revenue}} \times 365 \text{ days}$	$\dfrac{125}{1,540} \times 365 = 29.6 \text{ days}$
(6) Trade payables payment period	$\dfrac{\text{Trade payables}}{\text{Cost of sales}} \times 365 \text{ days}$	$\dfrac{140}{890} \times 365 = 57.4 \text{ days}$
(7) Gearing	$\dfrac{\text{Non-current liabilities}}{\left(\text{Total equity + non-current liabilities}\right)} \times 100$	$\dfrac{200}{710 + 200} \times 100 = 22.0\%$
(8) Working capital cycle	Inventory days + Receivable days − Payable days	$65.6 + 29.6 - 57.4$ $= 37.8 \text{ days}$

7.17 **(a)** **Notes for the Finance Director of Rudgard Ltd** regarding use of the company's cash resources.

The **inventory turnover** ratio is worse than the industry average.

- Rudgard Ltd sells its inventories more slowly (holds more inventories) than the industry average.
- Rudgard Ltd may have higher selling prices.
- Rudgard Ltd may have less effective inventory management systems/poorer marketing.

The **trade receivables collection period** is slower than the industry average.

- Rudgard Ltd is slower at collecting its debts
- Bad for cash flow
- Rudgard Ltd's credit control procedures may be less efficient than the industry average

The **trade payables payment period** is slower than the industry average.

- Rudgard Ltd is paying its trade payables slower.
- Good for cash flow.
- Not good for supplier goodwill.
- Rudgard Ltd may have difficulties with suppliers if it is seen as a slow payer.

The **asset turnover (net assets)** is worse than the industry average.

- Rudgard Ltd is using its net assets less efficiently to generate revenue, ie making poorer use of its assets than the industry average.
- It may have less sales revenue.
- More assets, or other companies may have assets that are working more efficiently in terms of generating revenue, or Rudgard Ltd may have revalued its non-current assets.
- The company may carry more inventories (see inventory turnover ratio), higher receivables (although the trade receivables collection period is better), and/or a higher cash balance.
- Current liabilities may be lower than other companies.

(b) **Recommendations** on how Rudgard Ltd's **trade receivables collection period** could be improved.

- Take credit references on all new customers.
- Credit collection procedures could be improved, eg sending reminders out promptly, telephone and email contact with customers' accounts payables departments.
- Shorter credit terms could be given to customers.
- Reduce credit limits.
- Possibly introduce settlement discounts to customers to encourage early payments – but ensure that the cost of doing this is worthwhile.
- Charge interest on overdue payments; take court action as necessary.
- Consider factoring of debts.

7.18 **(a)** **Relative performance of Gresham Plc**

Gearing is worse

- The percentage of non-current liabilities has increased in relation to the total equity and non-current liabilities.
- This is evidenced by the positive cash flow shown for 'Financing activities' which, although it could have represented a share issue, is more likely to be a loan raised.
- The higher the gearing percentage, the less secure will be the financing of the company and, therefore, the future of the company.
- The increase from 34% to 42% is below the 50% level, above which investors and lenders would become concerned, but could restrict the ability of the company to raise significant finance through loans in the future.

Asset turnover (non-current assets) is worse

- The efficiency of the non-current assets of Gresham Plc to generate sales revenue appears to have fallen.
- Revenue could be lower.
- The company may have purchased more non-current assets. This is supported by the 'Investing activities' section of the statement of cash flows which shows a large negative cash outflow.
- Furthermore, the purchase of non-current assets may have been made towards the end of the year, thus giving them less time to generate revenue for Gresham Plc and/or the new non-current assets could have been subject to initial teething troubles.
- The performance of the new non-current assets may improve in later years as they bed in.
- There could also have been a revaluation upwards of non-current assets.

Interest cover is worse

- Gresham Plc is more risky/there is less profit to meet interest payments.
- It may be more difficult to obtain finance in the future and there is likely to be a greater volatility of profits for ordinary shareholders.
- This could be caused by lower operating profits and/or higher interest payments.
- Gresham Plc may have taken out more loans during the year – this is a possible explanation for the positive cash flow shown for 'Financing activities' and the increase in the gearing percentage.

(b) **Advice to Nicola**

Nicola should, in the short term, be advised to sell her shares as she is receiving a lower rate of return and the company is more risky. Gearing, asset turnover (non-current assets) and interest cover have all declined.

In the longer term, Nicola might wish to consider keeping her shares as it appears that money has been raised to finance the acquisition of non-current assets which should hopefully improve the performance of the company in future years.

7.19

REPORT

To:	**Jake Matease**
From:	**A Student**
Date:	**December 20-1**
Subject:	**Interpretation of financial statements**

The purpose of this report is to assist in the interpretation of the financial statements of Fauve Limited. It considers the profitability and return on capital of the business for 20-0 and 20-1.

(a)   Calculation of the ratios

	20-1	20-0
Return on capital employed	$\frac{1{,}251}{8{,}430}$ = 14.8%	$\frac{624}{5{,}405}$ = 11.5%
Operating profit percentage	$\frac{1{,}251}{4{,}315}$ = 29%	$\frac{624}{2{,}973}$ = 21%
Gross profit percentage	$\frac{2{,}805}{4{,}315}$ = 65%	$\frac{1{,}784}{2{,}973}$ = 60%
Asset turnover (net assets)	$\frac{4{,}315}{8{,}430}$ = 0.5	$\frac{2{,}973}{5{,}405}$ = 0.6

(b)   Explanation and comment

Return on capital employed

- This ratio shows in percentage terms how much profit is being generated by the capital employed (total equity + non-current liabilities) in the company.

- The company is showing a higher return on capital employed in 20-1 compared to 20-0 and hence is generating more profit per £ of capital employed in the company.

Operating profit percentage

- This ratio shows in percentage terms how much profit from operations is being generated from revenue.

- The ratio has increased over the two years.

- This could be explained either by an increase in the gross profit margin or by a decrease in expenses, or both.

- It is also the case that the percentage of expenses to revenue has decreased from 39% in 20-0 to 36% in 20-1.

Gross profit ratio

- This ratio shows in percentage terms how much gross profit is being generated by the revenue of the company and thus indicates the gross profit margin on revenue.

- The ratio has improved over the two years with an increase in the percentage from 60% to 65%.

- The company is increasing its revenue without significantly cutting its margins.

- This may be due to increasing its selling price or reducing the cost of sales or both.

Asset turnover (net assets)

- This ratio shows how efficient the company is in generating revenue from the available net assets (total assets – current liabilities).

- The ratio has deteriorated between the two years – less revenue is being generated from the available net assets in 20-1 than in 20-0.

- Considerable new investment has been made in non-current assets and current assets in 20-1 and it may be that the investment has yet to yield the expected results.

(c)   **Overall**

The ratios show that the return on capital employed has improved in 20-1 and that the company is generating more profit from the capital employed. This is due to increased margins and to greater control over expenses, perhaps brought about by economies of scale. However, the efficiency in the use of net assets has deteriorated in 20-1 and this has reduced the increase in return on capital employed. It may be that the increased investment in assets that has taken place in 20-1 has yet to yield benefits in terms of a proportionate increase in revenue and that the situation will improve when the assets are used to their full potential.

The dividends for 20-1 are more than those for 20-0; nevertheless, the dividends are well covered by profits – there may well be scope for increased dividends in the future.

7.20

	Company A		Company B	
Return on capital employed	$\dfrac{200}{1,000}$	= 20%	$\dfrac{420}{2,800}$	= 15%
Operating profit percentage	$\dfrac{200}{800}$	= 25%	$\dfrac{420}{2,100}$	= 20%
Asset turnover (net assets)	$\dfrac{800}{1,000}$	= 0.8:1	$\dfrac{2,100}{2,800}$	= 0.8:1
Other possible ratios:				
Gross profit percentage	$\dfrac{360}{800}$	= 45%	$\dfrac{1,050}{2,100}$	= 50%
Expenses/revenue percentage	$\dfrac{160}{800}$	= 20%	$\dfrac{630}{2,100}$	= 30%

From the calculations we can see that Company A has the highest return on capital employed and the highest profit margin. It would, therefore, be the better company to target for takeover. However, the gross profit margin for Company B is, in fact, higher suggesting that the underlying business is more profitable. It is only because of the expenses of Company B in relation to revenue that it has a lower operating profit margin. If Company B could be made more efficient in terms of expenses by the introduction of a new management team on takeover, then, given that the underlying business is more profitable, it might be worth considering as a target for takeover.

7.21

REPORT

To: **Finance Director, Rowan Healthcare plc**
From: **AAT Student**
Date: **3 December 20-8**
Re: **Analysis of Patch Limited's financial statements**

Introduction

The purpose of this report is to analyse the financial statements of Patch Limited for 20-8 and 20-7 to determine whether to use the company as a supplier.

Calculation of Ratios

The following ratios for the company have been computed:

	20-8	Industry Average 20-8	20-7	Industry Average 20-7
Return on capital employed	$\frac{552}{5,334} = 10.3\%$	9.6%	$\frac{462}{5,790} = 8.0\%$	9.4%
Operating profit percentage	$\frac{552}{2,300} = 24\%$	21.4%	$\frac{462}{2,100} = 22\%$	21.3%
Acid test ratio	$\frac{523}{475} = 1.1{:}1$	1.0:1	$\frac{418}{465} = 0.9{:}1$	0.9:1
Gearing	$\frac{1,654}{5,334} = 31\%$	33%	$\frac{2,490}{5,790} = 43\%$	34%

Comment and Analysis

The overall profitability of the company has improved from 20-7 to 20-8. The return on capital employed has increased from 8% in 20-7 to 10.3% in 20-8. This means that the company is generating more profit from the available capital employed in 20-8 as compared with 20-7. The company was below average for the industry in 20-7, but has performed better than the average in 20-8. The operating profit percentage has also improved. It increased from 22% in 20-7 to 24% in 20-8. This means that the company is generating more profit from revenue in 20-8 than in the previous year. In both years the company had a higher than average operating profit percentage when compared against the industry average. From these ratios it would seem that the company is relatively more profitable in 20-8 as compared with 20-7 and that it now performs better than the average of the industry. This suggests that its long-term prospects for success are higher than the average of the industry.

The liquidity of the company has also improved in the year. The acid test ratio shows how many current assets, excluding inventories, there are to meet the current liabilities and is often thought of as a better indicator of liquidity than the current ratio. The acid test ratio in Patch Ltd has improved from 20-7 to 20-8. It has gone up from 0.9:1 to 1.1:1. This means that in 20-8 there were more than enough liquid assets to meet current liabilities. Again, the acid test ratio of Patch Ltd is better than the industry average in 20-8, and matched it in 20-7. We can conclude that Patch Ltd is more liquid than the average of the industry in 20-8.

There has been a considerable decline in the gearing of the company in 20-8 as compared with 20-7. In 20-7 the gearing was 43% and this has fallen to 31% in 20-8. This means that the percentage of debt funding has declined between the two years. High gearing is often thought of as increasing the risk of the company in that, in times of profit decline, it becomes increasingly difficult for highly geared companies to meet the finance costs of debt, and in extreme cases the company could be forced into liquidation. The gearing of Patch Limited was above the industry average in 20-7, making it relatively more risky, in this respect, than the average of companies in the industry. However, the gearing in 20-8 is considerably less than the industry average and hence may now be considered less risky than the average. There is thus less of a risk from gearing in doing business with the company than the average of companies in the sector.

Conclusions

Overall, based solely on the information provided in the financial statements of the company, it is recommended that Rowan Healthcare should use Patch Limited as a supplier. The company has increasing profitability and liquidity and a lower level of gearing in 20-8 than in 20-7. It also compares favourably with other companies in the same industry and seems to present a lower risk than the average of the sector.

CHAPTER 8: CONSOLIDATED FINANCIAL STATEMENTS

8.1   (d)   £52,000

8.2   (a)   £64,000

8.3   (a)   £870,000

8.4   (d)   £63,000

8.5   (b)   £100,000

8.6   **(a)**   **an acquiree** – the business or businesses that the acquirer obtains control of in a business combination

    (b)   **an acquirer** – the entity that obtains control of the acquiree

    (c)   **a business combination** – a transaction or other event in which an acquirer obtains control of one or more businesses

    (d)   **goodwill** – an asset representing the future economic benefits arising from other assets acquired in a business combination that are not individually identified and separately recognised

8.7   **(a)**   **Fair value** is the price that would be received to sell an asset or paid to transfer a liability in an orderly transaction between market participants at the measurement date.

    (b)   (1)   **Goodwill** is the cost of the investment in the subsidiary, less the fair value of the subsidiary's identifiable assets and liabilities

        (2)   **Post-acquisition profits** are affected where the use of fair value for non-current assets leads to a different depreciation charge from that based on historic costs

        (3)   **Non-controlling interest** is the proportion of the subsidiary owned, based on the fair values of the subsidiary's identifiable assets and liabilities

8.8   **(a)**   (1)   **A parent** is an entity that controls one or more entities

        (2)   **A group** is a parent and its subsidiaries

    (b)   **A subsidiary** is an entity that is controlled by another entity

    (c)   **Non-controlling interest** is the equity in a subsidiary not attributable, directly or indirectly, to a parent

8.9   Control is assumed to exist when the investor has power to direct the relevant activities of the investee, ie the activities of the investee that significantly affect the investee's returns.

Power to direct the relevant activities of the investee include:

- rights in the form of voting rights of an investee (eg more than half of the voting rights – although there may be circumstances where such ownership does not give power)

- rights to appoint, reassign or remove members of an investee's key management personnel who have the ability to direct the relevant activities

- rights to appoint or remove another entity that directs the relevant activities

- rights to direct the investee to enter into, or veto any changes to, transactions for the benefit of the investor

- other rights (eg decision-making rights specified in a management contract) that give the holder the ability to direct the relevant activities

8.10   **Exe Plc – Consolidated statement of financial position as at 31 March 20X1**

	£000
Assets	
Goodwill	230
Non-current assets	3,967
Current assets	2,530
Total assets	6,727
Equity and liabilities	
Equity	
Share capital	2,000
Retained earnings	914
Non-controlling interest	398
Total equity	3,312
Non-current liabilities	1,150
Current liabilities	2,265
Total liabilities	3,415
Total equity and liabilities	6,727

Workings

Goodwill	£000
Share capital – attributable to Exe Plc	–750
Retained earnings – attributable to Exe Plc	–420
Price paid	1,400
Goodwill =	230

Non-controlling interest	£000
Share capital – attributable to NCI	250
Retained earnings – attributable to NCI	148
Non-controlling interest =	398

Retained earnings	£000
Exe Plc	890
Lyn Ltd	*24
Retained earnings =	914

* £592 – £560 = £32 x 75% = £24

Note: for the consolidated statement of financial position, the inter-company transaction of £50,000 is deducted from both current assets and current liabilities

8.11   Carr Plc – Consolidated statement of financial position as at 31 December 20X0

	£000
Assets	
Non-current assets	
Goodwill	346
Property, plant and equipment	*6,530
	6,876
Current assets	4,090
Total assets	10,966
Equity and liabilities	
Equity	
Share capital	4,500
Share premium	500
Retained earnings	1,048
Non-controlling interest	558
Total equity	6,606
Non-current liabilities	1,240
Current liabilities	3,120
Total liabilities	4,360
Total equity and liabilities	10,966

*   £4,120 + £2,260 + £150 revaluation = £6,530

Workings

Goodwill	£000
Share capital – attributable to Carr Plc	−1,200
Share premium – attributable to Carr Plc	−320
Revaluation reserve – attributable to Carr Plc	−120
Retained earnings – attributable to Carr Plc	−544
Price paid	2,600
Impairment	−70
Goodwill =	346

Non-controlling interest (NCI)	£000
Share capital – attributable to NCI	300
Share premium – attributable to NCI	80
Revaluation reserve – attributable to NCI	30
Retained earnings – attributable to NCI	148
Non-controlling interest =	558

Retained earnings	£000
Carr Plc	1,070
Impairment	–70
Foss Ltd – attributable to Carr Plc	*48
Retained earnings =	1,048

* £740 – £680 = £60 x 80% = £48

8.12 **ALASMITH PLC AND ITS SUBSIDIARY**

Consolidated statement of financial position as at 30 September 20-4

	£000
ASSETS	
Non-current assets	
Goodwill	3,600
Tangibles 56,320 + 39,320 + 8,000 increase to fair value	103,640
Investments	–
	107,240
Current assets	
Inventories 13,638 + 5,470	19,108
Trade and other receivables 7,839 + 3,218	11,057
Investments	–
Cash and cash equivalents 1,013 + 1,184	2,197
	32,362
Total assets	139,602

EQUITY AND LIABILITIES

Equity

Share capital	25,000
Share premium	10,000
Retained earnings	43,088
	78,088
Non-controlling interest	17,280
Total equity	95,368

Non-current liabilities

Long-term loan 20,000 + 8,850	28,850
	28,850

Current liabilities

Trade and other payables 8,733 + 4,288	13,021
Accruals 450 + 543	993
Tax payable 1,059 + 311	1,370
	15,384
Total liabilities	44,234
Total equity and liabilities	139,602

Workings

1   The percentage of shares owned by Alasmith plc in Jones Limited is:

$$\frac{3{,}600{,}000 \text{ shares}}{6{,}000{,}000 \text{ shares}} = \underline{60 \text{ per cent}}$$

2   The non-controlling interest in Jones is 100% – 00% – <u>40 per cent</u>

3   At the date of acquisition (1 October 20-3), the non-current assets of Jones had the following values:

	£000
fair value	43,470
carrying amount	35,470
difference	8,000

4   As fair value is higher than the carrying amount, this increase must be recorded in Jones' accounts:

	£000	£000
debit non-current assets account	8,000	
credit revaluation reserve		8,000

5   Goodwill, non-controlling interest and retained earnings:

Goodwill	£000
Share capital – attributable to Alasmith plc	–3,600
Share premium – attributable to Alasmith plc	–2,400
Revaluation reserve – attributable to Alasmith plc	–4,800
Retained earnings – attributable to Alasmith plc	–11,880
Price paid	26,680
Impairment (note 6)	–400
Goodwill =	3,600

Non-controlling interest (NCI)	£000
Share capital – attributable to NCI	2,400
Share premium – attributable to NCI	1,600
Revaluation reserve – attributable to NCI	3,200
Retained earnings – attributable to NCI	10,080
Non-controlling interest =	17,280

Retained earnings	£000
Alasmith plc	40,248
Impairment (note 6)	–400
Jones Ltd – attributable to Alasmith plc (note 7)	3,240
Retained earnings =	43,088

6   Ten per cent of the goodwill is to be written off as an impairment loss:

     *4,000 goodwill on consolidation

      400 impairment loss for year to 30 September 20-4

     3,600 goodwill as at 30 September 20-4

 * from workings: 26,680 – (3,600 + 2,400 + 4,800 + 11,880) = 4,000

7   Post-acquisition profits of Jones are:

25,200 – 19,800 = 5,400

Of this 60% is attributable to Alasmith:

5,400 x 60% = 3,240

8.13 Tom Ltd – Consolidated statement of profit or loss for the year ended 31 December 20X2

	£000
Continuing operations	
Revenue	1,180
Cost of sales	−730
Gross profit	450
Distribution costs	−120
Administrative expenses	−140
Profit from operations	100
Finance costs	−30
Profit before tax	160
Tax	−60
Profit for the year from continuing operations	100

Attributable to	£000
Equity holders of the parent	90
Non-controlling interest (25% x £40)	10
Profit for the year from continuing operations =	100

Workings

Revenue	£000
Tom Ltd	800
Ben Ltd	400
Total inter-company adjustment	−20
Revenue =	1,180

Cost of sales	£000
Tom Ltd	500
Ben Ltd	250
Total inter-company adjustment*	−20
Cost of sales =	730

* purchases −20 = cost of sales −20

8.14 **Perran plc – Consolidated statement of profit or loss for the year ended 31 March 20X6**

	£000
Continuing operations	
Revenue	45,900
Cost of sales	−23,090
Gross profit	22,810
Distribution costs	−6,945
Administrative expenses	−4,745
Profit from operations	11,120
Finance costs	−2,020
Profit before tax	9,100
Tax	−2,480
Profit for the year from continuing operations	6,620

Attributable to	£000
Equity holders of the parent	6,100
Non-controlling interest (25% x £2,080)	520
Profit for the year from continuing operations =	6,620

Workings

Revenue	£000
Perran plc	36,450
Porth Ltd	10,200
Total inter-company adjustment	−750
Revenue =	45,900

Cost of sales	£000
Perran plc	18,210
Porth Ltd	5,630
Total inter-company adjustment*	−750
Cost of sales =	23,090

* purchases −750 = cost of sales −750

8.15   Fleet Plc – Consolidated statement of profit or loss for the year ended 31 March 20X1

	£000
Continuing operations	
Revenue	45,160
Cost of sales	−27,240
Gross profit	17,920
Other income	300
Distribution costs and administrative expenses	−13,700
Profit before tax	4,520

Workings

Revenue	£000
Fleet Plc	33,200
Drake Ltd	12,400
Total inter company adjustment	−440
Revenue =	45,160

Cost of sales	£000
Fleet Plc	19,400
Drake Ltd	8,200
Total inter-company adjustment*	−360
Cost of sales =	27,240

* purchases −440, unrealised profit 80+ = cost of sales −360

(+ unrealised profit is deducted from closing inventories; the effect of this is to increase cost of sales because closing inventories are deducted in the cost of sales calculation)

8.16 **Avon Plc – Consolidated statement of profit or loss for the year ended 31 March 20X1**

	£000
Continuing operations	
Revenue	90,240
Cost of sales	–60,260
Gross profit	29,980
Other income	200
Distribution costs and administrative expenses	–18,520
Profit before tax	11,660
Tax	–2,170
Profit for the year from continuing operations	9,490

Attributable to	£000
Equity holders of the parent	8,686
Non-controlling interest (40% x [£2,030 – £20 unrealised profit])	804
Profit for the year from continuing operations =	9,490

Workings

Revenue	£000
Avon Plc	60,240
Severn Ltd	30,180
Total inter-company adjustment	–180
Revenue =	90,240

Cost of sales	£000
Avon Plc	35,790
Severn Ltd	24,630
Total inter-company adjustment*	–160
Cost of sales =	60,260

* purchases –180, unrealised profit 20⁺ = cost of sales –160

(⁺ unrealised profit is deducted from closing inventories; the effect of this is to increase cost of sales because closing inventories are deducted in the cost of sales calculation)

8.17 **(a)**   An associate is an entity over which the investor has significant influence.

  (b)   Significant influence is the power to participate in the financial and operating policy decisions of the investee but is not control or joint control over those policies.

  (c)   The equity method of accounting is where the investment is initially recognised at cost and adjusted thereafter for the post-acquisition change in the investor's share of net assets of the investee. The profit or loss of the investor includes the investor's share of the profit or loss of the investee; the other comprehensive income of the investor includes the investor's share of the other comprehensive income of the investee.

8.18 (c)   2, 3 and 4

8.19 (a)   1 and 2

Appendix

These pages may be photocopied for student use
It is recommended that they are enlarged to A4 size.

These pages are also available for download from the Resources Section of www.osbornebooks.co.uk

The forms and formats are:

Statement of profit or loss and other comprehensive income for the year ended.........

	£000
Revenue	
Cost of sales	
Gross profit	
Distribution costs	
Administrative expenses	
Profit from operations	
Finance costs	
Profit before tax	
Tax	
Profit for the year from continuing operations	
Other comprehensive income for the year	
Total comprehensive income for the year	

Workings

Cost of sales	£000
Cost of sales –	

Select from the following list:

- Accruals
- Closing inventories
- Depreciation
- Opening inventories
- Prepayments
- Purchases

- -

Distribution costs	£000
Distribution costs =	

Select from the following list:

- Accruals
- Bad (irrecoverable) debts
- Depreciation
- Distribution costs
- Prepayments

Administrative expenses	£000
Administrative expenses =	

Select from the following list:

- Accruals
- Administrative expenses
- Bad (irrecoverable) debts
- Depreciation
- Prepayments

- -

Tax	£000
Tax =	

Select from the following list:

- Current year
- Previous year

Statement of changes in equity for the year ended . . . .

	Share capital *£000*	Other reserves *£000*	Retained earnings *£000*	Total equity *£000*
Balance at start of the year				
Changes in equity for the year				
Total comprehensive income*				
Dividends				
Issue of share capital				
Balance at end of year				

*'Profit for the year', if no other comprehensive income

Statement of financial position as at . . . .

	£000
Assets	
Non-current assets	
Current assets	
Total assets	
EQUITY AND LIABILITIES	
Equity	
Total equity	
Non-current liabilities	
Current liabilities	
Total liabilities	
Total equity and liabilities	

Select from the following list:

- Bank loans
- Cash and cash equivalents
- Debenture loans
- Inventories
- Property, plant and equipment
- Retained earnings

- Revaluation reserve
- Share capital
- Share premium
- Tax liability
- Trade and other payables
- Trade and other receivables

Workings

Property, plant and equipment	£000
Property, plant and equipment =	

Select from the following list:

- Accumulated depn – land and buildings
- Accumulated depn – plant and equipment
- Land and buildings – value
- Plant and equipment – cost
- Revaluation – land and buildings

- -

Trade and other receivables	£000
Trade and other receivables =	

Select from the following list:

- Accruals – trial balance
- Additional costs/expenses prepaid
- Prepayments – trial balance
- Trade and other receivables
- Additional costs/expenses accrued
- Bad (irrecoverable) debt
- Trade and other payables

Trade and other payables	£000
Trade and other payables =	

Select from the following list:

- Accruals – trial balance
- Additional costs/expenses prepaid
- Prepayments – trial balance
- Trade and other payables

- Additional costs/expenses accrued
- Dividends
- Taxation liability
- Trade and other receivables

- -

Retained earnings	£000
Retained earnings =	

Select from the following list:

- Dividends paid
- Other comprehensive income for the year
- Retained earnings at start of the year
- Revaluation reserve
- Total comprehensive income for the year
- Total profit for the year

Revaluation reserve	£000
Revaluation reserve =	

Select from the following list:

- Dividends paid
- Other comprehensive income for the year
- Retained earnings at start of the year
- Revaluation reserve at start of the year
- Total comprehensive income for the year
- Total profit for the year

Reconciliation of profits from operations to net cash from operating activities

	£000
Profit from operations	
Adjustments for:	
Cash generated by operations	
Net cash from operations	

Select from the following list:

- Adjustment in respect of inventories
- Adjustment in respect of trade payables
- Adjustment in respect of trade receivables
- Depreciation
- Dividends received
- Gain/loss on disposal of PPE
- Interest paid

- New bank loans
- Proceeds on disposal of PPE
- Profit after tax
- Profit before tax
- Profit from operations
- Purchases of PPE
- Tax paid

Statement of cash flows for the year ended . . . .

	£000
Net cash from operating activities	
Investing activities	
Net cash used in investing activities	
Financing activities	
Net cash from financing activities	
Net increase/decrease in cash and cash equivalents	
Cash and cash equivalents at beginning of year	
Cash and cash equivalents at end of year	

Select from the following list:

- Adjustment in respect of inventories
- Adjustment in respect of trade payables
- Adjustment in respect of trade receivables
- Bank loans repaid
- Dividends paid
- Dividends received
- New bank loans
- Proceeds of share issue
- Proceeds on disposal of PPE
- Purchases of PPE

Workings

Proceeds on disposal of property, plant and equipment	£000
Proceeds =	

Select from the following list:

- Carrying amount of PPE sold
- Depreciation charge
- Gain/loss on disposal of PPE
- PPE at end of year
- PPE at start of year

Purchases of property, plant and equipment	£000
Total property, plant and equipment additions =	

Select from the following list:

- Carrying amount of PPE sold
- Depreciation charge
- Gain/loss on disposal of PPE
- PPE at end of year
- PPE at start of year

Consolidated statement of profit or loss for the year ended . . . .

	£000
Continuing operations	
Revenue	
Cost of sales	
Gross profit	
Other income	
Distribution costs	
Administrative expenses	
Profit from operations	
Finance costs	
Profit before tax	
Tax	
Profit for the period from continuing operations	

Attributable to	£000
Equity holders of the parent	
Non-controlling interest	
Profit for the period from continuing operations =	

Workings

Revenue	£000
Parent	
Subsidiary	
Total inter-company adjustment*	
Revenue =	

* enter '0' if no adjustment needed

Cost of sales	£000
Parent	
Subsidiary	
Total inter-company adjustment*	
Cost of sales =	

* enter '0' if no adjustment needed

Consolidated statement of financial position as at . . . .

	£000
ASSETS	
Non-current assets	
Goodwill	
Property, plant and equipment	
Current assets	
Inventories	
Trade receivables	
Cash and cash equivalents	
Total assets	
EQUITY AND LIABILITIES	
Equity	
Share capital	
Share premium	
Retained earnings	
Non-controlling interest	
Total equity	
Non-current liabilities	
Current liabilities	
Total liabilities	
Total equity and liabilities	

Workings

Goodwill	£000
Goodwill =	

Select from the following list:

- Impairment
- Retained earnings – attributable to parent
- Share capital – attributable to parent

- Price paid
- Revaluation reserve – attributable to parent
- Share premium – attributable to parent

- -

Non-controlling interest (NCI)	£000
Non-controlling interest =	

Select from the following list:

- Current assets – attributable to NCI
- Non-current assets – attributable to NCI
- Retained earnings – attributable to NCI
- Share capital – attributable to NCI

- Impairment
- Price paid
- Revaluation reserve – attributable to NCI
- Share premium – attributable to NCI

Retained earnings	£000
Retained earnings =	

Select from the following list:

- Impairment
- Parent
- Revaluation
- Subsidiary – attributable to parent

Assessable international financial reporting standards

Tutorial note: this index lists the international financial reporting standards that are required for AAT's *Financial Statements* Assessment.

International Financial Reporting Standards (IFRSs)

International Accounting Standards (IASs)

362

Index